Critical Data Literacies

Critical Data Literacies

Rethinking Data and Everyday Life

Luci Pangrazio and Neil Selwyn

The MIT Press
Cambridge, Massachusetts
London, England

The MIT Press would like to thank the anonymous peer reviewers who provided comments on drafts of this book. The generous work of academic experts is essential for establishing the authority and quality of our publications. We acknowledge with gratitude the contributions of these otherwise uncredited readers.

This book was set in Stone Serif and Stone Sans by Westchester Publishing Services. Printed and bound in the United States of America.

Library of Congress Cataloging-in-Publication Data

Names: Pangrazio, Luci, author. | Selwyn, Neil, author.
Title: Critical data literacies : rethinking data and everyday life / Luci Pangrazio and
    Neil Selwyn.
Description: Cambridge, Massachusetts ; London, England : The MIT Press, 2023. |
    Includes bibliographical references and index.
Identifiers: LCCN 2023005535 (print) | LCCN 2023005536 (ebook) |
    ISBN 9780262546829 (paperback) | ISBN 9780262376617 (epub) |
    ISBN 9780262376600 (pdf)
Subjects: LCSH: Big data. | Personal information management. | Internet—Social
    aspects. | Internet literacy.
Classification: LCC QA76.9.B45 P33 2023 (print) | LCC QA76.9.B45 (ebook) | DDC
    005.7—dc23/eng/20230210
LC record available at https://lccn.loc.gov/2023005535
LC ebook record available at https://lccn.loc.gov/2023005536

10 9 8 7 6 5 4 3 2 1

Contents

Acknowledgments

The writing of this book arises from a number of research projects that we have carried out around the topic of datafication and everyday life. These include the Data Smart project, funded by the auDA Foundation (2016–2017); the Datos Inteligentes project (2018–2019), funded by the Uruguayan National Agency for Research and Innovation (ANII); and the Data Smart Schools project (2019–2022), funded by the Australian Research Council (DP190102286).

We would especially like to thank our co-researchers in these projects for all their ongoing conversations around digital technologies and datafication— especially Bronwyn Cumbo, Dragan Gasevic, and Lourdes Cardozo-Gaibisso.

We would also like to thank other research colleagues, including Julian Sefton-Green, Mark Andrejevic, Monica Bulger, Rebecca Eynon, Thomas Hillman, Carlo Perrotta, Sue Bennett, Cameron Bishop, Rebecca Ng, and members of the *Platform Pedagogies* reading group.

Prologue: Everyday Life in the Data Age: Three Short Tales

#1. Charmaine and Alexa

Charmaine wakes abruptly to the familiar sound of her phone alarm. It's 6:55 a.m. and a workday. By the time Charmaine gets to the kitchen, her home assistant "Alexa" has switched on the heating and the background chatter of breakfast radio. Perched at the kitchen counter, Charmaine begins to multitask . . . catching up on social media and email, eating breakfast, checking her calendar for the meetings of the day.

Being partially blind, Charmaine uses Apple's "VoiceOver" as a built-in screen reader across all her devices. Living alone with vision impairment can be difficult, but Alexa makes life easier as well as being "someone" to talk to. Charmaine asks Alexa whether she should pack a raincoat for her commute to work. "No rain is expected today," Alexa replies. As Charmaine tidies up the dishes and schedules in an Uber, the Food Reminder app connected to her smart fridge pings a notification—don't forget to buy milk!

Arriving at work, security cameras on the reception entry gate scan Charmaine's face to confirm her identity. All clear. Charmaine takes the elevator to her desk on the 14th floor. She "single signs" into a range of platforms to do her work, skipping between Gmail, Google Docs, Microsoft Office, and the company's rather more clunky work management system. Charmaine is soon sucked into another working day, and time quickly begins to slip by.

As the morning passes, Charmaine tries to snatch a few minutes when she can work covertly on her application to study law at a university. Being visually impaired, she wonders how she will complete some of the law school admission tests, but her GPA is solid, so she hopes her application will be reasonably competitive. Constantly diving in and out of the university website to look at things feels like a welcome respite from an otherwise boring day.

Charmaine feels a *little* bit guilty working on this while being paid to do something else, but everyone she knows is trying to leave this company. The hours are long, there are no work-from-home options, and the Key Performance Indicators (KPIs) are too stressful for the pittance of a salary.

After a busy day at the office, Charmaine decides to catch the metro home as the wait and cost for an Uber have surged far too much, even for peak hour. Luckily, she has an old travel card in her bag. Charmaine scrolls down and listens to a click-baity news item headlined "Amazon workers listen into your private conversations!" Charmaine feels a bit unnerved by the suggestion that whenever she uses the command "Hey Alexa . . . ," remote Amazon contractors might well be recording the conversation to improve their voice recognition software. She blushes at all the personal things she's disclosed to her Alexa over the years. What if an actual human was listening? She'd never imagined that was possible, but then again, she has never waded through all the terms of service before clicking "Accept." Charmaine's decision to purchase a smart assistant was driven primarily by her love of gadgets rather than a concern with data policies . . . and of course the fact that Alexa makes her life so much easier.

#2.   Andrei's 1,000 Daily Queries

Andrei's alarm clock starts beeping at 5:00 a.m. Eventually dragging himself out of bed, Andrei throws on some clothes, grabs a protein bar from the loudly humming fridge, and heads out to meet the bus. For once, the buses are running vaguely to schedule. As the bus trundles through the streets, all of Bucharest seems to be asleep. Certainly, the other shift workers on the bus are trying to get some extra rest. But there are only a few minutes left before Andrei has to wake himself up, step off into the freezing dark, and head into the large nondescript office block for today's nine-hour shift at Amazon.

Andrei realizes that he is one of the lucky Amazon employees in Romania. Rather than working in a vast warehouse, Andrei sits at a desk transcribing and resolving conversations that people have with Alexa—Amazon's highest-selling tech product. Although Andrei studied English language up to university level, he has had to work hard to get this job with Amazon. For five years, he worked in an Amazon distribution warehouse—ten hours a day, six days a week, rarely speaking to his coworkers, taking few breaks, and never appearing to be slacking off. That's how he got to be now sitting behind a desk—it's got nothing to do with his qualifications or luck! As Andrei steps off the bus, the dawn light begins to break over the sidewalk, and for a moment, he looks toward the sky to take in a little bit of natural light.

Without really thinking, Andrei trudges into the foyer and through the facial scanner. All his credentials are displayed for the security guard to glance at if she is so-minded—a fifty-three-year-old male, employed at Amazon for eight years, four months as an area manager, resident of Sectorul 3. For all the minor hassles of office work, this is much better than Andrei's warehouse work, which was physical, unrelenting, and far more stressful than it needed to be. In fact, Andrei was finding his current gig to be far more lucrative than most of his pre-Amazon work. Amazon pays good money, much better wages than any local company could.

That said, the work that Andrei is now doing is certainly mentally and emotionally draining. On a good shift, Andrei deals with around 1,000 short audio clips of people "asking Alexa." Most of these interactions are mundane in the extreme but certainly provide microscopic insights into people's private lives. Andrei spends his day listening to strangers around the world fighting, cooking, shouting for the emergency services, requesting music to cheer themselves up, asking advice on what to buy their elderly mother, seeking diet advice, or trying to purchase sleeping pills.

All Andrei needs to do is listen to the audio file dispassionately, read the automated transcript, and correct any errors that might have occurred due to accents, sound quality, or different idioms. This should be easy work, but Andrei is finding it all increasingly exhausting. It is difficult to simply focus on what is written on the screen and not also hear the emotions in the voices behind the words. Emotions are such an integral part of making sense of the commands; it is impossible not to register—if only subconsciously—people's joy, anxiety, fear, or laughter. Andrei occasionally finds himself wondering about the people behind these voices—where they might be from, what they might look like, and whether they eventually found what they were looking for. But most of the time, Andrei is able to snap himself out of such thoughts and remind himself that the less he cares, the better.

#3. Sandra and the University Admissions Office

Sitting in the admissions office of one of the state's higher-ranking universities, Sandra hears the ping and sees that she has finally been sent the

Demonstrated Interest reports for this year's law applicants. Last week, she was dealing with the arts degree intake, this week it is law, and next week undoubtedly there will be a deluge of late applicants for all of the most popular courses. At this time of year, each of these new emails always means that Sandra suddenly has a little more work to get through. While GPAs and test scores remain the headline data on which most admissions decisions are based, Sandra finds these Demonstrated Interest reports give her the final piece of the puzzle when it comes to the borderline cases.

Demonstrated Interest reports are something that the university has been using for a couple of years—providing administrators like Sandra with a sense of how committed a prospective student might actually be. Before the days of social media and website tracking, Sandra used to look if the student was recorded as lodging an inquiry card or perhaps had sent an email to the school. Another reasonably good indicator was if the student had made a visit to campus during a junior year. Now, however, these broad clues have been replaced by online behavior analytics.

In particular, Sandra's university now had a license for a platform that collects all kinds of online data to create applicant profiles. Did this person open all their admission emails and, if so, how soon after receiving them? How long did they spend reading each message in comparison to other applicants? Did the person bother to click through the links in the university webpage or watch the promotional videos?

Sandra marvels at all the data that this platform uses to compile each report—in some cases relying on over fifty different data points before assigning each applicant a traffic-light score. For an oversubscribed course like law, most applicants have brilliant GPAs and perform well on the admissions test. This can make it really hard for Sandra to do her job. But with these Demonstrated Interest scores, Sandra feels pretty confident that she can make a decent first cut of students for the law school faculty to then properly consider.

When Sandra had once casually mentioned these reports to a friend from outside the university, she was surprised at how enraged he had become. How can the university justify collecting that sort of personal data without the student knowing? Surely, the university should be interested in the student's intellectual capabilities, not how many links they clicked on? And what happens if word of this gets out to applicants—think how easy it would be for students to game these reports!

Sandra remained unconvinced by her friend's concerns. After all, since the university had started using these Demonstrated Interest reports, they had recorded considerably fewer student dropouts. Also, this is hardly personal data—just information on opening emails and clicking on websites. Anyway, she thought, why should a student be admitted to a prestigious law course when they can't even be bothered to watch the introductory video? I mean, how interested could a student be if they didn't watch a short video with all that important information? To Sandra, her job performance is judged in terms of getting the enrollments right. Anything that helps her select students who stay enrolled and don't drop out should be seen as a good thing. If the information is there, then why shouldn't the university be making good use of it?

1 The Rise of Digital Data in Everyday Life

Introduction

This is a book about data. In many ways, the reader might be forgiven for thinking that there is little new to be said on this topic. After all, humans have been living with "data" in the basic sense of the word for thousands of years. Archaeologists have found prehistoric tally-marks that were made over 40,000 years ago. Most of the world's ancient civilizations kept detailed records of trading and agriculture. There is nothing new about observing, measuring, collecting, and reporting information about things. More distinctly, however, this is a book about *digital* data and the increasingly important role that it now plays in our lives. The past 20 years have seen our engagements with data transformed by the rise of networked computers, the internet, digital sensors, cloud storage, and many other technological innovations. These developments now play key roles in how data is collected, circulated, calculated, and used. Crucially, many of these digital technologies also generate their own data streams and trails—much of which we do not get to see but is nevertheless used to make all sorts of inferences about who we are and what we do.

The three short tales presented in this book's prologue highlight the complex relationships that we now all have with data. These stories show that while some data might appear to be highly technical and of little general significance, many other forms of digital data play integral roles in determining our everyday lives and the shape of the societies in which we live. Each of these tales is based on real events. Amazon workers like Andrei are certainly "listening in" on the conversations that people have with their smart assistants to improve the quality of the voice recognition software. Similarly, some universities are looking at their Demonstrated Interest reports based on the "trace" data of unsuspecting applicants. While most people rarely think about the data that they generate online, every now and again, it can be used *decisively* by someone like Sandra in a university admissions office to determine possibly life-changing events, such as being accepted (or rejected) by one's preferred law school.

These brief glimpses into the realities of Charmaine, Andrei, and Sandra reveal how data not only connects our lives across continents and time zones but also creates new obstacles and impediments that can be difficult to overcome. How data is collected and used in our societies is determined by politics and economics, as well as the activities of "Big Tech" companies and the extent to which they are regulated. On the one hand, data can improve the quality of some people's lives, but it can also deepen inequality and injustice for others. Like many of us, the characters in these three stories are only somewhat aware of data, the consequences of which are often experienced in the future. In this way, data remains an abstract and illusive concept, which is why we all could do with some help in better "getting to grips" with it.

Digital Data—Why Everyone Should Be Concerned

While it might seem straightforward enough, getting to grips with the topic of digital data is a tricky (and seemingly never-ending) task. Part of the problem is the sheer breadth and depth of the topic—both in terms of the "digital" *and* the "data." For instance, most people have only a vague understanding of the digital technologies in their lives. While we may be aware of terms such as "artificial intelligence" (AI), "biometrics," "algorithms," and "machine learning," most nonspecialists have little idea of what any of these are, let alone what they do or how they function. The same goes for the billions of sensors, scanners, and other "smart" technologies that are embedded into everyday environments. Nevertheless, in a short space of time, all these technologies have become integral to our everyday lives. Most significantly, all these technologies are generating, processing, analyzing, and circulating data on a continuous basis.

The difficulty of getting to grips with digital data is compounded by the fact that many people would also not consider themselves to be particularly knowledgeable about math and statistics. As we shall see throughout this book, despite the exotic and esoteric connotations of AI and machine learning, data-driven computing is fundamentally a matter of advanced maths. Tellingly, many people (for a variety of reasons) have learned to see themselves as "not good" with numbers, statistics, or data of any sort. A few people might even see their innumeracy as a point of pride. Either way, not engaging with the roles that data plays in our lives ultimately puts us at a disadvantage.

These blind spots are compounded by the reassuring ways in which digital data is often talked about by those who stand to benefit most from data-driven society—as "nothing to worry about," a dry technical matter, or simply sets of neutral numbers. In our prologue, the lives of Charmaine, Andrei, and Sandra were unconsciously organized around data-driven digital technologies. The information technology (IT) industry and Big Tech companies make great efforts to reassure us that data-driven devices and technologies keep us safe, bring welcome conveniences, make societies run more efficiently, and connect people in new ways. And in many respects, such claims are all true. Take, for example, how digital technologies have helped people with vision impairments, like Charmaine, to maintain independence in their everyday domestic and working lives. Think about how machines can automatically process reams of data to reach decisions that would take a human many days, if not weeks, to make.

In all these ways, digital data continues to be celebrated as the "new oil" that is driving our societies into future prosperity. As such, general publics are encouraged to simply marvel at these developments and opportunities. In the same way that people are discouraged from giving too much thought to the sociotechnical complexities of driving a car or flying at 30,000 feet above the earth, we are not really encouraged to think about how our "free" social media services and apps actually function and are financed. Just ignore the terms of service, click on "AGREE," and then all the benefits of the data age can begin.

This book has been written to question the idea that data is nothing to be concerned about. In contrast, we suspect there is plenty that needs unpacking and problematizing. So, why might a new critical data literacies approach be helpful? Let's start with a brief pep talk. Picking up on some of the themes introduced in the prologue, here are three compelling reasons to reconsider any reservations that readers might have about developing a critical understanding of the digital data that underpins contemporary life.

You Do Not Have to Give Your Data Away

Many readers might well have reached the pragmatic conclusion that "giving your data away" is the price that one has to pay to use online services. This is what Nicholas Carr (2019) refers to as the implicit "bargain" struck between Big Tech platforms and their users. Indeed, most people believe they do not have much choice in the matter. For example, both Charmaine and Andrei have their faces scanned daily to enter their workplaces, essentially giving their biometric data away as a prerequisite for their employment. Often the only practical way to opt out of the data demands of an app or online service is to not use it at all or perhaps use it in a restricted way that undermines its full functionality and purpose. While people might resent being placed in such a predicament, it often feels like there is not much that they can do about it.

Feeling a sense of powerlessness around digital data is understandable, but this is no reason to give in to data processes and systems altogether. This book develops the idea of critical data literacies in the hope that it will offer an alternative to feeling trapped in a state of "data resignation" (Draper and Turow 2017). Developing critical data literacies allows us to see exactly how these unbalanced relationships are manufactured by those who design, develop, and market the online services and software that we rely on every day. Such insights can help people begin to question why this is, what is at stake, and how they might engage with digital technologies in alternative ways that do not simply advantage large transnational corporations. In short, having our personal data exploited for commercial gain is something to be resisted.

You Do Not Have to Be a "Numbers Person"

Some readers might shy away from the idea of a book about critical data literacies with the argument that "I don't do math." This response might have some credence if it is being used as justification for opting out of an advanced course on pure math but does not wash in terms of keeping up to speed with contemporary society. As this book will show, everyone living in a technology-rich society now needs to be a "data person" whether they like it or not. Data is being "done to" us all the time—whether in the form of small-scale decisions about what rate is charged for an Uber ride or big life-changing decisions about whether someone gets admitted to college or not. It is now essential that people develop good understandings of how data is being deployed to shape their everyday lives. That said, critical data literacies do not require us all to develop sophisticated statistical skills. Of course, it helps to have a basic level of numeracy and not glaze over when confronted with numbers. Yet, engaging critically with data does not require developing the advanced esoteric knowledge that an expert data scientist would have (Collins 2014).

Instead, it is much more important to develop a good awareness of the processes and practices that lie behind the data science that is increasingly shaping everyday life (see Burkhardt et al. 2022). For example, it can be very useful to have a basic understanding of what algorithms are and to be aware of the logics behind an algorithmic system. After all, not even the programmers who design algorithms can always explain exactly how they end up working in the way they do (Ivarsson 2017). Having an interest in what digital data is and how digital data works is a great start when developing critical data literacies—becoming a full expert is less important.

Your Data Is a Political Issue

Finally, some readers might also feel that focusing on data is simply a distraction from talking about deeper-rooted problems that underlie many of the contemporary social issues and controversies that relate to the (mis)uses of data-driven technologies—such as misogyny, structural racism, and other forms of straight-up injustice and discrimination. In short, it might seem that "data" is an unhelpfully slippery concept that ultimately distracts conversations away from talking about power and politics. Data is indeed difficult to define, and this can make it hard to know what to do about it. It is indeed difficult to regulate or manage something that is ambiguous. However, this sense of confusion surrounding what data is prevents people from examining its consequences and the implications these can have on marginalized groups. In this way, there is a danger that data becomes a red herring that prevents us from focusing on the underlying issues (Renieris 2019).

In this sense, engaging with the issues raised in this book can certainly feel overwhelming, confusing, and plain exhausting. Yet, again, this is no reason to avoid engaging with data-related issues altogether. While data is certainly the subject of much hype and abstract speculation, data is not a complete red herring when addressing matters of equity and social justice. In fact, it is becoming increasingly important to talk about data *and* power together. As this book will argue, at the heart of the critical data literacies approach is the idea of approaching data as a means of power, as well as developing an understanding of power as exercised through data. These two topics are not mutually exclusive. This is where critical data literacies can prove particularly useful.

Digital Data—Current Hopes and Fears

An important initial step in engaging critically with digital data is to spend some time unpicking the polarized ways that data is often talked about in popular discourse—what might be termed "data hype" and "data despondency." While these are obviously extreme positions, they nevertheless flag some interesting points of contention and useful lines of inquiry. Even if we disagree with what someone is saying about data, it is always interesting to consider *why* they feel this way and what lies behind their excitement or fears. In addition, it is always important to think about what is missing from any of these strident opinions. Any excessively positive *or* negative position will often obscure many of the nuanced ways that digital data plays out in societal, political, cultural and economic terms, as well as glossing over matters of history and difference. Digital data is neither wholly good nor wholly evil, and debates around the role that data now plays in contemporary society are not black and white. To borrow a cliché that arose from critical analysis of social media use during the 2000s, the most useful thought to keep in the back of our minds when talking about digital data is that "it's complicated."

Take, for example, what lies behind the common boast that digital data is the new oil of the twenty-first century. As with the oil boom of the twentieth century, digital data is certainly a source of considerable profit and wealth for those fortunate enough to own access to the means of its extraction and processing. Yet, for any balanced observer, it is difficult to see how the analogy stretches much further beyond this. Data is not a naturally occurring resource ready to be extracted from the ground. Instead, much of the most profitable forms of data is generated by everyday people going about their everyday business. Digital data is something that arises from the social rather than the natural world. Digital data is not mined, harvested, or collected. Rather, digital data is created.

In this sense, the "new oil" metaphor is often used to imply that digital data is of benefit to everyone involved. Indeed, throughout this book, we should not lose sight of the profound benefits associated with digital data.

For example, knowing that a mole is likely to become cancerous in 593 days' time is something that most people would like to know as soon as possible. As Evelyn Ruppert (2015) reminds us, even the most mundane data point has the potential to be "decisive" and significantly alter someone's social, educational, and economic fortunes. Similarly, information that is of use to one person can also be of use to others—especially the institutions and organizations that deal with large populations. For example, Charmaine's preferred law school has a vested interest in only admitting students who will see out their full course (and pay all the associated fees) and so have an incentive to use any means available to help make decisions on admissions. Similarly, if Amazon can develop a virtual assistant that is notably better at understanding what is being asked of it, then customers are going to make more use of it. Thinking beyond the stories that were told in the prologue to this book, there are many other companies that will pay handsomely for insights into someone's financial affairs, their medical history, or future shopping habits.

Yet, just as popular and political attitudes toward oil and other fossil fuels have shifted over the past fifty years, these are not good reasons for presuming digital data to be a wholly good—if not transformative—presence in our lives. In fact, it might be argued that many of the concerns now being raised around digital data stem from previous faith in the capacity for data to "solve" longstanding social problems—a variation of what digital technology critic and writer Evgeny Morozov (2013) has dubbed "technological solutionism." In this sense, we need to take care to steer a course between wholesale celebration and complete condemnation. Digital data is clearly an already established force in our lives but not always a force for good. Digital data might be advantageous for some people but can clearly be disempowering for many others. To borrow from French philosopher Michel Foucault, it is perhaps advisable to approach the topic of digital data as "dangerous"—that is, something that is not wholly bad and potentially sometimes useful . . . but certainly something that is not to be trusted. If things are dangerous, then we are primed to be alert and ready to act when necessary (Foucault, cited in Dreyfus and Rabinow 1982, 231–232).

The idea of critical data literacies therefore reflects this willingness to actively engage with the complexity of a topic such as digital data rather than striving to construct oversimplified "what works" explanations or despairing accounts of a passive descent into a data-driven dystopia. Of course, taking this circumspect line remains something of a niche position. Indeed, it is worth briefly considering why many commentators who engage with the topic of digital data tend to promote much more polemic positions. Why do so many people hold such strong views of either how wonderful *or* woeful they consider life in a data-driven world to be? And, what can we take forward from this data hype and data despondency?

The Hype and Hope of "Dataism"

While this is a book concerned with developing *critical* data literacies, we should not be altogether dismissive of digital data—particularly the potential for digital data to change our lives for the better. Over the past decade, it has been difficult to avoid the considerable hype around ideas such as big data, good data, and open data. These ideas and arguments are all worth taking stock of. While some of this talk quickly descends into self-interested hucksterism, behind the hype lies a number of compelling reasons that are worth bearing in mind as this book's discussions unfold.

That said, even the most enthusiastic depictions of digital data can often be frustratingly vague on exactly what the specific benefits are. A lot of people simply believe in the good of data, without giving clear actionable outlines for how and why data can *actually* be useful. In some areas of business and technology, this has led to a push for near-ubiquitous levels of data accumulation and hoarding. The idea of big data became a popular buzz-phrase during the 2010s as people enthused about the insights that could be gleaned from huge volumes of data being generated from the ever-increasing use of technology throughout society. From a technical point of view, this aligned with advances in computational power that allowed data scientists to tackle massive unstructured data sets that previously would have been too large to make sense of. At the point of peak data excitement, big data sets were described by corporate executives like Pearl Zhu (2014) as just the starting point to myriad computational possibilities. That said, as was the case with talk around big data in the 2010s, Zhu's description might sound impressive but sidesteps the question of exactly *where* this starting point is meant to be leading.

This belief in the inherent benefits of massive data accumulation and analysis persists into the 2020s. For example, a recent trend in business has been for companies to establish "data lakes"—vast repositories that can store all the possible data that can be generated and collated within an organization, regardless of how useful it might currently seem. This all-encompassing approach to data accumulation fits well with business mantras along the lines of "what gets measured, gets managed." Data gives a sense of control and insight into phenomena that are otherwise uncontrollable and unknowable. Critical media theorist Jose van Dijck refers to this sense that data is self-evidently good as "dataism." Dataism refers to the widespread trust and belief in objective quantification, thereby justifying and, in a sense, promoting tracking of all kinds of human behavior and interactions via digital technologies (Van Dijck 2014).

At this point, it is useful to dig a little deeper into the ideology of dataism and consider the reasons why the comprehensive and continuous generation and collation of data is seen as an inherent "good." One obvious set of expectations centers on the belief that data now being digitally generated throughout society can potentially drive new forms of knowing and action—benefits that sociologist Dave Beer has described as an inherently perceptive "data gaze." This raises the prospect of data-driven improvements along more "speedy, accessible, revealing, panoramic, prophetic and smart" lines (Beer 2019, 22). Such expectations certainly drive the ways in which datafied forms of society are talked about by policymakers and product developers. Take, for example, the logics that lie behind two much-used concepts associated with the development of data-driven technologies—the idea of "smart" environments and "precision" practices.

In this first instance, the idea of a "smart" environment relates to any setting infused by sensors, meters, monitors, and other computational devices that generate continuous data on changes in background conditions and events. This data can then be processed to adjust, alter, automate, and generally manage that environment. One common manifestation of this is the "smart home," where heating, lighting, and security are regulated and activated according to the data being collected by hundreds of sensors installed in and around the household. For example, a smart refrigerator can order more food when it detects that supplies are running low, home energy monitors can regulate heating and air conditioning according to low tariff rates, and security can be managed by smart locks and data-driven surveillance systems.

Running throughout these innovations is the belief that the complex responsibility of household management can be delegated to data analytics and household automation ("domotics" as it is sometimes called), which are assumed to do a far better job than any human "head of household." Similar logics are evident in the design of smart hospitals, smart schools, smart prisons, and even smart cities. The idea of data being generated at all times within the environments in which we live and work is understandably appealing. These places can suddenly become far more responsive to personal behaviors and routines, optimize the use of resources, and be made more secure and sustainable. As critical tech scholar Jathan Sadowski (2020) argues, these forms of smart tech are all based on the promise of an infinite array of new capabilities and conveniences, all powered by the network of data and algorithms.

This idea of data being used to fine-tune, adjust, optimize, and tightly control our everyday environments leads onto the second logic of data-driven "precision." This relates to the use of fine-grained personal information to better direct the ways in which services are provided to individuals. Perhaps most well-known is the idea of the "precision medicine," which reimagines health care treatment and medical services in an era where vast amounts of data are recorded and stored about individual patients. This includes DNA and genetic data, lifestyle data (much of which might be self-tracked through devices such as Fitbits), and even data relating to people's broader living conditions. Precision medicine anticipates the use of all this data to develop bespoke treatment and prevention strategies, in contrast to the "one-drug-fits-all" approaches of mass medical provision. This logic is being applied to other areas of society—from precision policing to precision education. In all these forms, "precision" services embody the logic of using data to tailor services to best fit each individual—allowing doctors, teachers, and other professionals to move beyond blanket approaches, guesswork, and trial and error.

Such promises of living "smart" and "precise" lives tell us much about what many people have come to expect (or desire) from data in ideal circumstances. Regardless of the type of decision being made, the basic premise is that digital data now allows us to know more about our societies, our organizations, our communities, and ourselves. Crucially, the vast amounts of digital data being generated within any social setting raise the possibility of having continuous real-time information that can provide comprehensive insights into what is going on *and* what should be done next. This promise of enhanced knowing is certainly reflected in how data-driven technologies are marketed and sold (e.g., sentient, smart, precise, predictive, and personalized). Such phrases suggest an accuracy, an efficiency, a flexibility, *and* a convenience that are otherwise lacking in traditional analogue ways of doing things. Who wouldn't want such benefits in their day-to-day lives?

Data Despondency and the "Techlash"

These idealizations of smart, precise uses of data are all very well, but an obvious counterargument is that very few people live in such ideal circumstances. While hyperbole persists around big data, the data age, and a general enthusiasm for "better living through data," the 2020s are proving to be a time of growing pushback against these enthusiasms. Of course, some of these criticisms were leveled against the initial hype of big data. From the beginning of the 2010s, various critics were challenging ideas of big data with arguments that it was destined to lead to little more than an overwhelming data deluge. Indeed, by the mid-2010s, even staunchly business-centered publications such as *The Economist* were proclaiming a backlash against big data.

Perhaps the most insightful voices in this initial wave of critique were professional data scientists. Indeed, at the height of the 2010s' hype around big data, a few prominent statisticians felt obliged to temper expectations of their craft. In a high-profile *New York Times* op-ed, Gary Marcus and Ernest Davis (2014) outlined a number of compelling "problems with big data." For example, they reminded readers that while data science can discern otherwise unseen correlations among different data points, working out why these correlations exist and what they mean is far more difficult—as the saying goes, correlation does not mean causation. These authors also made the point that even the most "robust" data set will have large gaps, skews, and biases—especially data drawn from online populations, which are distinctly different from general populations. There is also a risk of seeing patterns where none exist, either due to errors of chance or simply the human tendency toward apophenia. Marcus and Davis pointed out that data scientists like themselves were well aware of the limitations of what they are able to do and were therefore keen to make this clear to nonspecialists who had recently become converts to the big data trend.

These contentions—particularly questions relating to the representativeness, reductiveness, and robustness of data—recur throughout this book. Yet, there are plenty of other reasons to be skeptical of the supposed benefits of digital data—not least the serious social harms that people increasingly see arising from a data-driven society. These include concerns over erosions of personal privacy, algorithmic bias, and the ways in which discrimination appears to be baked into many data systems. Such issues—and how we might be able to encourage data fairness, accountability, and transparency—will be returned to throughout this book. Key here are questions of trust, particularly the extent to which we trust the institutions and organizations in our lives that get to oversee the ways in which data is generated and used. As Jose van Dijck (2014, 198) acknowledges, "Dataism also involves *trust* in the (institutional) agents that collect, interpret, and share (meta)data culled from social media, internet platforms, and other communication technologies."

In this sense, we need to pay close attention to the political debates around data that are taking place across the world. In recent years, many people have come to not fully trust governments, corporations, and other key actors to do the right thing with their digital data. Indeed, public pushback against data and "dataveillance" has been a prominent part of the notable "techlash" against Big Tech and the machinations of the digital economy. This started in earnest in the aftermath of the Edward Snowden revelations during the 2010s regarding the National Security Agency, the Cambridge Analytica scandal, and various other ways in which citizens using digital technologies came to learn that their technology use was not completely free or private. Since then, whistle-blowers and data activists continue to remind us that there is very little impetus for these institutions to alter their ways. A decade later, the misuse of personal data remains a largely unchecked concern.

Indeed, many of these points of concern have been well publicized through high-profile books, films, and TV programs over the past few years. This included Harvard Business professor Shoshana Zuboff's book, *The Age of Surveillance Capitalism: The Fight for a Human Future at the New Frontier of Power* (2019). Here Zuboff introduced her readers to the rise of dataveillance and the economic logic of continuous data sharing and big data computation. She outlined how during the 2000s, burgeoning tech companies such as Google discovered the value of various forms of "collateral" system data that was produced inadvertently through people's interactions in online environments. These data-logs of clicks, locations, and other "digital breadcrumbs" could be used to produce remarkably robust (and profitable) predictions of future user behavior. Zuboff showed how collecting and "hunting" this data from people's everyday online activities has now become the key business model for tech companies—ideally with only a minimum level of implied consent from their customers. Crucially, Zuboff drew attention to what she termed the "radical indifference" of our data infrastructures (what she characterizes as "Big Other" rather than "Big Brother"), making the point that these are systems that do not care what we do, as long as we are producing data.

The uneven relationships that most people have with the digital technologies in their lives and the data that these technologies generate were
the focus of the 2020 film *The Social Dilemma*. Alongside focusing on digital
"addiction" and the mental health implications of social media, *The Social
Dilemma* also tackled the role of algorithms in political manipulation and
the spread of misinformation and "fake news." For many audiences, this film
provided an introduction to concepts of data mining (especially the tracking
and recording of how individuals are using devices and apps) and the deliberate design of social media to use this data to predict user behaviors and target
advertisements. *The Social Dilemma* proved to be a critical and commercial
success and was praised for bringing such issues to mainstream attention.
Notably, it featured critical reflections and *mea culpas* from ex-technology
developers, executives, and entrepreneurs. This included a few particularly
repentant technologists, such as Google's ex-design "ethicist" who has since
pivoted to run a Center for Humane Technology.

While viewers might have been heartened by Silicon Valley executives
belatedly recognizing the need to repent their ways, *The Social Dilemma* was
criticized in some quarters for relying on the testimony of what Maria Farrell
(2020) termed "The Prodigal Techbro"—the young white male "tech execu-
tive turned data justice warrior [who] is celebrated as a truth-telling hero."
In contrast, another film from the beginning of the 2020s notably presented
the work of a more diverse range of critical voices tackling issues of dataveillance and data justice. In many ways, the film *Coded Bias* presented a sharper
critique than *The Social Dilemma*—drawing on a range of nonwhite, non-
male perspectives on the oppressive and discriminatory characteristics of the
digital economy. One of the key arguments developed in this film was that
data-driven technologies are inevitably biased and discriminatory. This is primarily because technologies are "trained" on data sets and design assumptions that are rooted in our unfair and discriminatory societies and, second,
because they are then deployed in what are inherently unfair and discriminatory societies. If one accepts the premise that no society can ever be wholly
fair, then it is hard to believe there could ever be a fair AI, facial recognition,
algorithm, or other data-driven technology.

Coded Bias powerfully illustrated this logic through various situations,
such as the opening of the film where MIT computer scientist Joy Buolamwini finds that the facial recognition algorithm she is working with does

not recognize her own face unless she puts a bright white mask on. As she subsequently discovers, the algorithm being used has been trained on data sets that contain primarily light-skinned male faces. As Buolamwini states in the film, "AI is based on data, and data is a reflection of our history." The film then goes on to show how these inherent data-driven biases impact decisions made about social housing, police arrests, employment, and credit—usually to the disadvantage of marginalized and nondominant groups. All these examples leave any claims for digital data being a universally beneficial starting point looking increasingly implausible and out of touch.

Taking a Balanced Approach toward Digital Data

There is a lot that this book can take from these "data-hype" and "data-lash" perspectives. Clearly, even if the possible benefits of living in a data-driven world are only even *partially* realized, then it is still worth taking seriously the question of "what data might do for us." Many people might welcome the convenience of having things tailored toward their individual needs and preferences—even if these are derived from broad-brush data profiles that do not *perfectly* match who we might consider ourselves to be. From an institutional perspective, the prospect of having greater insight and knowledge about core processes is clearly appealing—especially in terms of identifying problems and opportunities that might have been missed previously when anticipating what might lie ahead. In terms of making people's everyday lives run a little smoother, the "data is the new oil" analogy might still hold a little weight.

On the flipside, there is also much from the "data despondency" point of view that also merits attention. Clearly, we need to explore further the limits of mathematically modeling social phenomena—in short, exactly what can (and what cannot) be represented in numbers? While our brief glimpse into the working life of Andrei suggests that he was ranked as outperforming his peers in the Amazon warehouse, these metrics do not (and, many would argue, cannot) show how his work was impacting his mental health or family relationships. All data needs to be interpreted within such broader contexts. Clearly, we need to ensure data analysis does not become reductive but instead be prepared to question the robustness and rigor of what is being claimed (and what is being overlooked) in any data analysis.

Alongside these questions of whether we can trust the institutions and organizations that are using our data are more basic concerns over whether we have any realistic sense of who these actors are. This also raises questions over how much of our online activities are being monitored and tracked . . . and exactly how this is being used to manipulate and "nudge" our behaviors. This, in turn, raises concerns over erosions of personal privacy, algorithmic bias, and the ways in which discrimination appears to be baked into many data systems. Underpinning all of this is a general unease and uncertainty over the impact that this increased prominence of digital data is having on societies—from misinformation through to miscarriages of justice.

At this point, it should be clear that there is no easy or clear-cut way to be thinking about digital data. This is not something that it makes sense to be completely opposed to *or* completely enthusiastic over. As such, the rising prominence of digital data might be seen as a fundamental dilemma of our times. On one hand, there is much to look forward to. Many people might welcome the convenience of being recommended a surprisingly decent movie that they would never have otherwise come across. Many people might certainly welcome the reassurance that their home is more secure and that their doctor is alerted to a potential medical condition. In return, many people might be prepared to turn a blind eye to the occasionally "creepily" relevant advertisements that pop up alongside their videos, messages, and news feeds. Yet how might you feel if these adverts inadvertently revealed that your teenage daughter was pregnant? How might you feel if a job applicant algorithm decided that you might not fit well with a company based on your race, gender, age, or various intersections therein? How convenient, speedy, and pleasantly surprising would that feel?

In case these scenarios come across as overly alarmist, then all of the scenarios just raised in the previous paragraph (as with all the examples in this book) are based on actual real-life events. Any fears we might have about unfair automated job rejection were illustrated in Amazon's development of job-hiring software, which relied on algorithms trained on a data set of thousands of resumes that the company had used in their previous job hire decisions. By mathematically modeling the ideal types of applicants that the company had hired previously through human interview panels, the algorithm was faithfully reproducing the (un)conscious bias in decision-making that disproportionately favored male engineers. As was reported at the time,

Amazon's system taught itself that male candidates were preferable and eliminated or penalized résumés that included the word "women"—for example, as might be detected in the phrase "women's chess club captain" (Dastin 2018). To paraphrase an old computer science adage, this was a case of "prejudice in, prejudice out." This is a clear instance of the "coded bias" that Joy Buolamwini and colleagues were warning us about.

Yet, even when it is possible to identify and describe the real-life problems that exist with such data-driven processes, the challenge of working out what to do about it remains. Often, proposed "solutions" to these issues are not viable for many people—many are highly technical, require particular expertise, or are somewhat impractical for anyone wanting to continue making use of digital technologies and leading a relatively "normal" life. For example, *The Social Dilemma* helpfully ends with a list of possible countermeasures that viewers might consider adopting. These include suggestions such as uninstalling social media services, ditching Google searches in favor of search services that do not store and share personal data, or not allowing young people to use smartphones or social media until they are at high school. These are highly individualized recommendations that fall into a well-worn path of prescribing abstinence and avoidance. Why should each of us have to take personal responsibility for the wider problems of the data economy? Why should we have to stop using powerful and useful technologies? In short, if this is a society-wide issue, should we be also collectively developing society-wide responses?

Developing "Critical" Perspectives on Digital Data

This book aims to get its readers thinking about all these issues, positions, and possibilities in a careful, circumspect, and constructive manner. This is what we mean by critical data literacies. Time will be taken to introduce the broader critical literacy approach (and indeed, the longstanding precedent of the literacy tradition) and how it can be applied to digital data in detail across chapters 4 and 5. Chapter 2 will also take time to explore the specific approach of critical data studies. In anticipation of these discussions, then, the remainder of this chapter will spend a little time exploring the broad idea of taking a critical approach to a topic such as digital data.

As is evident in talk of critical literacy, critical data studies, critical theory, and so on, there are a number of ways in which one can take a critical stance toward digital data and its part in contemporary society. On one hand, taking a critical approach toward digital data can be seen simply as a counterpoint to the orthodoxy that data-driven processes and practices are an inherently good thing—what we described earlier as "dataism" (Van Dijck 2014). In this sense, taking a critical approach does not have to involve a rigid, dogmatic adherence to a particular political viewpoint or specific philosophical tradition. Indeed, there is much to be said for simply pursuing what prominent educator Thomas Popkewitz (1987, 350) describes as "critical intellectual work"— that is, attempting to move beyond the assumptions of the status quo and problematizing the categories, assumptions, and practices of everyday life.

That said, being critical is not an outright dismissal of digital data. This is the difference between approaching data as dangerous as opposed to outright bad. In this sense, taking a critical approach toward data also means looking for instances and cases that we might consider to be worthwhile, meaningful, and of value. Being critical involves a willingness to be surprised and look for better alternatives. This is especially important in light of the recent techlash and popular turns toward digital detoxes, digital dieting, and a nostalgic return to analogue ways of living. Digital data is not a completely bad thing anymore than it ever was a completely good thing. Our thinking and discussions around these issues need to be sophisticated and self-aware. This echoes Evgeny Morozov's (2020) observation that any critique of digital technology needs to be approached along the same lines as literary criticism. As is the case with literature, we should be critical of digital data because ultimately, we believe it to be important enough to merit critique. So, while we might passionately dislike (or distrust) most of the forms of digital data that currently prevail, this does not mean that we are completely opposed to any use of digital data at all.

In many ways, this book is committed to developing an open-minded criticality when it comes to digital data—that is, being objective, producing detailed and contextually rich analyses, engaging in objective evaluation, and taking time to investigate any situation in terms of its positives, negatives, and all areas in between. This requires us to be inherently skeptical but to be always mindful of not slipping into outright cynicism. This involves being prepared to ask difficult questions of how what we might consider problematic forms of digital data have nevertheless found a place in our own everyday routines and wider society. Importantly, a critical approach also involves speaking up for, and on behalf of, those voices usually marginalized in discussions of data and society. As educational theorist Michael Apple (2010, 97) contends, perhaps the most useful role that we can strive for is to act as "critical secretaries" of "the voices and struggles of those who on a daily basis face the realities of life in societies so deeply characterized by severe inequalities."

Most important, this mode of being critical involves doing more than simply explaining why things are the way that they are (usually, why we consider things to be imperfect and unequal). As French philosopher Bruno Latour (2004) pointed out, it is very easy to fall into a trap of debunking received wisdoms and established ways of doing things. Many critical commentators do little more than complacently point out problems that they presume to be otherwise hidden to others lurking beneath the surface of society and then offer up their predetermined explanations. This might be personally satisfying for the person unveiling such revelations (they can never be wrong per se) but is usually of little practical insight for anyone else. It is important to point out that Google harvests your data, that algorithms increase inequalities, and so on—but if this is all that we do then, we will only fuel a weary sense of resignation and hopelessness. As Latour (2004, 243) concluded, "Are you not all tired of those 'explanations'? I am. I always have been."

In this spirit, then, one of the key questions underpinning this book's approach is thinking, "How might things be otherwise?" What alternate forms of data use in society might be more desirable and/or beneficial than those currently on offer? What is required for these data processes and practices to be designed, developed, and taken up? What alternate data futures might we hope for? Of course, there is plenty to be pessimistic about, and many of the ways that digital data is currently being deployed in society remain deeply problematic and distinctly dangerous. Nevertheless, we need to retain an underpinning hope that things can be better than they currently are. Being critical also involves being hopeful that there are better ways of doing things than are currently found in the world (Amin and Thrift 2005).

Crucially, we hope that this book's application of a critical approach to digital data is of practical value. Indeed, remaining hopeful about digital data does not simply involve speculating on ways that things might be different, dreaming of better futures, or drawing up blueprints for desired change. As will be seen in later chapters, there are growing numbers of people striving to actually build and maintain alternate data systems, data infrastructures, and what media archaeologist Lori Emerson (2016) describes as "other networks." The end goals of critical data literacies can therefore be substantive and material—building new apps or visualizations, playing with code, and hacking around the edges of the data economy. Building alternate data systems therefore requires bringing together groups of people with the requisite technical skills, social consciousness, and political imaginations. When it comes to emerging data-driven technologies, as cultural anthropologist Genevieve Bell (2021) contends, "it is as much about critical doing as critical thinking."

Introducing the Critical Literacies Approach

All these ideas, issues, and imperatives will be fleshed out in much more detail over the next seven chapters. For the time being, this chapter concludes with a brief introduction to the idea of interacting with data in terms of literacy and, more pointedly, in terms of critical literacy. In essence, then, where will we be going across the next few chapters? What is literacy? And what are critical *data* literacies?

The idea of literacy is applied to all manner of topics—from financial literacy to emotional literacy and even physical literacy. Indeed, it seems that efforts to improve any aspect of our everyday lives can be construed as a new kind of literacy. So, what is literacy and why has it become so prevalent in contemporary society? In a basic sense, literacy refers to an individual's capacity to understand information and the social norms and conventions that surround it. The idea of literacy also refers to the ability to demonstrate this knowledge through writing and/or through one's actions. For example, financial literacy refers to the ability to understand the basics of how finances work *and* then use financial skills to manage personal finances, budgets, and investments. What makes the idea of literacy so appealing is the twin dynamics of reading *and* writing, interpreting *and* acting. Taking a literacies approach toward any particular topic therefore culminates in tangible outcomes as a consequence of developing understanding.

Despite this proliferation of literacies across contemporary society, the idea of literacy has a long history, and different uses of the term tend to reflect the social politics of the eras when it has been prominent. For example, during much of the twentieth century, when the idea was first developed, an instrumental or skills-based approach to literacy was largely understood as the norm. This involved literacy being understood as the acquisition of a "uniform set of technical skills" (Street 2001, 2). Children learned to read, write, and then apply this to their schooling (and perhaps later in their working life). However, during the late twentieth century, the new literacies approach emerged (Street 1995; Gee 2000), which was quite different from this earlier instrumental approach.

This foregrounded the idea of literacies (plural)—reframed as a part of everyday life rather than something that is only learned in school to pass a course or gain accreditation. This broader approach highlighted the various forms of understanding and knowledge required to navigate experiences at home, at church, within extended families, at cultural ceremonies, and in local neighborhoods. New literacies and new literacy studies stressed that all these experiences, practices, and routines form an individual's social literacies and should be acknowledged and respected as equally as important as any formal literacy learning. In this way, learning to read the back of a cereal packet or a train timetable is as much a literacy "event" as taking a vocabulary test or sitting a comprehension examination (Heath 1982). Literacy therefore relates to a range of everyday activities, including enacting identities, achieving goals, and facilitating social relations.

Seen along these lines, then, there is not just one literacy that is acquired through formal instruction but rather a variety of languages, texts, and ways of expressing meaning that contribute to literacies. Crucially, there are a multitude of contexts within which meanings can be made. Indeed, the new literacies approach stressed the importance of using the plural form "literacies" to acknowledge the diversity of practices that are possible to make sense of everyday texts. In this sense, the idea of data literacies reminds us that there is no one *right* way to be "data literate." Instead, data literacy involves different people embracing and exploring how their own everyday cultures, practices, and technologies can be applied to data in new and creative ways. It also means starting from the personal, including the affective and embodied responses people have to data, so that cognitive and critical understandings are developed in relevant and meaningful ways.

Importantly, this book is not just about data literacies but more specifically about *critical* data literacies. While we have already introduced the critical stance in this chapter, the notion of critical literacies has a quite specific meaning—stemming from the work of Brazilian educator Paulo Freire in the 1960s, perhaps best known to English-speaking audiences for his book *Pedagogy of the Oppressed* (1970/2006). Freire sought to free people of all ages from oppression and coercion by enabling them not just to read texts but to deconstruct the underlying messages and motivations involved in the production of these texts. In doing so, he highlights the power of literacy to raise *conscientization*—in other words, a critical consciousness of the social and political contradictions in society. Freire, for example, taught illiterate peasants to read in order to address the cycles of oppression that had existed for over five hundred years in Brazil since Portuguese colonization. For Freire, then, critical literacy has the overarching goal of achieving a more socially just society.

In some ways, this book's discussion of critical data literacies is continuous with other critical literacies in that they refer to a competency or capability to unpack the politics of a particular topic, field, or issue—in this case, digital data. However, just as the notion of data is difficult to define, so too is setting out what might constitute data literacies. However, the critical literacies tradition offers a useful starting point, pushing us to see critical data literacies not just in terms of people learning to work with and understand data and datafication processes but also to identify and analyze the array of social, cultural, and economic forces that shape how data is used and why. As this opening chapter has already begun to explore, contemporary forms of data are clearly entangled with a vast digital economy and complex cultural politics. In this way, our approach to critical data literacies aligns with what Emejulu and McGregor (2019) call a "radical digital citizenship," which seeks to rethink and reconsider dominant ideas about technologies as well as our relationship to them, with the overarching goal of advancing the common good.

Conclusion

This opening chapter has covered a lot of ground. We have shown just how quickly our lives have become entwined with the use of digital technologies that are inherently implicated in the generation and processing of data. According to the companies and corporations responsible for their development and scale, these data-driven devices and technologies offer us convenience, keep us safe, make our societies run more efficiently, and connect us in new ways. We have discussed how digital data is now thought of by many people in powerful positions as a form of "new oil" that might advance our societies toward future prosperity. Yet for many others, this analogy between data and oil does not hold. Data is not a natural resource mined from beneath the ground like oil. Instead, data is generated by us—everyday people going about our everyday lives. Moreover, data is unlikely to lead to unparalleled wealth for all but a minority.

Having justified the advantages of developing a critical data literacies approach, we now need to carry on with the next steps in outlining what it might be to develop understanding and awareness of what digital data is. This is a complex topic that requires a careful and considered approach. The next chapter therefore introduces some key terms, processes, and procedures associated with data and datafication.

2   What Is Data?

Introduction

As argued in chapter 1, developing a critical understanding of data does not require an advanced degree in data science or sophisticated statistical skills. Instead, we simply need to be interested in what data is and remain open to finding out more about data-driven processes and practices—that is, a general sense of what data does. In this spirit, our second chapter aims to develop a working knowledge of some of the basic data-related terms, processes, and presumptions that underpin the idea of critical data literacies. For example, in order to develop a critical understanding of algorithmic discrimination, it helps to first have a broad understanding of what an algorithm is. Similarly, to have a critically informed view on AI, it helps to have a broad understanding of the basic tenets of how AI works—what the technology can and cannot do. In fact, engaging with the basic tenets of data science quickly exposes the limitations of hype around big data, AI and similar—just as Gary Marcus, Ernest Davis, and other professional data scientists were quick to point out, as discussed in chapter 1. Indeed, most data experts are very mindful that their work is not some sort of modern-day magic but rather an ad hoc and understandably messy process.

This chapter considers some of the key definitions, descriptions, issues, and questions that relate to data and datafication. This should give us a better sense of what critical data literacies involve, as well as perhaps unsettling a few preconceptions about data science and data-driven computing. The chapter starts by going back to some basic definitions and considering the first notions of data long before the emergence of the search engine and smartphone. We then reflect on the ways in which digital data is distinct from preceding analogue forms of data—particularly in terms of the massive scale of digital data production, as well as the rapid processing and continuous circulation of digital data that drives the fast-growing data economy. We conclude with a few questions and caveats that are often raised in terms of what can (and what cannot) be done with data. For example, how raw, comprehensive, representative, and neutral should we presume data to be? As these definitions and questions suggest, digital data is not a straightforward, easily definable phenomenon.

Basic Definitions of "Data"

Chapter 1 started with a throw-away definition of data—what we described as "observing, measuring, collecting, and reporting information about things." This is a reasonable start but merits a little more thought and elaboration. First off, then, it is helpful to consider the origins and history of the term "data." Most readers will probably already be aware that "data" is the plural of the Latin word "datum." Yet, as geographer Rob Kitchin observes, it is perhaps less well-known that "datum" is a word widely understood to mean a "thing that is given." This is an interesting contrast if we consider the ways in which digital data is often taken from individual technology users without their knowledge or consent. Regardless of these classical origins, the notion of data really came to prominence during the Renaissance period with the rise of scientific experimentation, trade, and bureaucracy— all of which relied on measurement and statistical techniques. Then, with the emergence of computers and computing during the twentieth century, data became the basis of computer operations and began to be used to refer to information that could be transmitted and stored by computers. At this point, people began to talk of data entry, data processing, and the storage of data in databases. While these are all now familiar derivations of the word for contemporary readers, from a historical perspective, they are all relatively recent adaptations.

Crucially, these latter computational understandings position data as something that is "pre-factual and pre-analytical in nature; that which exists prior to argument or interpretation" (Kitchin 2021, 26). This aligns with popular distinctions that continue in some areas of information science and knowledge management among data, information, knowledge, and wisdom. In this sense, a piece of data can only become information with context and meaning-making. For example, whereas "151" is data, the statement "I am driving a car at 151 km per hour" provides context, turning data into information. To make meaning, this information is further contextualized until it becomes useful knowledge—for example, "I am driving at 151 km per hour, which is illegal in this country." A further level above this would be understanding, where knowledge is analyzed, synthesized, and built upon to make a decision or create new knowledge—for example, "As I am driving at 151 km per hour, I should slow down to prevent getting arrested."

In essence, what data scientists now refer to as raw data can be numbers, characters, and other symbols that make no sense (and have no real meaning) until they are contextualized. The logic here is that something has to be done to data before it can be of use to either humans or machines—hence the need for data *processing*. In data science terms, data is assumed to be raw in the sense that it has no meaning until it is interpreted by a data-processing system. This logic might be extended to presume that data has no meaning in everyday life until it is processed by humans.

That said, the computational understanding of data as raw and operational is only one way of approaching data and something that this book will strive to look beyond. For example, data can just as easily be taken to refer to information of some kind (i.e., something that already has some context and meaning as well as a set of consequences). This supports, for example, the idea from the field of information theory that information is something that reduces uncertainty. Alternately, from an epistemic point of view, data can be seen as facts that can provide the basis for further reasoning or else constitute empirical evidence (Kitchin 2021). Both these latter definitions suggest that we need to consider data as more than just abstracted numbers and symbols with no meaning in and of themselves. This is especially the case when it comes to talking about digital data.

The Distinctiveness of Digital Data

While we often think of digital as relating to modern computerized technologies, strictly speaking, the term "digital" also refers to data—more specifically, discontinuous data that takes the form of two distinct states of off or on (or 0 and 1) with no value in between. In a technical sense, even the most sophisticated computer is capable only of distinguishing between these two values of 0 and 1 and then uses binary codes to combine zeros and ones into large numbers and other symbolic forms of information. This is why we talk of *digital* technology and why illustrations of anything digital often feature fast-moving streams of seemingly random numbers, or simply a lot of zeros and ones.

That said, in this book, we use the term "digital data" in a broader sense to refer to the ways that data has been transformed over the past 20 years or so through the rise of powerful, networked digital technologies—from advanced parallel computing and voluminous data servers to smartphones and social media. This book has already touched upon various digital devices and services (such as Alexa, Siri, Facebook, and YouTube) that have become so familiar that they rarely tend to be thought about as digital. Chapter 1 also touched upon a number of devices and services that many people are perhaps not aware of at all—from a bank's credit-scoring system to facial detection cameras embedded into smart billboards in a local shopping mall. While the rise of these technologies is often described in terms of the digital society and a digital age, all of these shifts are intrinsically entwined with data. Gaining a good understanding of how digital technologies and data come together is therefore an important initial step in developing critical data literacies. Here are three different concepts to consider.

Digital Data and Digital Technologies

In one sense, critical data literacies is primarily concerned with the ways in which data is now processed, analyzed, stored, transferred, and transmitted by digital technologies. For example, while a doctor might have previously recorded a patient's new medical condition by writing into that person's paper medical records, this is now done on computers. A patient's medical record is no longer kept in only one form and one place (e.g., a manila folder in their doctor's filing cabinet). This information no longer needs to be physically transported somewhere else by a nurse or courier. This information no longer needs to be duplicated into additional physical forms—copied out longhand, Xeroxed, or perhaps sent by fax. Instead, as soon as the doctor inputs the note into their tablet or laptop, it can then be sent in various forms to various places almost instantaneously. This is a very different form of medical data.

That said, our interest in digital data extends well beyond using computers to record, store, process, and transmit facts and information that were previously being recorded, stored, processed, and transmitted in analogue forms. We also need to understand the ways that digital technologies are now used to capture and record new forms of data in ways that humans and analogue machines previously did not (and mostly could not) record. A diverse range of digital technologies now exist to generate such data—from small sensors installed in a smart home to detect humidity to smart cameras that stream video to detect the presence of objects or people. These devices (and the software systems that they are part of) embody the data gaze promises of speed, scale, precision, and insight discussed in chapter 1. An airport security guard cannot count all the people who walk into JFK on a single day while also picking out the faces of anyone on the FBI and Interpol most-wanted lists. On the other hand, this is precisely what facial recognition technology is now being used for in airport departure gates around the world.

Perhaps one of the most significant forms of digital data that will be discussed repeatedly throughout this book is the data that is generated through people's personal uses of digital technologies (see Burgess et al. 2022). For example, every smartphone or laptop user provides a lot of data to the devices and software that they use daily. Every time someone types a query into an internet search engine, sends a text message, or clicks "Like" on a video, they are generating data. Alongside the data that is inputted directly into devices and systems are a range of other less direct (and less discernible) forms of data. Every device and piece of software relies on continuous flows of data in order to keep functioning, as well as producing diverse forms of data themselves. For example, the central processing unit of a laptop computer is continuously uploading and downloading data to ensure that it continues to function—continually monitoring device temperature, checking for any keyboard or mouse use, and other forms of technical data.

Much of this data is purely technical and used to ensure that the device and its software run smoothly. Often this data is also collected by technology companies to help refine and improve their products—to streamline code or monitor how software is actually being used. Yet, this data is often of interest to other parties for additional reasons. For example, a smartphone is designed with a GPS chip inside to give off geolocation data—signals that are picked by GPS satellites to provide geographical coordinates that can locate where the device is. This "position fix" is integral to each smartphone deciding which cellphone mast or Wi-Fi network to connect to for the best signal. Less obvious, perhaps, this geolocation data is also used to geo-tag photographs taken on each phone (i.e., identifying where the photo was taken). This is an example of metadata—additional information that is attached to original content. A photograph might also include date and timestamps, information about the device that was used, and what camera settings had been selected, along with more esoteric information such as the phone's accelerometer reading to show how much the device was shaking. All this is known as EXIF metadata (Exchangeable Image File Format) and is used for various technical purposes, including deciding on file compatibilities and allowing printers to work out what resolution the image can be printed out as.

The important point to be aware of when it comes to geolocation data is that our phones are continuously giving off a data trail of such information whether we are aware of it or not. Indeed, the volume of data and metadata being produced by even the most basic smartphone is such that some people refer to it as data exhaust—a metaphor intended to draw attention to the vast amounts of metadata produced by every interaction that a person has with their smartphone (including the act of simply carrying it around). In principle, the generation of such data is not simply a sneaky move on the part of technology companies. Rather, the generation of this data is essential to the way that these technologies function. Furthermore, every smartphone user will have already consented to this information being generated and used by accepting the terms of service straight after unboxing their smartphone. For example, every iPhone user will (in theory) have read and agreed with the following statement: "*Sharing or synching photos through your Device may cause metadata, including where and when the photo was taken, and depth information, to be transmitted with the photos.*"

While this does not constitute the illicit extraction of data, it is useful to draw a distinction about people's awareness of what data is generated through their interactions with digital technology. Social psychologist Sonia Livingstone and colleagues (2019a) make the distinction between "data given" and "data given off" to highlight the difference between people's conscious and unconscious generation of data through their engagements with digital technologies. Similarly, Rob Kitchin (2021) distinguishes between data footprints (i.e., data that people choose to create or are at least directly cause to appear) and data shadows (i.e., data that is created and captured whether someone wants it to be or not). These are all important distinctions to be thinking about as this book progresses.

Digital Data as Fluid and Flowing

These ideas of data trails and data shadows highlight the fact that for most people, digital data remains often out of sight and out of mind—regardless of the constant circulation and flow of digital data around the world. In this sense, while we have tended to talk so far in broad terms about the transmission and transfer of data, a second characteristic that is important to be aware of relates to the specific ways in which data is mobile.

First, it is worth thinking about *how* data is circulated and *where* it travels to—what might be described as the material infrastructures of data. In their most basic physical form, the "zeros and ones" of digital data often take the form of electromagnetic pulses transmitted through copper wires and fiber-optic cables. In this sense, most people will probably be aware of the wires and routers required to get their home internet up and running. However, far less familiar is the thousands of miles of undersea trunk cabling that connect continents and countries together to physically form the "internet." Also crucial are the thousands of data centers spread around the world in places such as Ashburn in Virginia, Hohhot in Inner Mongolia, and the remote municipality of Ballangen in Norway. Data centers are the huge physical warehouses where data is stored—full of thousands of computers and servers, as well as supporting data management software. While we might like to think of data storage in ephemeral terms of "the cloud" or "data lakes," the realities are more likely to resemble large nondescript warehouses in industrial parks. All the data that is generated and inadvertently given away through the use of digital technologies will all be routed around these physical networks of cables, pipelines, trenches, and warehouses at very high speeds and very low costs.

These global movements and flows of data are worth thinking about in a little more detail. First, digital data is infinitely replicable. In this sense, we are not talking about one piece of data moving from point A to point B. Any individual's credit card details might be transmitted, processed, and analyzed by various different organizations for different purposes in literally hundreds of different ways at the same time. Second, digital data can be infinitely combined. Putting different data points together to form a new piece of data is a key part of data science. In this sense, at this very moment, someone's credit card transaction history might be combined with their geolocation to produce a new data point relating to their likelihood to move house within the next twelve months. In this sense, it is common in the field of data management to hear talk of the data life cycle. This involves various stages, including data creation and cleansing, processing and analyzing, data storing and archiving, data sharing, and accessing and reusing. This sense of continuous motion gives a good sense of the perpetual circulation of data. To emphasize the flow of data and its societal consequences, some social scientists describe data as "lively" (Lupton 2017) or having a "social life" (Beer and Burrows 2013).

The Scale and Scope of Digital Data

A third way in which digital data is distinct from predigital forms relates to what can be done with it. We have already discussed the massive increases in the volumes of data that can now be stored on computers, alongside the increasingly powerful forms of data processing arising from advances in parallel computing—where data tasks can be broken into separate sections and processed simultaneously by multiple computers. This has led to the development of powerful forms of data analysis that were simply too big, complex, and time-consuming to have been attempted before. Now, however, data scientists have the computational capacity to address highly complex challenges such as the mathematical modeling of financial markets and the analysis of DNA sequencing.

Two key elements of this enhanced analytic capability involve the role that digital data now plays in supporting increasingly complex data visualizations, alongside the development and use of algorithms. In this first instance, then, digital data has undoubtedly transformed the ways in which data can be communicated to nonexpert audiences in easily understandable visual forms—leading to highly innovative, interactive, and creative forms of "data viz" (as data visualization is often called). For example, medical imaging technologies such as computed tomography (CT) and magnetic resonance imaging (MRI) scans have transformed the ways that nonmedical experts now think about brain functioning and disease, while modeling complex phenomena such as climate change has become reliant on visual features such as warming stripes and heat gradient mapping. Recently we have seen increasingly sophisticated dashboards, streamgraphs, and other techniques that present dynamic representations of data in forms that are easily recognizable and understood.

Often these visualizations constitute the main form that most nonexpert audiences encounter data—in contrast to the sophisticated algorithmic computations that underpin them. Second, then, another important theme that will recur through this book is the relationship between digital data and algorithms. In basic terms, an algorithm is a finite sequence of specific steps—instructing computers on what to do with data in order to perform a calculation or solve a problem. In this sense, an algorithm can be understood like a set of mathematical formulas that is used to transform "input" data into a set of different "outputs." One of the obvious practical benefits of digital data is that these algorithmic calculations can be incredibly complex and replicated at high speeds. Indeed, algorithms lie at the heart of how digital data has transformed data analysis, allowing data scientists to easily apply complex computational algorithms to large data sets, which would otherwise be impossible to perform—such as the Monte Carlo method, which makes use of random sampling to solve problems. We discuss algorithms in greater detail in chapter 5.

A crucial aspect is the use of algorithms is to take digital data and follow sequences of steps to solve problems or reach decisions. In this sense, one broad but useful metaphor for understanding algorithms is as a precisely defined recipe (Lewis et al. 2018). The object of these algorithms is to set out the procedural steps that underpin forms of automated reasoning or automated decision-making. Algorithms therefore lie behind all computer systems and software and certainly all of the real-life examples that have been described in this book so far. For example, algorithms lie at the heart of how banks will calculate their account holders' credit scores or how a university can use webpage and video click data to calculate students' Demonstrated Interest scores. In these examples, algorithms replicate the reckoning that previously would have fallen to a bank manager or university admissions officer. In very simple terms, a university admissions officer might have previously weighed all of the following information in judging a new applicant:

If the prospective student has a GPA of 4.45 or above, and they have replied to all our emails within a week and watched all five promotional videos then they are likely to accept our offer of a place.

In algorithmic terms, this can be codified as follows:

if GPA ≥ 4.55 and VIDEO_COMPLETED $= 5$ and
$\bar{x}$ (RESPONSE_TIME) < 10080 then LIKELY_ACCEPT $= 1$

As such, the act of converting any rule of thumb that a human administrator might have developed over time into a codified logic therefore means that a university's computerized system can instantaneously sort and rank thousands of prospective students in terms of their demonstrated interest. Crucially, the administrator whose rule of thumb is being replicated no longer needs to have oversight of each new application as it arrives. Instead, the college admittance process can be automated. Returning to the first of our prologue stories, Charmaine might have the required GPA but, being visually impaired, might not have prioritized the promotional videos. Does this mean she is automatically deleted from the list of offers? How do these systems account for differently abled people and the differentiated circumstances many of us find ourselves in?

Such forms of data-driven automated systems are a key part of how digital data is now being used across various areas of everyday life—from smart home systems deciding whether to lower the room temperature to schoolteachers using automated essay-grading software. Of course, some of these tasks, decisions, and problems are quite tricky to codify. For example, it is relatively straightforward to codify an automated grading system for a multiple-choice test with a set of "closed" questions that has only one "correct" answer. In contrast, it is extremely difficult to specifically set out how a teacher might reach a decision on grading a 2,000-word written essay.

This brings us to a further advantage in using digital data—the use of previously collected data sets on a particular task to train an algorithm to act along similar lines in the future. This is a key element of statistical forms of AI based on observational techniques. This means that systems and software do not have to reply on preprogrammed automations but can learn from observing previous data sets and then self-correct, refine, and even improve the algorithms. In essence, statistical AI involves the development of algorithms that are designed to learn from large data sets by following approximated understandings of how the human mind operates. As such, this form of AI allows the development of automated systems that do not "blindly" follow preprogrammed sets of rules and logics. Instead, these systems are designed to calculate odds and probabilities in humanlike ways—for example using heuristics or through continuously repeated forms of trial and error. Contemporary forms of AI therefore involve computers being provided with an expert knowledge base and codified reasoning required to make decisions.

Needless to say, AI and other forms of computer-based automation rely on large sets of digital data. Indeed, perhaps the most important aspect of this work is based around the concept of machine learning—the process of extracting information from data patterns. This takes the form of algorithms being trained to parse large amounts of data relating to real-life topics in order to learn how to make informed decisions and perform tasks relating to that real-life topic. So, for example, an essay-grading system might learn about how human graders decided on grades by looking at a data set of thousands (or ideally millions) of previously graded essays—looking for patterns in terms of how the data representation of each written text correlates with the human marker awarding a particular grade.

Until recently, machine learning required the guidance of programmers to steer an AI system toward correct calibrations. However, the 2010s saw machine learning take on a more powerful guise—what is termed "deep learning." This relates to the application of machine learning techniques to artificial neural networks modeled on the structure of biological brains. In this manner, a deep learning system is theoretically able to train itself to refine the accuracy of these algorithms, until it is capable of reaching accurate conclusions. In essence, these are software systems that can self-correct and come up with their own ways of doing things. Awareness of these advanced uses of digital data is therefore an important aspect of critical data literacies—notwithstanding the mathematical complexity of such operations.

The Promise of Digital Data

The scale and scope of these different uses and applications explain the profound significance that many people attach to digital data as facilitating genuinely world-changing technologies. In principle, at least, digital data can produce speedy large-scale insights and predictions, can lead to greater efficiencies, and perhaps identify otherwise imperceptible patterns and trends. As we have just outlined, any transformative qualities of the data gaze are primarily technical and infrastructural in nature—based on complex mathematics, sophisticated computing, and thousands of miles of cabling. Yet, a few additional qualities to the growth of digital data also deserve our close attention. First, is the idea that large quantities of digital data are attributed and attached to individual and identifiable people (i.e., what is termed "personal data"). Second is the idea that much of this personal data can be combined and processed in order to make inferences about these individual people—who they are, what they are likely to do, what should happen to them. Third is the idea that being able to know so much about people and events has become a hugely profitable business. In short, another set of key critical data literacies relates to the notions of personal data, data profiling, and the broader data economy.

Digital Data as "Personal"

People will often try to puncture the considerable hype around social media and other online apps and services with the cautionary saying, "If something is free, then you are the product." This cliché rose to prominence in the early 2010s as a reminder that even though digital platforms like Google and Facebook were ostensibly provided to the consumer free of charge, their business model depended on buying and selling users' personal data. Certainly, digital data that can be associated with a specific individual is particularly valuable, and the rise during the 2010s of mass-user platforms such as Facebook meant that large quantities of personal data could be processed and commodified at any given time. As sociologist Deborah Lupton (2020, 4) explains, personal data refers to any "digitized information generated by [the] entanglements of people with digital devices, apps, sensors and online platforms." This means personal data can be drawn from a wide range of software and hardware sources and can take a variety of modes, including numbers, characters, symbols, images, electromagnetic waves, sensor information, and sounds (Kitchin 2014).

Despite these relatively straightforward definitions, identifying personal data is far more difficult than it might first appear. As digital studies scholar David Golumbia (2018) explains, personal data is in fact a "much larger and even more invasive class of information than the straightforward items we might like to think." Personal data includes not only what users input into digital apps and platforms about themselves but also what is able to be inferred from what people do on and around these platforms.

In this sense, it is helpful to think about the different types of data that users generate both consciously *and* unconsciously through their digital interactions and engagements. For example, Martin Abrams (2014), an information and policy officer at the Information Accountability Foundation, outlines four different types of personal data:

- **provided** data: originating from actions by the individual that they are fully aware of;

- **observed** data: includes an enormous range of data points from anything that is observed and recorded about the user online, such as what they look at, how often, and for how long;
- **derived** data: data that results from manipulation of existing data but then becomes a new data point related to the individual; and
- **inferred** data: created through probability-based analytics and then attributed to the individual.

While it is tempting to think of personal data as relatively recent, personal data is certainly not a new and newly powerful phenomenon (Bouk 2017). Indeed, personal data has long been collected to create populations and enact power. The vast Domesday Book survey of English and Welsh households in 1086 was intended to record the taxable values of every citizen's possessions and holdings. In the nineteenth century, personal information was collected for the purposes of economics, in the form of taxation and medical insurance. Prior to this, the extraction of personal data from subjected populations served a more directly oppressive purpose in the creation of administrative nation-states and the colonialist expansion of empires into new territories. Thereafter, personal data was used by all sorts of organizations and agencies to calculate and create aggregates that could be used to place or categorize individuals, with quite profound effects on the ways in which people began to conceive of society and each other (Hacking 1990). As such, the recent forms of digital data that this book is primarily concerned with allow all these established processes to continue at greater scale and speed. However, the rise of personal digital data also allows for significantly different forms of profiling individuals, with these representations now being used in unprecedented ways.

Digital Data as "Profile-able"

The idea of the data-driven profile therefore constitutes one such new significant characteristic of digital data. In a basic sense, this will often take the form of personal data being used to create profiles about technology users in order to bring insights into their tastes, interests, and purchasing habits. Data profiling involves accumulating a range of different data relating to an individual and then attempting to make connections and relations among these different data points *and* the data profiles of other people. For example, two separate data points relating to (1) a person's age and (2) how long they spent on the Amazon website do not mean much when seen in isolation. However, once put together, these data points can be used to establish a consumer profile that might bring insights into that person's personality, interests, and histories. Profiles therefore provide representation of individuals for companies, organizations, and institutions to connect with.

This logic can be illustrated through the example of a seventy-six-year-old who goes online to browse Amazon listings. Given their age, this behavior might be seen as justifying a label of being an insomniac or someone kept awake through poor health. Conversely, a twenty-two-year-old who browses in the mid-evenings and at weekends might be deemed as uninterested in going out and socializing in bars, restaurants, and nightclubs. These profiles provide a representation of people for companies, organizations, and institutions to connect with. John Cheney-Lippold (2017, 87) describes this as a process of continual "profilization," which he defines as "the intersections of categorical meaning that allow our data, but not necessarily us, to be gendered, raced, and classed."

While vast quantities of personal data are now generated through people's technology use, much of it remains surprisingly inaccurate. As Golumbia (2018) points out, data collectors are aware of the fact that the information they have on any specific individual is only an approximation. Indeed, the significance of personal data lies in its scale and the capacity to find patterns in large data sets that can be used to predict and shape future behaviors. As Viljoen (2020) explains, "The most powerful technology companies are primarily aimed at deriving population-level insights from data subjects for population-level applicability." In other words, accuracy at the level of individual is not essential. So, while great efforts are made to render digital data *personal*, it is perhaps not personal in the way that might be assumed. In fact, if someone was to see the personal data attributed specifically to them by data collectors, then they might have trouble recognizing it as their own. In some ways, this might offer some comfort—Big Tech is not interested in you as an individual, but rather as part of an aggregated category or set of individuals.

Nevertheless, regardless of their approximate nature, there is something that feels intimate and genuinely personal about these data practices. A study by ProPublica in the mid-2010s (Angwin, Mattu, and Parris 2016) revealed that Facebook had constructed more than 52,000 unique attributes in order to classify people with Facebook accounts. This was achieved by combining platform data with additional information purchased from data brokers about these Facebook users' offline lives. These created categories of interest that were assigned to individuals. Many of these categories were quite specific, such as identifying an individual's propensity for "Pretending to Text in Awkward Situations" or "Breastfeeding in Public." Facebook's rationale for producing such categories was to sell this data to marketers to give them the opportunity to target advertising at increasingly niche groups of individuals. Such data profiling is used for a wide array of purposes, including not only commercial judgments about selling, securing, and assessing risk but also judgments around personalizing learning and health care outcomes.

Digital Data as Profitable

As such examples suggest, these large-scale exercises in data extraction and data profiling are most often pursued for profit. Indeed, the promise of being able to predict future behaviors has led to the emergence of a thriving data broker economy that is estimated to be worth US$200 billion annually (Lazarus 2019). But what are data brokers, and what do they do? As Crain (2016) points out, "data broker" is an imprecise term but generally refers to companies that specialize in the collection and trading of personal data. Data brokers not only extract information directly from consumers but also buy information from companies and government agencies, as well as trawl information on property records, motor vehicle registrations, and similar public records. This information can reveal much about an individual's wealth, cultural and religious background, purchasing patterns, and education. Once aggregated, these large data sets are algorithmically sorted to identify and extract patterns, which can then be used to predict future behaviors.

Developing a good outsider understanding of the data broker industry is not easy. The majority of firms are not public facing but instead serve a range of large- and small-scale institutional clients, including companies, nonprofits, and government agencies (Crain 2016). These are not companies that necessarily want the general public to know of their existence, let alone their business models. Nevertheless, it is generally understood that there are three main types of data broker companies. The first of these are "people search sites," where clients can request information on a particular individual by providing the company with their name or mobile phone number (Grauer 2018). People search sites either are free or require a small fee from clients, who are then provided with a wealth of information that can be used for a variety of reasons—some of which might be perfectly legitimate (e.g., connecting with an old friend) and others that are more questionable (e.g., doxing).

A second category of data brokers is involved in marketing—selling profiles of individuals to marketers so they can better tailor advertisements (Grauer 2018). These data brokers work to place consumers into categories based on their age, ethnicity, education level, income, number of children, and interests and then sell these dossiers to clients. Axciom, one of the largest data broker companies in the world, is thought to have over 3,000 pieces of information on every adult consumer in the United States and has insights into approximately 700 million consumers worldwide (Christl 2017). However, whether targeted advertising is as effective as data brokers would have us believe is another matter. A study commissioned by eBay in the early 2010s found that search advertisements (adverts that are placed at the top of an internet user's list of search results) have no measurable benefit, as users are more likely to click on the "natural" results (Hern 2014). Also, it has been noted that any preponderance of reviews, comments, and other content on a webpage tends to dilute the impact of online advertising altogether (Thompson 2014). Nevertheless, as with all marketing and advertising, the hope of reaching large audiences continues to drive this area of the data brokering business.

The final category of data brokers is involved in assessing risk, offering products that verify identities and help detect fraud. For example, a health insurer may be interested in whether a particular demographic group is more at risk of diabetes or heart attack, or a bank may be interested in the likelihood of a particular sociodemographic defaulting on their loan. In addition, when it comes to social security payments, ID analytics can be used to ensure individual accounts are not associated with a deceased person or fraudulent activity (Grauer 2018). That said, as previously acknowledged, personal data is not always accurate and decisions such as these can be difficult to correct. For this reason, assessments that are made in regard to insurance premiums, social security payments, and identity verification can have significant implications for individuals. As Virginia Eubanks (2017) demonstrated in her book *Automating Inequality*, datafying processes and automating decision-making with regards to welfare payments and insurance run the risk of intensifying and extending any systematic errors, biases, and inequalities that previously existed in that system. This mirrors the example from chapter 1 of previous biases in human interview panels being baked into automated recruitment systems. Examples such as these highlight the limitations of the promise of digital data, not least the importance of having a good understanding of social context.

Such limitations notwithstanding, the multibillion-dollar data broker industry continues to thrive as the 2020s progress. Aggregated data sets based on ever more intimate and sensitive information continue to be automatically processed by algorithms that discover and extract patterns that can be used to predict behaviors. Yet this is clearly not an exact science. The data broker industry is based on personal data that is inferred from other data points or created through probability analytics, meaning much of it is erroneous. It is for this reason that Jathan Sadowski (2020) suggests the data economy is perhaps better described as data manufacturing rather than collection or extraction. In chapter 3, we investigate how different academic fields and disciplines have theorized the problems associated with personal data and what they believe should be done about it.

Digital Data: Challenging Some Basic Assumptions

So far, the issues that have begun to emerge throughout this chapter highlight the need to be circumspect when it comes to making sense of data. While it is easy to get carried away with the scope and scale of digital data now being generated through digital technology use, alongside innovations in automated reasoning, deep learning, and the data economy, it is useful to consider the limitations, caveats, and questions that accompany the "data turn." Digital data is undoubtedly a defining aspect of contemporary society, but it is by no means unproblematic. Before we move on to the next chapter, we can first highlight and return to a few basic lines of questioning that have already emerged in the opening chapters of this book.

There Is No Such Thing as "Raw" Data

Jathan Sadowski's (2020) assertion that we need to see digital data as manufactured provides a sharp counterpoint to the ways that data is usually talked about. We began this chapter by noting that it remains popular to think of data existing in an original unprocessed state—something that can be taken and used. In this sense, data is often talked about as some sort of naturally occurring resource that can be processed. The idea of data as "the new oil" certainly compounds this idea, as does talk of data collection, gathering, mining, extraction, and so on. Instead, it is much more accurate to talk about data being generated or manufactured—either through the direct actions of humans or by computational processes that at some point originate from the action of humans. Either way, data is always the product of human action.

In this sense, it can also be helpful to make the distinction that data is always "cooked" from its inception, rather than ever existing in a precooked "raw" state. This viewpoint reflects what can be termed an "epistemic" perspective on data, rather than a "computational" perspective, and is especially important when talking about data that relates to people and social issues. Seen in this light, any data point results from someone making a choice about what needs to be measured and how it should be measured. By making such choices, they are also inadvertently deciding what does *not* get measured. While the idea of raw data can be useful, as statistical scientist Nick Barrowman (2018, 131) explains, it can be misleading. Instead, every stage of identifying something as data and then working to collate it involves intentions, assumptions, and values that can become a kind of preprocessing.

Data Will Usually Contain Gaps and Omissions

While the hype over big data tends to celebrate the inherent advantages of data quantity, far less attention is usually given to issues of data quality. Most data sets will have gaps and omissions. A temperature sensor might cut out for a very short period of time, a video camera might flicker, or a customer might leave a field blank. Many data sets will also contain inadvertent errors or deliberate misreporting. A temperature sensor might report high numbers because it is located in a parking lot, a video camera might not pick up the presence of an object, or a customer might deliberately enter a bogus ZIP code or a false age. As such, the quality of any data set will rarely ever be perfect, and its coverage will rarely ever be comprehensive. While data scientists strive for the highest ratio of signal to noise possible, it is acknowledged that data will always contain glitches and gaps (see Pink et al. 2018).

In a basic sense, the components of data quality are completeness, consistency, timeliness, and accuracy. Data scientists pay great attention to the ratio of complete versus incomplete records to gauge the viability of the data. More technically, the idea of data consistency refers to the extent to which all the data records conform to the same format and structure. Within a data set, even a slight variation of one character can render a data record incompatible and unusable (e.g., entering a date as 01/02/23 as opposed to 01/02/2023). The timeliness of data generation is also a key sticking point—in terms of both data currency (how long since the data was last generated) and data volatility (how frequently the data point is updated). Regardless of how "accurate" we might consider a piece of data to be, if it was generated a long time ago, then there are obvious limitations.

All of these aspects of data processing might seem deeply uninteresting and unexciting, yet provide the bulk of work for data analysts, data scientists, and others who work with data. Indeed, the main task in any data analysis is usually what is termed "data cleansing"—methodically checking data sets for errors, gaps, and inconsistencies and then making amendments and adjustments that allow the data to be used. This involves making choices over what data to correct (and how it might be corrected) and what data to discard or ignore. Often, data errors can be countered by applying other statistical techniques—such as weighting particular data points to give them more credence or glossing over occasional instances of measurement error by combining multiple measurements and using averages. Often, data analysts will opt to automate these acts of cleansing through data-wrangling tools or computer scripts that can standardize or correct large volumes of data. Nevertheless, as with the initial process of generating data, any subsequent act of data cleansing is highly subjective, creative, and contextually constrained—another instance of how data is cooked.

Data Is Rarely Fully "Representative"
Finally, as was argued in chapter 1, any claims about the capacity of data to enhance understandings, insights, and knowledge need to be tempered by the realities of data science and the data sets that are being worked with. This therefore raises fundamental questions of the extent to which any piece of data can fully capture what it purports to represent. As mentioned earlier, data scientists will often consider these issues in terms of data accuracy or validity—that is, the extent to which a data point or measurement corresponds with the real-life entity that it represents. Again, this is a reasonable approach for things where direct measurements are available (such as someone's height or weight). However, this is less clear-cut for things that do not have a comparative measure (such as someone's happiness or their determination to go to college). Sometimes this is recognized in talk of data credibility, transferability, or trustworthiness—terms that acknowledge the approximation of what is

being represented. As such, the idea of data as a representation should not be conflated with the idea that data is *fully* representative.

This leads to the argument that anything that data and data-driven systems can claim to "know" about many social entities and issues is inevitably going to be reductive of the actual issues. In part, this relates to the question of whether social data is inaccurate, incomplete, poorly chosen, or simply a weak indicator of what it supposedly represents. These gaps and omissions are especially important in terms of modeling the social world and what humans do within it. For example, even the most basic aspects of someone's "happiness" are highly complex. Conversely, even the most complex models of something that appears to be reasonably quantifiable (such as household expenditure) contain significant gray areas. In particular, the core claims of data analytics to precision, clarity, and predictability feel at odds with the many areas of everyday life that rely on dealing with constant ambiguities and uncertainties.

We might therefore conclude that many elements of everyday life and wider society cannot be fully captured and expressed through data processing—even if technically sophisticated approximations are possible. Of course, as mentioned earlier, the field of data science relies on the use of proxy indicators. Nevertheless, many laypeople tend not to treat the data they are presented with as "proxies" or even "indicators." Instead, it is often presumed any data is a direct measure—especially when presented conclusively in the form of simple and striking visualizations. These concerns stretch well beyond conventional notions of data validity and instead challenge the appropriateness of using data to model societal processes and social practices.

Most Aspects of Society Cannot Be Directly Measured

Related to these latter concerns is the fact most of the social facts, characteristics, and issues that everyday data relate are often unquantifiable. Very few things in our societies have a direct measurement (such as using centimeters to measure height). Instead, most of the social issues that have featured so far in this book can only be represented in some sort of abstraction. For example, we have talked about data points that measure a person's determination to go to college, their creditworthiness, or their performance at work. All of these are highly complex and contingent qualities, characteristics, and dispositions that are entwined with people's circumstances, local contexts, and current mental states. These data points are impossible to verbalize, let alone capture in a neat label or number. As such, these sorts of data are extensively cooked—relying on abstractions, representations, and what data scientists refer to as proxy measures (a concept we shall return to throughout this book). Proxies are measurements that can stand in for things that cannot be measured—for example, using unemployment rates as a proxy for the overall state of the economy or the newspaper that someone regularly purchases as a proxy for their social class.

All of this means that most forms of data relating to people and their everyday lives are socially constructed—more specifically, derived from guesswork, approximation, and improvisation on the part of data scientists, analysts, and programmers. In this sense, data science can be seen as much of a creative art as an objective science. This is particularly the case when it comes to working with imprecise and messy sets of social data. For example, think of the diverse ways that someone's social class might be gauged. On a day-to-day basis, we might be happy to make rough distinctions between someone being middle class and working class. Market researchers might like to talk of ABs, C1s, C2s, Ds, and Es. Sociologists might make more nuanced distinctions between submerged middle class and working poor. An extensive UK study during the 2010s found that when given a free choice, the general public came up with seven distinct new categories of social class, including New Affluent Workers, Emergent Service Workers, and the Precariat. While most people might consider that social class is an important data point to include in any model or calculation, there is clearly no correct way to do this. Moreover, these measurements from a class-ridden ex-colonizing country such as the United Kingdom would make little sense when applied to other countries and contexts where the notion of social class is notably different. As social statisticians will tell you, many things are simply not comparable or even worth trying to quantify.

Data Is Not Neutral

All of these latter points therefore cast doubt on the argument that data is somehow neutral. Instead, it seems more accurate to contend that any piece of data results from a series of choices—some implicit and some acknowledged. The personal data that these opening two chapters have paid particular attention to might sometimes result from choices that people make themselves but more often also from choices that have been made for them (often by remote entities that they have little or no awareness of). Even if a data scientist considers themselves to be completely objective or working in nonpolitical ways, they are making a subjective (and political) choice. As Barrowman (2018, 132) puts it, the objectivity of data is in the eye of the beholder—"when people use the term 'raw data' they usually mean that *for their purposes* the data provides a starting point for drawing conclusions."

This idea of data processing as an inherently subjective process holds true for even the most tightly controlled use of data by scientists. While we might like to imagine a detached scientific rationality that is free from subjective decisions, the data that scientists see as important to use (alongside all the other data they *do not* use) results from presupposed theories or the hypotheses they are trying to test. In this sense, it is important to pay attention to *who* is making these choices (and therefore who is doing the "cooking"), even if this is a far distant system programmer or product designer who decided many years previously that height should be measured in centimeters rather than millimeters or that the log-in page should ask users if they are MALE/FEMALE rather than a spectrum of self-identified genders or even not asking the question at all. What are the values, assumptions, blind spots, desires, and agendas that these people hold? What were they anticipating would be done with this data, and how did that shape their decisions?

As noted earlier, it is also important to consider the context of any data point—the conditions under which it was generated, the way in which it was cleaned, processed, and presented for use. Just like people, any piece of data has an extensive back story or biography that can help gain a sense of its character and capabilities. The context of data is an integral part of making sense of it—why it was collected, how it was collected, and how it was processed? To reiterate a point made throughout this chapter, there is no such thing as raw or context-free data, which also means that data cannot attain perfect objectivity in the way that is sometimes imagined (Barrowman 2018).

Conclusions

This chapter set out to define and describe what data is. However, even this initial step in developing critical data literacies highlights that data is not a clear-cut concept. That said, this chapter has also explored obvious tensions, limitations, and gaps between the rhetoric of the data gaze and the reality of inconsistent data points, incomplete data sets, and questionable choices.

This chapter has laid out some of the fundamental characteristics of digital data that we can take forward into the remainder of this book. For example, we have highlighted the fact that even the most complex applications of algorithms and artificial intelligence are nothing more than very complicated mathematics, rather than any sort of magical autonomous process. We also discussed how the rise of digital data has made data increasingly personal (i.e., directly related to our individual lives) *and* also highly impersonal and used for broad-brush profit-making by marketers and other companies. Perhaps one of the key points arising from this chapter is that there is no such thing as raw data. Instead, data is generated in ways that are predetermined and highly contextualized. Moreover, we need to pay attention to who gets to "do" data—who makes the choices over what is measured and what is not. Ideally, we want to ensure that all these processes are conducted in open, transparent, and appropriate ways. As informatician Geoffrey Bowker (2005, 183) puts it, "Raw data is both an oxymoron and a bad idea; to the contrary, data should be cooked with care."

Looking back to what we described in chapter 1 as developing a critical mind-set on these matters, there are many other issues arising from the questions and arguments arising from this chapter. These questions, concerns, and criticisms are a key element of critical data literacies and therefore demand our further attention. Already, readers might be thinking along similar lines. For example, the idea of personal data raises immediate thoughts of people's rights to some sort of privacy. Similarly, the idea of big corporations profiting from the data that is produced from people's technology uses raises questions over the possible regulation of these firms and what oversight and governance might provide an effective check to their power. The idea of technologies being programmed to make decisions based on inevitably incomplete data sets raises issues of possible errors and biases—and how this might make data-driven processes unfair, if not discriminatory, to people who might not be well represented (or might even be blatantly misrepresented) in data sets.

In the next chapter, we therefore look more closely at how to make critical sense of what it means to be living with datafication. This chapter draws on everyday uses of data to explore the different aspects of datafication and highlight the main theoretical advances from across the social sciences that have emerged to make sense of such shifts. From data-driven customization and intelligent assistants to geolocational sensors and the internet of things, the chapter details the processes of datafication and highlights the creep of data into all spheres of life. We introduce some theories and concepts that will then help us establish a critical approach to data. By exploring the movements of data justice, data feminism, and sociomateriality studies, we survey the array of critical approaches toward data and therefore establish a strong basis from which to build critical data literacies. There are lots of different ways to begin to think critically about the issues raised so far in this book—we now go onto consider some of the most important (and interesting) approaches.

3 Thinking Theoretically about Data

Introduction

Given all the issues and problems raised over the past two chapters, there is now understandable interest in thinking about digital data in more circumspect, critically aware terms. In particular, the past ten years or so has seen the steady growth of what has become known as critical data studies. This work reflects the recent growing sense among social scientists and others working in the humanities, law, politics, and arts that "something important is going on with data" (Couldry and Mejias 2019, 336). Such writing and thinking therefore provides an ideal backdrop to our own interest in critical data literacies.

In this chapter, we introduce some of the core themes, concepts, and approaches that have emerged within this broader critical data studies turn. These approaches—developed by writers working in areas ranging from infrastructure studies to data feminism—all offer specific takes on what data is and point to different issues of concern (and possible change) that need to be taken on board. In this chapter, we identify different connections between these approaches and the literacy tradition that we can take forward into developing the fundamental components of our own critical data literacies framework. At the same time, it is also important to think about what gaps there might be in this existing work (and what a literacies approach might add), as well as how literacies can be used to operationalize or put some of these ideas into action across society. While we have a lot of work to do, there is *already* a lot of work that can be drawn upon.

The Recent Rise of Critical Data Studies

As with lots of discussions about digital technology and society, critical data studies is a messy, eclectic endeavor—perhaps best described as a loose research theme rather than a tightly focused research field. In this spirit, geographer Craig Dalton and colleagues (2016, 1) suggest that critical data studies simply is "three words cobbled together, imperfectly signifying diverse sets of work around data's recursive relationship to society." That said, the idea of a distinct critical data studies certainly pushes us to look beyond the big data and "data as the new oil" hype outlined in chapters 1 and 2. As such, critical data studies usefully brings together disparate critical work from across the social sciences, humanities, legal and policy fields, arts, and design—all with a shared interest in speaking back to the hubris and technological determinism that tends to pervade popular understandings of digital data and instead focus on nuance and contingency (Dalton et al. 2016).

Several characteristics of critical data studies might fit particularly well with our own interest in critical data literacies. First is critical data studies' declared interest in *digital* data (i.e., data that is digitally generated and/or digitally circulated). This builds upon some of the core ideas developed in chapters 1 and 2. For instance, critical data studies pays close attention to the masses of data "traces" generated through everyday uses of personal devices, software, systems, and other technologies, alongside the data produced by technologies that are otherwise out of sight (such as sensors, digital video cameras, and other technological forms of monitoring). In addition, critical data studies pays close attention to data that might not have originated from digital technologies yet is quickly digitized and then processed, analyzed, circulated, and recombined in digital forms. Above all, critical data studies is primarily interested in the computational processes that lie behind the *digitization* of data and the outcomes arising from this digital data, rather than simply the creation of the data itself.

Another significant feature of critical data studies is recognizing that this digital data is primarily what Dalton and colleagues (2016, 2) term "human subjects data." In other words, this is digital data that is (in essence) *produced by* people and nearly always consists of information *relating to* people. This challenges the idea that digital data is naturally occurring and instead allows us to explore how data is artificially generated and manufactured. It also focuses attention on how this artificially generated data is used to infer things about people. Key here are the ways in which these data inferences can often become productive rather than representative (i.e., ways in which the data becomes constitutive of the events they purport to represent). For example, while the idea of genuinely "accurate" computer-based emotion monitoring based on facial expressions might well be highly contestable (see, e.g., Crawford 2021), the use of facial detection software to approximately detect emotions may well end up rationalizing the *measurement* of a particular emotion being present and then trigger subsequent actions accordingly. In this situation, it does not matter how a person is actually feeling, as everything is based on what the data reports the person as feeling.

A third important concept within critical data studies is the idea of the data assemblage. This is a heuristic that brings together all of the varied technological, social, political, and economic apparatuses and elements involved in the generation, circulation, and deployment of data (Iliadis and Russo 2016). Rob Kitchin and Tracey Lauriault (2018) point to a range of different technological, political, social, and economic apparatuses that underpin how any data assemblage functions. These can include the bringing together of various people, places, processes, and practices, as well as systems of thought, forms of knowledge, and underpinning materiality and infrastructures. Good examples of such data assemblages might include a social media platform such as Facebook, the online production of global university rankings, or a national police force's crime anticipation system. Each of these relies on key people, particular technologies, specific ideas and understandings, institutional policies, ways of processing data, and so on. Crucially, critical data studies pay close attention to the fact that any assemblage is constitutive of the data that it is concerned with producing. In other words, data and its assemblage are "bound together in a set of contingent, relational and contextual discursive and material practices and relations" (Kitchin and Lauriault 2018, 8).

Critical data studies encourage us to detail and document the constituent elements and apparatus of any data assemblage—paying close attention to the connections that form between these apparatuses, as well as the connections that form with broader data regimes. In many ways, the most interesting characteristics of these data assemblages is not their different elements per se but how these elements are held together (Macgilchrist 2021, 3). As such, critical data studies are never intended to be simply a process of describing different elements of a data assemblage—rather the main interest is on working out relations and connections between these different elements.

A fourth feature of the critical data studies approach involves extending these ideas of human subjects data and data assemblage into examining the ways in which digital data functions in contemporary society as a form of power. This leads critical data studies scholars to pay close attention to ways in which data is used to "permeate and exert power on all manner of forms of life" (Neff et al. 2017, 86)—not least the power structures that lie behind (and are advanced by) digital forms of data generation and processing. In this sense, critical data studies also encourages close attention to the influence of digital data on contemporary governmentality and social organization, as well as the ways in which data is used to make subjects. Also of significance are the ways in which the *absence* of datafication might form a source of power for some people in some circumstances (i.e., giving them the power not to be seen), while constituting a lack of power for others.

Ideas and Issues from Critical Data Studies

As this brief introduction has already highlighted, critical data studies foregrounds a range of important questions, concerns, and avenues for inquiry. Although covering a broad array of different approaches, critical data studies certainly offers a set of distinct epistemological and ontological positions from which to make sense of the role of digital data in contemporary society. So, in what ways might this tradition of thinking about digital data inform our own interests in critical data literacies? We now go on to present brief outlines of seven different sets of issues and concerns that emerge within the critical data studies paradigm. In particular, we consider how these different lines of thought might fit with the critical literacies tradition and therefore help refine our own conceptualization of critical data literacies.

Materiality and the "Stuff" of Data

First is the idea of paying close attention to material aspects of digital data. While we often talk about data as if it is abstract, ethereal, and without any physical substance, critical data studies reminds us that various tangible aspects of data need to be kept in mind. Of course, in a literal sense, the materiality of digital data is manifest in physical forms. For example, it is possible (at least, under particular laboratory conditions) to "see" pulses of light transmitted through a fiber-optic wire or magnetic atoms stored on a thin film of ferromagnetic material in a computer's hard drive. It is also possible to detect the modulation of electromagnetic waves through a "wireless" connection. Yet, the idea of seeing data in material terms stretches well beyond these physical and chemical properties. Data is manifest in a number of different material forms—all of which can help us think about data in diverse and revealing ways.

For example, critical data studies reminds us to pay close attention to data **infrastructures**—that is, the "backstage" mess of wires, routers, devices, code, and people that are integral to the production and circulation of digital data. These aspects of data are often hidden away behind locked doors, ceilings, and underground trenches, yet there is much that can be gained from analyzing these "submerged" elements of datafication. As such, there is growing interest among critical data scholars in what Geoffrey Bowker (1994) terms as "infrastructural inversion"—that is, focusing on the inner workings of data infrastructure, with a particular focus on the relational aspects of what people are doing around and through these components.

Points of interest here include the invisible labor that is required to keep digital data infrastructures working. This includes the routine maintenance work of technicians to instances of situational repair and problem solving when infrastructures break down, go wrong, or malfunction. Data infrastructures also include thinking about various incursions into our natural and built environments—from the deep-sea trenches that house international internet cables to the various boxes, masts, and wires that clutter our sidewalks and rooftops. Data infrastructures also include thinking about the integral role of software in supporting any aspect of data work, as well as how institutions and end users shape the nature of what this software is. As such, seeing data in infrastructural terms reminds us to pay close attention to the kinds of practices that are involved in software composition, including the associations, interactions, and performances between and among individuals, groups, organizations, and code (DiSalvo 2019).

Approaching data in infrastructural terms also prompts us to think about the ways that data is represented in new forms within different contexts of everyday life. This focuses our attention on the various ways in which digital data is now represented in the form of online data visualizations, dashboards, and other indicators. As designer Laura Forlano (2019) observes, these new online material forms "are clickable, taggable, searchable, and indexable; as such, they have new associations with one another as well as with networks." At the same time, there are also all manner of physical materializations of data—from printouts and reports to noticeboards and display screens. All these different forms draw attention to the ways in which data is "performed" in a number of unremarkable (but highly revealing) ways. These are all aspects of everyday digital data that are worthy of our attention.

Alongside these different facets of data infrastructure are other ways in which digital data can be understood as a material object (Dourish and Mazmanian 2011; Dourish 2017). A key concept here is that data should be understood in sociomaterial terms. This emphasis on the sociomateriality of digital data therefore recognizes that every piece of digital data is a result of social organization as well as technical processes. Echoing the earlier idea of the data assemblage, any piece of data derives from networks of people, technologies, and physical objects, all of which are entangled in social practices, interactions, language, and other forms of representation. This prompts us to think about data in terms of entities and artifacts—that is, as something that results from the interactions among people, places, and technologies. For example, this way of thinking about data prompts us to consider the ways in which the materiality of data is evident in the social practices that give rise to data production and the subsequent ways that cultural values shape the forms that the data eventually takes (Bates et al. 2016). One example of this is the still frequent encoding of gender along strictly binary lines of M/F. In this case, a distinct set of sociocultural values around what gender is has been encoded into the materiality of the data that is subsequently generated. A binary understanding of gender is therefore reinforced in this process of data generation.

It is also useful to think of the material consequences of digital data. This includes the ways in which the spatial arrangements of buildings are altered and adjusted to accommodate the physical aspects of data infrastructure. This also includes thinking through how digital data is associated with practical consequences and instantiations. For example, the scheduling of meetings in a "smart" office building might be guided by analysis of the previous year's room occupancy data, while an automated window blind will be opened and closed by changes in meteorological data. Thinking about digital data in all these terms is a useful way of making sense of how data is "done" in everyday settings and with what outcomes. In particular, thinking about the materialities of data prompts us to consider how digital data is entwined with the (re)configuration of power relations. As Tara Fenwick (2010, 104) reasons, investigating sociomaterialities can reveal important insights into how subjectivities are created through work by focusing on the circulation and sedimentation of knowledge as well as how power configures and reconfigures practices.

In all these ways, then, seeing data in terms of sociomateriality and infrastructure offers lots of different ideas and angles through which to critically think about digital data from a literacies perspective. First, what is data and how is it apprehended by people in their everyday lives? Taking cues from infrastructure studies and sociomateriality theory means seeing beyond the visualizations of data on dashboards, bar charts, and metrics and thinking about how data manifests in the physical environment through routers, cables, and hardware. Another consideration is how visualizations of data encourage and instigate particular practices, values, and beliefs with implications that are experienced or felt by many. Digital data is unlike other kinds of texts encountered in literacies. Typically, data is represented on platforms, apps, dashboards, and dials through graphs and visualizations, but these are far removed from the actual *physical* phenomena of data (e.g., as magnetic atoms on a material film). The goal of critical data literacies is to consider and interpret data not only as an analytic phenomenon through visualizations and representations but also as an emergent infrastructure with social and physical implications for society.

The Idea of Things Being Made into Data

A second tradition of documentation studies is also prevalent within critical data studies—focusing on the ways in which individual phenomenon are "made into" data and are then considered representative of that individual phenomenon (Buckland 2015). This expands on the ideas of data profiling and "profile-able" data outlined in chapter 2 and raises a number of broad questions over how such data representations are constructed. For example, what specific sources and selections of data are being used? In whose interests do these data analyses serve? What heuristics are used to justify the actions that the data analytics inform? Do different people share a common or diverse sense of how this data is useful?

This idea of data being made also prompts us to ask where particular forms of data originate from and whether they are part of a broader corpus. Also significant is how the data was created—for example, what data-cleansing processes and subsequent calculations were involved? Were these processes purposely planned, or was the data manipulated in an ad hoc manner? Perhaps most interesting are the questions that can be asked about the human and nonhuman actors involved in these processes. For example, who is directly and indirectly involved in generating data (and are they also involved in using the data)? It is also important to ask questions about the nonhuman actors involved in these processes. For example, what is the role of algorithms and artificial intelligence models in shaping and refining the data's characteristics?

Similarly, the idea of people being considered as these data also raises a number of important (but not always obvious) questions. For example, how are data relating to people used to provide evidence about who a particular person is? How is it possible to verify the veracity of this evidence? What ends do these data profiles serve, and what value does this data have in terms of social, cultural, or political outcomes? Perhaps most significant are questions of morals and ethics—are these uses of data morally justifiable? Can the data be ethically accessed and used? How does the existence of this data create harms?

Seeing data along these lines therefore raises various critical concerns over the growing use of digital data across different aspects of society. These can also feed into our emerging sense of critical data literacies in a number of ways. First is the notion of data fallibility—particularly how administration and bureaucratic interests shape the processes of making individuals into data and "effectively reduc[e] them into fragmentary representations" (Jones and McCoy 2019, 52). Second, are concerns over digital data-led apophenia—that is, the identification of patterns that do not actually exist. This relates to the broader concern over data being analyzed without the involvement of individuals for whom the data represents or relates to. Third are critical concerns over the construction and use of data doubles. Questions raised here include how we know what data is actually included in the makeup of any profile or representation (i.e., its provenance), whether policies exist to specify what data should be included in official records or profiles, and who or what can access these records and for what purposes.

As such questions suggest, the documentation studies approach aligns with a number of broad concerns that have long been addressed within literacy studies. For example, questions of who is creating data and how it is being used align neatly with critical literacy questions around author (i.e., who is creating a text) and audience (i.e., who a text is being created for). Typical literacy investigations into textual production pay close attention to how a text is created. Indeed, following a critical literacy approach, understanding how a text has come into existence is a key part of the reading process. As literacy scholar Ernest Morrell (2003, 6) reminds us, reading is not simply decoding messages that fit with hegemonic curricula and dominant media narratives but rather asking critical questions of how the text is created and who stands to benefit from its production.

It makes sense, then, that critical data literacies also involve disentangling the various social and political dimensions that lead to not only the creation of particular data texts but also assumptions around how these should be interpreted and understood by everyday individuals. As we shall see throughout this book, exploring these aspects of digital data is no easy task—not least because of the opaque nature of data processing. Nevertheless, these are issues that deserve our attention, if only to highlight what elements of the data assemblage are *not* known, cannot be found out, and/or being deliberately kept hidden.

Data and New Forms of Social Order

A third set of useful concepts relates to thinking about how data plays a part in reconfiguring the overall order of social life. This raises questions about the politics of datafication and the forms of power that are enacted through data assemblages. Media and communications theorist Nick Couldry (2020) describes this in three interlinked ways. First is how datafication might alter established (predatafied) ways in which what counts as social knowledge and who/what counts as an input to social knowledge. Here, we might consider the example of traditional understandings of poverty as a socially caused phenomenon that is best addressed by giving the poor more favorable terms. In an era of big data, however, this knowledge is likely to be reconstituted along data-driven lines. For example, the category of being poor might start to be calculated and determined in terms of a person's previous credit-related behavior, rather than their actual material circumstances. This may lead banks and companies to deny a person services because their credit profile is designated poor and poses a commercial risk. Whether one is considered poor or not, then, becomes a matter of data profiling rather than actual material circumstances.

Second are how these shifts in the inputs of social knowledge might begin to change how we make sense of society as a whole. While automated and algorithmic knowledge is unlikely to replace existing social knowledge altogether, these new datafied models of social knowledge are already beginning to marginalize older forms of expertise and judgment in important ways. In this sense, popular and political conceptions of what constitutes society might begin to follow these data-driven forms of social knowledge. Following on from this is a third set of questions about how these new forms of social knowledge begin to constitute practical understandings of what is socially actionable. We should, therefore, pay close attention to how people come to accept the logic that new forms of social knowledge are grounded in data-driven and machine interpretations of the world ("what the computer says"), rather than human interpretations. This can already be seen in the growing belief in IT industry claims that machines are able to "know" more about humans than humans know about themselves. While human expertise and judgment will not be done away with altogether, these forms of knowledge may no longer be the primary driver of how things are done.

All told, these questions of how digital data is altering what is known about societies and peoples is another issue that we can add to our efforts in thinking about critical data literacies. For example, how can we anticipate ways in which data becomes an organizing principle across different aspects of society? How can we make sense of the ways in which corporate and government actors contrive to build different types of social order through datafication? What are the values and moral dynamics of the data-driven processes that lie behind these reorganizations? All these questions encourage us to think about "processes of social formation themselves on the largest scale" (Couldry 2020, 1146). This certainly moves us away from an instrumental approach to understanding data that focuses solely on using data and living within datafied systems, rather than questioning the construction of this data. Again, clear links can be made with the critical literacy tradition—not least the emphasis placed on examining how practices and objects come to have value and how they shape the way see ourselves and others. In this sense, critical data literacies need to take into account the way in which social phenomena are both constructed and represented through data, as well as challenge the dominating logics associated with big data.

Data as a Form of Capital

A fourth set of ideas to consider relates to the changing political economy of digital data. Key here is making sense of data as a form of capital—in particular, the idea of data being taken from people and machines by third parties.

This approach therefore builds on the notion of digital data being created through an ongoing process of "dispossession" (Dalton, Taylor, and Thatcher 2016). This is not dispossession in the sense of people being suddenly deprived of something that they previously possessed and subsequently are not able to access. When personal data from a social media post is extracted by third parties, the original social media post does not disappear. Instead of data being taken away from individuals, it is perhaps more accurate to talk of data being transferred. In other words, digital data is a form of property that can be appropriated in multiple, replicable forms (Gray 2021).

These distinctions raise the point that digital data is not a commodity per se. Instead, data is more usefully seen as an asset—that is, something that has zero marginal costs, is nonrivalrous in consumption, and is not profitable in its raw form *but* highly profitable when aggregated at scale and analyzed (Komljenovic 2021). This has prompted some commentators to talk of a "rentier" form of data economy—where the value of online platforms and digital devices derives from the data that they generate. An individual does not "own" the devices, software, and platforms that they use and certainly does not benefit from the value of the data that is extracted from these sources of data generation. Instead, value can only be extracted from large amounts of data that can be aggregated and analyzed at scale. Seen in these ways, then, data can be understood as a specific form of capital—as Jathan Sadowski (2019, 1) puts it, "Data [is] a core component of political economy in the 21st century."

These are various approaches to thinking how this data capitalism might develop over the next few decades—from Shoshana Zuboff's (2019) description of surveillance capitalism to more dystopian and oppressive visions. One useful recent line of thinking—especially in terms of expanding our terms of reference beyond the (over)industrialized Global North—is the idea of data colonialism (Ricaurte 2019; Daly, Devitt, and Mann 2019; Couldry and Mejias 2019). In one sense, the parallels between territorial colonialism and data colonialism are obvious. The political economy of data can be said to involve predatory extractive practices, the violent imposition of a particular worldview, the exploitation of human beings as raw material, and relentless expansionism in terms of geographical space *and* the social lives of human subjects. Yet, the idea of data colonialism is also meant to signal a step-change in terms of a new social order and new forms of capitalism—reconfiguring the exploitation of people through *labor* relations into the appropriation and exploitation of their *social* relations. In other words, data capitalism involves the extraction of value from many aspects of social life and society that were not previously subject to being appropriated and exploited by capitalism. Couldry and Mejias (2019) refer to this as data relations—new types of human relations that enable the extraction of data for commodification. This idea of data relations therefore draws our attention to the ways in which people are conditioned to accept (if not expect) data-based tracking as a permanent and totalizing feature of everyday life.

So, what can critical data literacies take from this stand of thinking? How can we take into account the different affective, political, and relational dimensions involved in datafication? The short answer is that while it will likely be always impossible to grasp the full extent of such complex systems, we should nevertheless not let this lead to apathy, powerlessness, and exploitation. Indeed, critical literacies have a long history of being used to address issues relating to living in capitalist societies. For example, culture jamming has been used in education for decades to draw attention to the power of media and its influence on our values and views toward consumerism. Culture jamming involves providing people with popular images, typically advertisements, and analyzing and modifying them to create meaningful critiques of capitalist society. In this spirit, one way forward might be found in the critical literacies tradition of starting with personal experiences and engagements with data capitalism and using this as a way into the broader issues involved in data extraction. In doing so, people are encouraged to trace datafication from themselves back to the systems and processes involved so that personal experiences and histories act as a kind of guide in examining the politics and power of data. There may well be some discomfort involved in confronting these systems. However, a key part of critical literacies thinking is that discomfort can be a powerful pedagogical tool in motivating change.

Data-Driven Forms of (In)Justice

A fifth set of ideas from critical data studies relates to the challenge of making the use of digital data more equitable, empowering, and fair. This is an increasingly popular focus, with critical data scholars keen to extend their academic interest in issues of power, disadvantage, and oppression to develop practical ideas such as data justice and data feminism. Such approaches make a deliberate attempt to move beyond seeing data as an individual problem and responsibility. Instead, data is framed as a collective concern that is enmeshed with broader patterns of injustice and structural inequalities.

These approaches focus attention on the connections between data and broader structural issues of societal inequality, discrimination, and oppression. First is the idea that social justice issues around digital data are not purely technical and/or organizational problems with likely technical and/or organizational solutions. Instead, digital data needs to be seen as entwined with longstanding social problems such as discrimination, social immobility, and the social reproduction of inequality (Dencik et al. 2022). Given that these issues are social, cultural, political, and economic in their origins, any responses to address them also need to be social, cultural, political, and economic in nature. Second is the idea that data-driven social justice issues are not an individual concern that arise from an individual's personal choices or individual biases. Neither are individuals ultimately responsible for dealing with these problems. Instead, the idea of data justice reminds us that these issues are primarily structural in nature and form. As such, any moves toward data justice require collective responses that involve a wide range of peoples, groups, and interests who can work together to articulate the challenges that datafication poses to them and also what local responses might be appropriate.

Third, framing datafication in terms of (in)justice prompts us to consider broader political responses and direct actions. For example, viewing data issues solely in terms of "rights" can often result in responses relating to improving individuals' consumer rights (e.g., clearer and fairer terms of service), recommendations for direct consumer action (e.g., individuals deleting their Twitter or Facebook accounts), or pushes for stronger regulatory and legal protections. In contrast, the notion of data justice prompts us to think about what might be achieved through direct collective actions. Issues of data justice are not likely to be solved by the market or by better regulation. Instead, these are issues that might well require protest, confrontation, disobedience, and disruption.

One notable strand of thinking is what has become termed "data feminism." As Catherine D'Ignazio and Lauren Klein (2020) explain, many of the social issues of our time are about power—who has it, how it is wielded, and upon whom. Through this lens, feminism is not about women or even gender but rather about the different dynamics of power. Data feminism takes a lead from Black feminist notions of intersectionality—foregrounding the idea that gender interlocks with other systems of oppression (such as race and class), prompting different people to experience different forms of benefit/harm from data regimes depending on their background and circumstances. Data feminism can help us to rethink ways in which this power can be both challenged and changed. For example, a middle-class, white, disabled woman is likely to have very different interactions with data-driven systems than a Black, working-class, abled-bodied man. As such, data feminism moves conversations away from somehow "getting rid of" data injustices and instead working to rebalance them. The data feminist approach raises a number of pertinent issues and ideas that can be used to inform our notion of critical data literacies. These include disrupting the use of data to produce essentializing categories (such as false binaries and hierarchies) and instead embracing data as a means of highlighting pluralism and foregrounding conflicting viewpoints and multiple perspectives.

All of these goals of data justice and data feminism resonate with earlier critical approaches to literary theory—especially the idea of identifying what is *not* being said and examining the gaps and silences in texts. Gaps can be thought of as instances where ideas and concepts are not explicitly connected in a text but rely upon commonsense assumptions and logics to make the connection. In this way, readers unconsciously reproduce these ideas when making meaning of a text, which, in turn, naturalizes these discourses and ideologies. Similarly, the idea of silences refers to the social and cultural values that are *implied* within the gaps of a text. For example, particular minority groups are spoken on behalf of, so their experiences, practices, and values are assumed. These gaps and silences are therefore key questions to ask when interpreting digital data, especially in terms of developing critical understandings of how proxies and correlations in data sets lead data scientists to conclusions. With this in mind, a useful starting point for critical data literacies may be alerting people to the fact that these conclusions are in a sense foretold by the construction and organization of the data (or text), rather than the actual phenomena that it purports to represent.

Data as a Site of Resistance

A sixth approach to thinking critically about digital data also takes the ideas of digital justice in a radically confrontational and resistant direction. This includes ideas arising from queer data, Black data, and crip technoscience

(McGlotten 2016; Hamraie and Fritsch 2019)—all of which strive to develop radically minded approaches toward countering harms that arise from dominant data regimes. Many scholars working in these areas make deliberate use of the term "minoritized" to describe the groups most disadvantaged and oppressed by dominant uses of data that have historically privileged white, European, male interests. One starting point for these approaches is acknowledging the double bind of how digital data renders minoritized groups hypervisible within oppressive systems of surveillance and control, while at the same time other data-driven systems that might be of benefit often struggle to "fit" minoritized people. If digital data serves to both misrecognize and oppress minoritized groups, then digital data is something to be wholly rejected and resisted.

This spirit of rejection and resistance runs strongly throughout ideas of queer data (Guyan 2022). In one sense, the prospect of queer data raises a blunt challenge to the legitimacy of data science. How can data science ever fully represent identities, experiences, and political positions related to gender and sexuality that defiantly resist dominant societal norms? More important, queer data also raises questions of intent and effect. In other words, even if it were possible, queer history shows how attempts at quantification constitute acts of control, regulation, and marginalization of the identities and desires of queer people (Gieseking 2018). These acts of data misidentification and misrepresentation can often result in what Dean Spade (2011) terms administrative violence on the part of social institutions, software companies, and other authorities. At the same time, the process of being misidentified can also result in personal harms. For example, Sasha Costanza-Chock (2020) describes the data-driven "dysaffordance" where a system forces individuals to misidentify themselves in order to continue the interaction. In queer terms, then, digital data is not something that is to be trusted or welcomed.

Similar ideas run throughout discussions of "Black data" (McGlotten 2016). This critical scholarship is focused explicitly on the inherently racialized dimensions of data culture, economics, and politics—in particular, challenging the ways in which "whiteness" is continually affirmed as normative across the most dominant features of datafication (Chun 2021). As with the idea of queer data, discussions around Black data also start from the premise that any attempt to datafy people along lines of race is deeply problematic for a number of reasons—not least the fact that race is not a hard-and-fast variable relating to biological traits but a socially constructed notion. In this sense, Black data scholars remind us that digital racial profiling directly links back to historical forms of racialized profiling—long discredited and seen as discriminatory.

Key themes within the Black data literature include how data-driven systems are used to misrepresent and segregate people along lines of race in ways that lead to outcomes that discriminate and oppress. Indeed, the racialized nature of computational processes and algorithmically determined encounters is a growing area of concern within critical data studies. Critical scholars have long noted racial differences in terms of algorithmic visibility (Introna and Nissenbaum 2000) and what Oscar Gandy (1993) terms the "panoptic sort" of online data. Here it is argued that data-based practices designed to classify, sort, and evaluate populations inevitably reproduce existing racial inequalities, while then going on to generate new modes of racial discrimination through the cumulative recirculation and recombination of already racialized categories—what Gandy terms a "matrix of multiplication." In this vein, critical data scholars have begun to detail algorithmic racial exclusion on online dating sites (Albury et al. 2017), the biases inherent in the construction of facial recognition software (Stevens and Keyes 2021), and the racist misrecognitions that are naturalized into the coding processes informing Google's search engine algorithms (Noble 2018). All these studies confirm the suspicion that computer-generated models and calculations are compromised by "hidden assumptions that frequently encode racist perspectives beneath the façade of supposed quantitative objectivity" (Gillborn et al. 2018, 158).

This fundamental incompatibility between the prevalence of digital data and the everyday experiences of Black, queer, crip, and other minoritized groups therefore leads to the provocative move of rejecting conventional assumptions around digital data and data science. Instead, a focus is placed on exploring ways of challenging and resisting expectations and norms that currently surround data and datafication—particularly in terms of challenging how digital data is entangled with power relations and the politics of oppression (Jakobsen 1998). Key here is the understanding that none of these dominant conditions of data use can be easily altered for the better. Instead, these ideas foreground the idea of radical rejection and resistance toward dominant data practices and products. This is reflected in the growing academic (and activist) interest in vernacular resistance to data collection and analysis (see Siles 2023). Here, the act of actively disrupting the generation and processing of data is legitimized and encouraged as a powerful means of increasing minoritized groups' agency and autonomy, as well as reducing their visibility through what McGlotten (2016, 269) describes as "blackboxing ourselves to make ourselves illegible to the surveillance state and big data."

At the same time are attempts to reimagine data along more confrontational and adversarial lines. Writing from a critical race perspective, Crooks and Currie (2021) advance the idea of agonistic data. This involves using data to highlight difference, raising (rather than resolving) questions and stimulating grassroots political involvement and engagement with developing alternative forms of data. These ideas have clear precedents in critical literacy traditions that have long focused on providing those who have been silenced with the opportunity to speak. As Paulo Freire (1970/2006, 69) reasoned, "Those who have been denied their primordial right to speak their word must first reclaim this right and prevent the continuation of dehumanizing aggression." Taking this sentiment forward in terms of (re)claiming the language of data to raise awareness and mobilize action over longstanding issues of oppression and marginalization should be a primary goal of critical data literacies.

Data as a Source of Social Good

A final set of ideas from within the critical data studies literature explores the possibility of digital data as a form of social good. The idea of technology "for good" is a popular concept in current discourses around emerging technologies—in practice, the use of digital technologies to support humanitarian or environmental crises response to applications related to culture, the arts, and entertainment. Such efforts have been rightly criticized for falling into a vague "know it when you see it" approach to deciding what constitutes social good (Green 2021). That said, the notion of "good" data tends to be a little more specific, while remaining optimistic about possible better uses of data. These discussions are less interested in detailing the current data "harms" and are instead more concerned with positive alternatives and a hopeful vision of alternate forms of datafication. The focus here is on considering how digital technologies can be used in "good ways" for "good purposes." As sociolegal scholar Angela Daly and colleagues (2019, 9) suggest,

"If digitization and data are inevitabilities, then we have to (re)imagine the kind of digitized world and data we want to see rather than only offering a naysaying critique of the status quo."

One interesting line of thought centers on establishing alternate forms of democratic data processes and practices. This shifts attention away from seeing data generation and data governance along individualized lines and more in terms of population-based relations. As Salome Viljoen (2020) reasons, data about individuals only has value when aggregated on a mass scale with data about other people. As such, the social value and social harms that arise from digital data stem from the ways in which data puts people into population-based relations with one another. Seen along these lines, it seems important to rethink data in terms of supraindividual interests. For example, how can communities (and perhaps even whole societies) properly be involved in public, collective, and fundamentally democratic forms of governing data production and use?

A range of "good data" practices embody these principles. For example, the idea of data sovereignty offers one way of holding digital data accountable to the governance structures, cultural interests, and knowledge structures relating to the communities and cultures where it originates (and to which the data relates). In particular, this has sparked interest in issues of Indigenous data sovereignty and postcolonial forms of data—that is, alternate forms of data processes and practices that are rooted in Indigenous beliefs and value systems, epistemological approaches, and ontological assumptions. As Walter and Suina (2019) note, this requires fundamentally different types of data assemblages that produce data that is disaggregated and that disrupt deficit narratives, in order to advance Indigenous people's and First Nations' rebuilding agendas. These arrangements are rooted in access to this data being controlled by Indigenous representatives.

Another example of "good data" thinking is developing democratic forms of data stewardship and data-sharing approaches to creating value from data—shifting focus away from economic revenue to public good, social solidarity, and citizens' self-determination (Micheli et al. 2020; Williams 2022). These principles are evident in the growing trend of establishing data cooperatives by civic organizations—aggregating individuals' data in the form of data trusts, data-sharing pools, and other forms of data commons that can then be used for socially just purposes that are collectively decided upon. At a municipal level, public bodies can establish public data trusts—collating citizens' data to better inform policymaking and promote the idea of data as a public infrastructure.

Critical Data Concerns—The Socially Contested Nature of Datafication

All these various critical data concerns clearly raise interesting and challenging lines of thinking to take forward into the rest of this book. For example, these critical lenses remind us that data is primarily a matter of people and material things just as much as it is about mathematics and computational procedures. These critical lenses raise questions about representation, identity, and inclusion—what is lost when social issues are translated into data and what cannot be quantified at all. These critical lenses raise questions about ownership, oversight, and curation, moving on from questions of privacy to more complex concerns over dataveillance, ethics, and justice. In some cases, then, this foregrounds serious concerns over issues of exploitation and oppression—highlighting the further disadvantaging of minority groups and interests in an age of averages, sorting, and profiling.

Above all, these alternate approaches certainly offer useful counterpoints to the hype of big data, data as oil, and other takes on data that we have covered in the book so far. Running throughout all these specific issues and questions, then, is a fundamental concern over issues of how data-driven digital technologies, processes, and practices are implicit in the reshaping of our social world. As Arne Hintz and colleagues (2019, 6) put it, this foregrounds questions of "how the epistemological and ontological implications of data collection and data-driven processes may (re)constitute both knowledge and subjectivity." Indeed, these issues can be expanded through four guiding concerns common to the various critical data studies lenses just outlined:

- **How does data alter reality?** Digital data is now a key factor in setting the conditions, parameters, and expectations of everyday life. This raises the need to explore the ontological implications of digital data—in other words, the ways in which digital data now shapes how we know the world in which we live.

- **What are the values of data?** Data science and the computational mindset have long been argued to be distinct ways of understanding the world. In this sense, it is perhaps useful to approach the rise of the data-driven society as ideological in nature—conveying specific sets of values, logics, interests, and agendas. If so, what are these values? Does digital data inherently favor certain types of value and value systems? For example, how might dominant forms of datafication foreground the economic over the social and/or favoring the individualized rather than the intimate and genuinely personal?

- **What shifts in power are associated with data?** The capacity to "do" data is becoming a key source of power in society. As such, what individuals and institutions are becoming (more) empowered by their jurisdiction over digital data? At the same time, to what extent can we say that data and data-driven processes are becoming new powerbrokers in their own right? For example, while algorithms are authored and maintained by humans, they are increasingly left alone to make and adjudicate decisions. In this sense, to what extent can we talk about algorithmic power and algorithmic governance?

- **What are the social/political consequences of our data-driven society?** Underpinning all these concerns are basic questions around outcomes and impact—to put it bluntly, "So what?" For example, what lines of reasoning and argumentation is datafication reinforcing over others? To what extent does the datafication of society constitute a radically different state of affairs, as compared to merely extenuating established power relations and the status quo?

Above all, these four sets of questions reflect an overarching concern with data and power. In this sense, critical data studies pushes us to pay close attention to the structural barriers that impinge on individuals' capacity to benefit from digital data—barriers that can often be said to result from the corporate ownership of personal data and the generally disproportionate influence that Big Tech interests seem to currently hold over legislative and public debates around data use in society. As a result, perhaps the most useful points to take from all these different critical data approaches relate to questions of agency and empowerment—especially how unequal distributions of agency are between (1) individual users and (2) those who process the personal data of these individual users. As has been increasingly suggested over the past decade or so, a new power dynamic has clearly emerged between those individuals who provide personal data (data "have nots") and those large companies and states who own, trade, and control it (data "haves").

When developing our account of critical data literacies, then, we need to remain mindful of those who are able to do data and those who largely have data done to them. In contrast to claims of data being objective and neutral, the issues, concerns, and perspectives highlighted in this chapter suggest that data is certainly not fair or empowering for all.

Conclusions

As this chapter has shown, there are already numerous existing critical approaches to the increasing datafication of society. In this sense, we have much to draw on in developing our own take on critical data literacies. Indeed, there are many points of natural alignment between these critical data studies concerns and the critical literacy tradition, which also foregrounds questions of voice, agency, and dialogue as powerful strategies for enacting change. The arguments, writing, and research outlined in this chapter throw up a wide range of issues, ideas, warnings, and inspirations that we can take forward into the coming chapters. These are all different ways of making sense of the ways in which digital data has become intrinsic to the logics that drive contemporary society and the repercussions for everyday life. For example, what is the most productive way to conceptualize data in order to build people's knowledge and understanding of datafication processes? These approaches point to the ideological underpinnings of datafication—especially in terms of a new economic rationality. They also begin to make sense of the practical consequences of living in times when "objective" data-driven approaches to understanding the social world predominate. Some of these lines of thought also point to possibilities for alternate uses and resistant practices. They remind us that other forms of digital data are possible.

That said, many of these questions and concerns might be seen as remaining rather abstract, academic, complex, and/or speculative. For example, how does one begin to engage with the machinations of data capitalism or data colonialism, let alone actively seek alternatives to the ongoing extraction and exploitation of one's personal data? One important motivation in recasting these questions and concerns into the form of critical data literacies is therefore to provide a framework for their practical use. How can these concerns be made meaningful to broader publics *beyond* the niche of academic critics currently raising these points and the experts working in and around the data industries? While this chapter has made some speculative connections between critical data studies and critical literacies, in chapters 4 through 7, we begin to consider these issues in much more detail. So, having set up the imperative for critical data literacies, where do we take things from here? What might critical data literacies look like, and how does a literacies approach add to thinking critically about data and datafication? The next chapter lays out the critical data literacies framework.

4 Toward a New Approach: Critical Data Literacies

Introduction

The first three chapters have explored different aspects of datafication, including the challenges and opportunities presented by the growing prominence of data in the digital age and the various concepts and theories that are emerging in response. This chapter justifies the need for an explicit critical literacies approach to understanding digital data. The chapter begins by examining the main *practical* responses to data and datafication that have developed over the past few years. Some of these involve top-down regulation of Big Tech, while others involve bottom-up grass roots movements striving to help people keep personal data private. All of these responses rely on an awareness and understanding of data and datafication processes. For this reason, we make the argument that educational responses are key to empowering individuals to ask critical questions of data. Indeed, even the most comprehensive legal, technical, and tactical responses require some kind of education about data if they are to be effective.

While a range of educational responses to data already exist, we argue that most educational responses to data are instrumental in their approach. In other words, the usual goal of data education tends to be preparing individuals to learn, work, and contribute to the goals of a datafied society—rather than encouraging them to ask critical questions of data and datafication processes. In this sense, a more organized educational response is required to prepare people to ask the critical questions of data, such as how it is constituted and collected, who it benefits, and how these processes might be reimagined. This is what we are calling critical data literacies. With this in mind, the bulk of the chapter then focuses on sketching out the critical data literacies framework. This starts with an overview of the literacies paradigm and its tradition of learning to both read and write in a given mode. The literacies paradigm therefore provides a helpful way of sharpening our understandings of data and providing a helpful framework for scaffolding a critical disposition toward it by identifying and discussing the key components to developing knowledge and understanding. All of this is used in generating a framework of critical data literacies that can be used throughout the rest of our discussions.

Current Responses to Datafication—Regulatory and Technical Approaches

Any idea of critical data literacies joins a range of existing ways in which digital data is being addressed across various parts of society. Indeed, the past ten years or so has seen growing acknowledgment among policymakers, publics, and some professionals that datafication should not be allowed to continue unchecked. This realization has tended to come primarily from governments, civil society, and other actors not directly involved in the IT and data industries. A range of responses have emerged from different sectors and organizations around the world, which fall into three broad categories: (1) efforts to regulate data, (2) efforts to impose technical limits on data, and (3) efforts to increase public understandings of data. Our own interest in critical data literacies fits most closely with the third of these categories—education. As such, we will discuss existing educational responses in more depth. Before that, however, it also worth considering the other two forms of response— that is, regulation and technical responses to data and datafication.

Regulatory responses to datafication seek to use the law and other legal avenues to prevent unequal power relations that place the individual in a vulnerable position. This has seen the idea of human rights—particularly digital rights—invoked as a response to the issues raised by datafication. In simple terms, digital rights can be described as human and legal rights that allow individuals to access, use, create, and publish digital content on devices such as computers and mobile phones, as well as in virtual spaces and communities (Reventlow 2017). Currently, digital rights tend not to be seen as a distinct set of rights in and of themselves but are usually related to other human rights, such as freedom of expression and the right to privacy (Hutt 2015). In this sense, digital rights when it comes to data have often been expressed in terms of people's right to privacy, as too often the implications of using a particular platform or app are buried in the terms and conditions of use.

Recently, calls to protect the digital rights of the child have gained considerable support. This movement has prompted the 1989 UN Conventions on the Rights of the Child to be brought to bear on digital contexts. For example, it is now accepted that digital rights for children and adults should cover both participation and provision, as well as protection. One outcome from this campaigning and advocacy has been the introduction of the Children's Code in the United Kingdom. This code of practice for tech companies is the first of its kind and requires tech companies that provide online services (such as apps, games, connected toys, and devices and new services) to act in the best interests of the child. Also known as the Age Appropriate Design Code of Practice, the changes prohibit tech companies from using a number of design features that have become standard to online services. For example, the code prohibits "nudge" techniques that encourage the sharing of personal data, prevents geolocational tracking, minimizes automated data collection, and ensures that software and platforms offer children privacy options that default to maximum security. It also aims for greater transparency by providing privacy information to children in language that is easy to understand.

In addition, regulations such as the right to be forgotten and consumer protection offered by the General Data Protection Regulation (GDPR, introduced May 2018) and the Online Eraser Law for minors in California (introduced in 2016) allow individuals to take control of their own data. However, these interventions are not without their critics. For example, the GDPR has been criticized as a highly individualized response that fails to adequately recognize the difficulties of human decision-making in the digital domain. People must be well informed about data processing if they are to take control. However, the daily amount of information that people are required to take notice of across multiple platforms and devices is overwhelming. This makes it very difficult to achieve the informed consent that laws such as GDPR depend on (Van Ooijen and Vrabec 2019). Indeed, Renieris (2023) argues that laws focused on data protection and data privacy, data security, and data ownership have failed to protect core human values, including privacy.

Despite such concerns, many commentators see regulatory responses as a potentially powerful means to redress violations of personal data privacy, as well as some of the main data justice issues outlined in chapter 3. However, any notion of rights and regulation remain framed by principles of law that operate in regard to the individual, meaning it ultimately remains up to the individual to understand what their rights are and when they are being breached. Thus, in terms of many of the critical data studies arguments raised in chapter 3, regulatory responses do not align naturally with the collective, communal, and democratic principles that many consider essential to rectifying data-related injustice and harm and instead rely on official structures and procedures to support individual action.

While regulatory responses use legal means to address privacy issues and information asymmetries, various technical solutions are now also being offered to help people exert some control over their personal data. A range of products have emerged that are designed to increase the transparency of data processing, anonymize and encrypt personal information, and block data extraction by third parties. For example, Blacklight is a website privacy inspector that helps users better understand the implications of using popular digital platforms by enabling them to see who is tracking and watching them as they use the internet. Similarly, TrackMeNot is a browser extension that generates random search queries to create misinformation or noise that hides the users' *actual* browser history.

The development of such products has provoked reactions from some Big Tech companies and platform operators who are keen to retain their commercial access to personal data. For example, some platform and software providers have attempted to reassure users of their corporate responsibilities toward data privacy by installing private or safe browsing modes in their products or even adding dashboards that display what the platform "knows" about them through personal data. The aim is to alleviate user concerns through increased transparency of data collection. However, these commercial features could be seen as a rather strategic (if not cynical) response from tech companies. On the surface, these features may allay users' data privacy concerns, but their overarching goal is to keep them on the platform for as long as possible so they can continue to generate personal data.

Another technical response emanates from regulatory interventions that maintain that users "own" their data. Following this logic, software has been designed and developed to enable people to choose which companies and brands their personal data is sold to. Apps like People.io and CitizenMe provide people with a technical means of collecting all the personal data they have generated through their device and software use and then trading it in the data broker economy. In exchange, users are offered personal insight into their digital identities and interactions and remuneration for brokering their data with companies and brands of their choice. Such software is designed to liberate personal data by making the insights that can be gathered from such information available to individuals.

Current Responses to Datafication—Educational Responses

This book's focus on critical data literacies contributes to a different type of response—what can be described as educational responses to datafication. The legal and technical responses just described rely on individuals having awareness and understanding of data and datafication processes. Without an understanding of how data is being generated, processed, and used—and, most important, the problems and injustices that occur as a consequence—there is little motivation for someone to act, either legally or technically. In this sense, educational responses are fundamental to *all* responses to datafication. Educational responses strive to make datafication processes visible for everyone to develop understandings of—especially understandings of how they can take action to improve data-driven circumstances and outcomes. Educational responses should also bring together and organize the array of responses to data that already exist (including the legal and technical responses just outlined), while also providing people with the knowledge and awareness required to act.

Critical data literacies is by no means the first educational response to datafication, so it is important to consider the types of educational responses that already exist—from data science to protectionist methods of cybersafety. Each of these has particular audiences in mind. For example, data science tends to be directed toward professionals (such as journalists, civil society, and civic coders), while data safety stems from the cybersafety movement and is therefore typically directed at children and young people. A third educational approach involves the direct operationalization of critical data concerns put forward in chapter 3. These initiatives work with minoritized groups to intervene in the ways that data is used in (and on) their communities. What follows is a brief overview of each of these educational approaches. While they are each quite different in orientation and application, they are all concerned with increasing people's skills and raising data awareness and understanding. Each of these is therefore of direct relevance to how we might begin to imagine critical data literacies.

First are educational programs designed to support people in developing basic skills and competencies to work with and manipulate data. These efforts do not require people to reach the level of "proper" data science students or professionals. Rather, they aim to provide nonspecialists with basic awareness and what might be described as street-level data science. Many of these data education approaches center on reading, comprehending, and analyzing sets of open data that have been collected by governments and organizations for various purposes. Examples of such programs include Software Carpentry's *Data Carpentry* and the School of Data's *Data Expeditions*. In addition, some universities offer data science bootcamps as "tasters" for the more advanced data science degree courses. All these educational offerings are based around hands-on pedagogical approaches—ranging from basic skills of data interpretation to complex statistical data analysis and the principles of software development. While sometimes labeled data literacy, these data science approaches usually align more closely with numeracy than literacy—typically involving "statistics, or the systematic study of the organization, properties, and analysis of data and its role in inference" (Dhar 2013, 64).

Open data science approaches are often justified as developing skills to improve society and empower citizens. Despite the rhetoric of democratization promised through "open" data science, some critics argue that there are inherent contradictions in the notion of governments and other vested interests supporting meaningful forms of openness, open access, and open data (Halford, Pope, and Weal 2013; Langlois, Redden, and Elmer 2015). Indeed, even those *within* the discipline argue that data science can lead to new forms of power that can be used to police and surveil populations in discriminatory ways (D'Ignazio and Klein 2020). Other criticisms include the overly instrumentalist nature of many of these courses—lacking any meaningful engagement with the social consequences and politics of data use. This is not to undermine the importance of data science and its ability to empower people. Indeed, as we shall see in later chapters, there are promising signs that data science principles can be used to address some of the data justice issues mentioned in chapter 3 that use data for good.

Another educational approach is the more protectionist idea of data safety—based around giving people the skills to protect the dissemination of personal data (Office of the eSafety Commissioner 2020). This extends the idea of cybersafety—long popular in elementary and high school education—by focusing on the development of skills to manage and control the data trails and traces left behind when using digital media. This is often described in terms of someone's digital footprint (Roddel 2006). Data safety approaches focus primarily on personal data that people have voluntarily uploaded to devices and platforms, rather than examining the broader ecologies of data and the data broker economy. In this way, data safety approaches might focus on minimizing the personal details entered signing up for a digital platform, while typically overlooking the data that is generated and collected by tech companies through geolocational tracking.

This approach to data education is most often directed at children, young people, and their families and adopts a didactic approach, which typically presents a clear right and wrong way to do data. Data safety approaches tend to present the responsibility for data protection as lying with the individual, and these skills are often promoted most vigorously by advocacy groups and educational institutions through classroom-based programs and websites. These are based around normative strategies that can be enacted within a device or system, such as adjusting security settings within the platform or reading the terms of service attached to a particular platform. While these are certainly important understandings and skills to have, they inadvertently reinforce datafication as the status quo.

In contrast to the relative popularity of data safety education, there are decidedly fewer educational programs working in the critical tradition. One of the earliest and most prominent is the *Digital Defense Playbook* by the US "Our Data Bodies" collective. This program is targeted at minoritized communities with the overarching goal "to shift who gets to define problems around data collection, data privacy and data security" (Lewis et al. 2018, 6). This approach foregrounds story sharing and critical reflection, with a focus on participants mapping and itemizing the various ways that data shapes their everyday lives. The underpinning ethos of data self-defense seeks to foster a sense of "power rather than paranoia" when it comes datafication. Other programs such as the *Data Literacy Guidebook* by the Data Justice Lab in Cardiff seek to raise critical understanding and awareness of datafication and its impacts, with a strong focus on examining algorithms, bias, and fairness (Brand and Sander 2020). This guidebook provides an overview of the tools currently available to develop critical understandings of data, including workshop resources, interactive learning tools, and guides for data protection.

There are also guides specifically directed at young people, such as the *My Data and Privacy Online* (Livingstone, Stoilova, and Nandagiri 2019b), which emphasizes the importance of knowing your data rights.

These critical data education programs tend to focus either on raising awareness of datafication processes or encouraging critical reflection on personal data practices. For example, the *Digital Defense Playbook* focuses on critical self-reflection, while the *My Data and Privacy Online* concentrates on developing awareness of data mainly through short instructional videos. The scope of each program is quite focused and therefore bounded to specific situations and contexts. Data science and datafication are rapidly evolving fields with processes that adapt and change "in the wild." Even for specialists, then, it can be difficult to stay abreast of the features and implications of algorithms and automation.

Limitations of Current Responses to Datafication

Most of the responses outlined so far are based on the presumption that individuals are inherently compelled to act. This is not always the case. Datafication is deeply intertwined with our personal lives and the ways in which our societies function. As Taina Bucher (2021) puts it, in many parts of the Global North, people's lives have become oriented toward platforms like Facebook, meaning the presence of these technologies (and their data demands) is "felt everywhere" (9). Personal data processing can improve search results and recommend friendship connections and entertainment—all of which is indispensable given the vast amounts of digital content we navigate online. Conversely, the fact that the more negative implications of datafication are not easily recognized by individuals can make it difficult to motivate people to become data literate. For example, it is unlikely (or perhaps even impossible) for a college applicant to know that the reason they did not get into their chosen course was because they did not open all the links in an email sent by the university. For these reasons, one-off tactical interventions and education programs that are not contextualized or developed over time are unlikely to change practices in the long term.

Similarly, while data science and data-hacking approaches might be thought of as supporting "deeper" forms of understanding, they also remain limited—especially in terms of personal data. Most data science programs work with open and anonymized data sets curated by governments, institutions,

and organizations. Successfully engaging in these approaches requires technical skills that nonspecialists typically do not possess and can often only be
partially developed through courses and programs. In addition, data science
and data hacking are not typically focused on managing and protecting one's
own data but instead support people to work with data sets that have been put
together to answer particular questions, problems, and agendas.

A further limitation is that all these existing responses tend to operate in
isolation from each other—meaning that it is difficult to develop a unified
approach that enables people to progress to higher forms of knowledge and
understanding. Critical understandings and skills need to be systematically
deployed to connect with what people already know about technology and
data, as well as how they feel and experience data in their everyday life.
For example, Deborah Lupton's (2020) research into how people engage
with self-tracking devices is a helpful reminder that data is not "out there"
but entwined with people's sensory experiences. Lupton found that people
draw on their own strategic knowledge of data to interpret and act upon
the data visualizations and materializations they encounter through self-
tracking devices. For this reason, it makes sense to start with what people
know and experience—using this as the foundation for any critical and
reflexive understandings of datafied systems. There is no point in introducing concepts such as algorithm and automation if participants have not yet
experienced and reflected on the implications firsthand. Like other literacies, critical data literacies need to be developed over time. What is required,
then, is an educational approach that not only scaffolds *all* people to more
sophisticated and complex understandings of digital data but also provides
them with the skills, opportunities, and alternatives to do data differently.

Introducing Critical Data Literacies

Given the variety of existing responses to data just outlined, it is important
to differentiate critical data literacies from other ways of working with and
managing digital data. Here, we now return to the new literacies approach
introduced in chapter 1 to make sense of digital data as a part of the cultural
and material practices of daily life. The tradition of new literacies has grown
in prominence over the past thirty years to offer a significantly different take
on what counts as literacy. From the new literacies perspective, everyday practices such as decoding traffic signals and street signs are treated as significant

meaning-making processes that count as literacy events and practices (Heath 1982). A new literacies approach highlights the importance of the context or environment in which these texts appear in the meaning-making process. In this way, literacies are always socially and culturally situated, and they are used in a wide range of everyday activities. Given the ubiquity of digital data in everyday life, it makes good sense to apply the idea of new literacies to develop critical awareness of data.

In simple terms, then, the new literacies approach recognizes the benefits of being able to unpack the politics of everyday texts and, most important, for these understandings and dispositions to inform people's digital practices. In this respect, a useful guide is literacy theorist Allan Luke's definition of critical literacy, which outlines the cultivation of increasingly sophisticated and critical engagements with texts. It consists of three components (Luke 2000, 72):

- the *metaknowledge* of "meaning systems and the sociocultural contexts in which they are produced and embedded,"
- the *technical skills* to negotiate these systems, and
- the *"capacity to understand* how these systems and skills operate in the interests of power."

This simple three-point definition belies the complexity involved in developing critical literacy, particularly when applied to digital data. For example, the meaning systems of any aspect of digital technology use are often developed by platform operators, and these processes are designed to be deliberately opaque, therefore making it difficult to develop metaknowledge. That said, Luke's definition also points to the need to understand the sociocultural contexts of everyday texts, alongside the ideologies that underpin them. A new literacies approach to data therefore focuses our attention on the ways in which it is constructed (written) and interpreted (read) by different social actors within data assemblages. This encourages critical reflection on the representativeness of data, as well as the role of data scientists in creating and analyzing data sets. It also encourages critical consideration of how data-driven insights are acted upon by those in positions of power and authority. In line with some of the critical data studies approaches outlined in chapter 3, digital data is seen as not only producing knowledge but also shaping realities (Bowker 2013; Renzi and Langlois 2015).

Approaching digital data along these lines therefore draws attention to how the realities created by data are internalized and often in unconscious ways. A new literacies approach would therefore begin by attempting to open the black box of datafication—that is, identifying and understanding when and how we are generating digital data through our everyday engagements with digital devices and systems. Like Allan Luke's (2000) scaffolding toward more complex engagements with texts, critical *data* literacies are therefore also about providing opportunities to increase people's capacity to do data differently. As digital practices are so intricately entwined with our social lives, this cannot be achieved through didactic approaches and instructing people what to do (see Buckingham 2003). Instead, critical data literacies begin with the individual's own data experiences and practices, scaffolding them toward more critical understandings and awareness of how these fit into the bigger picture of datafication.

Above all, then, the starting point for critical data literacies is that digital data needs to be identified and interpreted *in context*. This marks an important difference from existing data science and data safety approaches, which tend to focus on general insights rather than the emergent and contextual meanings that individuals bring to digital data from their own experiences. As we have noted in the past three chapters, digital data is almost always generated under the assumption that it represents or indicates something about the wider phenomena from which it is drawn. In this way, understanding and interpreting digital data in context is crucial for turning information into knowledge (Boyd and Crawford 2012). Similarly, what might be considered useful, beneficial, good, or ethical use of digital data depends on the context and norms within which the flows of data are situated.

Up to this point, then, the idea of critical data literacies can be seen as similar to any other critical literacy. That said, we need to more thoroughly consider the ways in which we might make sense of digital data as a distinctive "text." Indeed, a few inherent tensions between the literacies paradigm and digital data require careful consideration.

Seeing Digital Data as "Text"—from the Page to the Platform

The literacies tradition—and education more broadly—depends on concepts and phenomena being presented in tangible forms so they can be apprehended and interpreted. For example, one only needs to consider how the visual representation of abstract phenomena such as the water cycle or the periodic table are crucial to building knowledge and understanding. Like similar scientific and philosophical phenomena, digital data is largely immaterial, abstract, and behind the scenes. How digital data is represented is therefore crucial to the kinds of understandings that can emerge and develop. A literacies approach requires data to be presented in textual forms that can be engaged with, taught, and described in terms of models, frameworks, and knowledge content. Furthermore, the *critical* literacies approach also assumes a set of practical strategies and tactics that individuals can experiment with to operationalize their newfound awareness and understanding of the "text" (Pangrazio and Sefton-Green 2020). Critical data literacies therefore encourages us not only to decode and interpret data when it is represented as lexical, visual, or graphical information in dashboards and analytics but also to consider the other parts of the data infrastructure involved in its production.

In basic terms, text in the new literacies sense is "a collection of semiotic elements that can function as a tool for people to take social action" (Jones et al. 2015, 5). As such, conceptualizing digital data as a text marks a point of departure from the models outlined earlier in which data was not seen as providing opportunities for social action but primarily as information to be individually protected and managed. Rather than focusing on isolated skills for data manipulation, management, or security, a literacies approach promotes the idea of data as a text that is a part of not only social practices *but also* tools for action. This resonates with the "good data" approaches discussed in chapter 3. However, critical literacies also consider the construction of the text. Seen along these lines, then, the role played by digital platforms in the generation and processing of digital data also has particular significance.

As such, it is important to acknowledge the role of digital platforms in the constitution of digital data as a text for analysis. As touched on in earlier chapters, platforms now play a key part in how we engage with digital contexts—from Facebook to TikTok, AirBnB to Uber. Through their design, these platforms determine which data is collected as well as how it is used and interpreted. Furthermore, these platforms present processed data back to users through analytics, dashboards, and metrics. In many respects, then, the platform interface is how the results of black-boxed data processes are presented to the end user. Crucially, because what is measured by the platform is what people who are using the platform learn to value (Pangrazio 2019), platforms also determine what is deemed important or significant when it comes to digital identities and interactions.

With this in mind, platforms and platform architectures present several challenges when thinking about data as text. First, people are often not aware of the data being generated about them through their engagements with a platform and the kinds of inferences that are drawn from this information. Second, people are not aware of how this data is processed and used after it is collected. Finally, when people do encounter data on a platform through analytics, dashboards, or metrics, its representative form is entirely determined by the platform. In one sense, discerning the text of digital data is easier through platforms due to the public display of metrics and dashboards. Yet, in another sense, deconstructing the text of digital data, as well as understanding how it might be reconstructed, is more difficult due to the hidden nature of platform processes. In this way, we need to give further thought to how digital data is rendered interpretable and therefore might be engaged with to develop critical data literacies.

(Re)constructing the Text—Three Ways That Digital Data Is Generated

The first step in developing critical data literacies is to identify how digital data is brought into existence. Chapter 5 extends on this by discussing the different types of digital data that are generated within datafied systems. For the time being, we can begin with three broad ways that digital data is generated, including data that people "give" to devices and systems, data that devices and systems extract from people, and data that systems process on behalf of people. What follows is a brief description of each of these processes of digital data generation.

Giving Information to Digital Devices/Systems
The first way that data is created is when people voluntarily *give* information to devices and systems. This might include self-tracking information, social media data (including videos, pictures, texts, and tweets), emails, and videos. The proliferation of social media platforms such as Facebook, TikTok, Instagram, and Twitter has increased the quantity of personal data that people consciously give to devices and systems, especially in terms of data-rich photographs and video content. The practices enacted through these

platforms are often expressive and emotive, resulting in what are seen as rich and detailed sources of personal information.

Information that relates specifically to people's behaviors and performance can also be generated through activities that take place in work and educational settings. Using a learning management system in university, for example, involves students accessing and uploading learning resources, contributing to discussion forums, and completing quizzes and assessment tasks. While these activities are ostensibly supporting learning, they also generate data on each individual student, which can be processed and analyzed to predict and optimize future use of the system. Crucially, these forms of volunteered data are often linked to other forms of data that users are less likely to be aware of. For example, all the data points just described will have attached technical details and various other forms of metadata that represent "unstructured and finely granular information" (Peacock 2014, 2) about each person using a platform, which can be processed to make predictions about performance or to incentivize particular behaviors.

Devices/Systems Extracting Information from People

Another means of data generation is the extraction of information from people by devices and systems. This includes information that is extracted without the person knowing—a form of background soft surveillance involving the continuous harvesting of people's device use, online searches, and transactions (Lupton 2017). Crucially, given that this data is brought into existence through its collection, the company, organization, or institution that extracts this data can claim ownership and control (Hearn 2010). By contrast, the person whose actions trigger the extraction of this data has no control over its generation or how companies, governments, researchers, and scientists subsequently seek to process and reuse any collected information. However, if these details are outlined in the terms of service (even in vague and/or ambiguous terms) and a person has agreed to these, then this is considered to be legal use of their data. However, whether terms of service agreements can cover all the possible ways in which data might be reused is doubtful (see Andrejevic 2014).

Devices/Systems Creating Data on Behalf of People

Data is also created when information is processed on behalf of people to provide information of relevance to companies, institutions, and individuals.

Individuals often have little or no exposure to this data, as it is used to inform system processes and institutional procedures, often in the form of data doubles that are used to organize people into groups and categories that can be usefully deployed for, among other things, marketing and security purposes. That said, some forms of this data are fed back to people via digital platforms and apps. Many social and/or consumer platforms aggregate and process data generated through platform participation and then (re)present it back via dashboards, metrics, and other analytics pages. For example, Twitter provides detailed information on a user's tweets, including the number of impressions your tweet received, profile visits, and mentions by other Twitter users. However, identifying and interpreting processed data can be challenging (see Roberts et al. 2016). In addition, what is shown to every platform user is a small and simplified subset of the much larger and more complex field(s) of data the company would have. Crucially, which data is collected, how it is processed, and what is represented back to users is determined by platform operators, who are driven by very specific profit-driven motivations.

Developing a Framework for Critical Data Literacies

Given everything that has just been discussed, if we approach digital data as a text that is generated from these different sources, how might we begin to develop critically minded ways of interpreting it? How can we think about the data assemblages that sit beneath the platforms, devices, and other aspects of our everyday lives? In the remainder of this chapter, we sketch out a framework of critical data literacies, drawing together everything discussed in the chapters so far. There are five domains to this framework:

- Data Identification
- Data Understandings
- Data Reflexivity
- Data Strategies
- Data Tactics

While these stages of the framework do not have to be engaged with in a linear and sequential manner, they are constructed around increasingly advanced levels of critique. Each domain of the framework is critical in orientation—even the simple act of identifying where digital data is generated is an inherently critical act. Put together, then, these different stages describe what it might mean to engage with digital data through critical literacies. For example, someone trying to find a particular address might decide to turn on the geolocational settings on their mobile phone to find out where they are using a "Maps" application. Being data literate means understanding the implications of changing this setting, as well as having the technical skills to do so.

Data Identification

The first domain of the framework—Data Identification—is fundamental to developing critical data literacies. To explain this further, we return to the three ways that data is generated: information that people *give* to a digital system, information that devices and systems *extract* from people's digital engagements, and data that is *processed* on behalf of people. Some practical examples of how these types of digital data might be identified in relation to the framework are as follows:

- Someone *gives* information to a system when they upload a photo to Instagram or post on a discussion forum.
- A mobile phone *extracts* geolocational information when its location services are switched on.
- *Processed* data is presented back to someone who is using a system through an analytics dashboard, providing insights into their social media practices, learning, or work habits. Some *processed* data is traded in the data broker economy without the individual's knowledge.

A crucial element in establishing this as a *critical* framework for data literacies is identifying or revealing the ways in which digital data is surreptitiously extracted from people without their knowledge. So too, is examining the ways in which analytics, dashboards, and evaluations are constituted from particular types of personal data (while excluding others). This first step in the critical data literacies framework essentially involves identifying where and how the data was generated. This might sound straightforward, yet as we shall see in chapter 5, data identification is a complex and challenging step.

Data Understandings

Once identified, data can then begin to be read by considering things like the context in which it was generated and the method by which it was captured. This domain of the framework also considers the ways in which the data is likely to be processed and used by other parties. However, data infrastructures are opaque, making it difficult to analyze how data was captured and how it will be processed. Even more difficult is anticipating the ways in which data might be processed and used in the future. This second part of the framework therefore involves informed speculation based on an awareness of possible (re)uses of one's data. There are some practical tools that can help with this. For example, some open-source web browsers and search engines now use enhanced tracking protection, which not only blocks trackers but also enables users to see who has been tracking and tracing their searches. The big advantage of this tracking protection is that unlike other blocking software, it does not compromise the sites' functionality. In regard to processed data, this domain of critical data literacies would involve understanding and interpreting visual representations (e.g., dashboards, graphs, indicators) of data, as well as understanding the source data underlying these representations. It might also involve understanding the basics of data science, such as what an algorithm is and how data sets are constituted.

Data Reflexivity

Thinking about how digital data is being used and analyzing the implications of data processing is the goal of the next domain of the framework Data Reflexivity. For example, people might think about information that they give to digital platforms and how this becomes social data that can be used to profile or predict behaviors and interactions. For example, a Facebook user might reflect on the consequences of commenting on a friend's post—such as how this action then influences what they will see subsequently on their Newsfeed and the kinds of social connections that are created on the platform. They may also consider the implications of their actions on Facebook in terms of their subsequent experiences on other platforms, such as friend recommendations and advertisements. Regarding a data breach or infringement of digital rights, the reflexivity stage of the framework encourages the individual to reflect on how this occurred. For example, was the breach the result of signing up to a new platform or engaging in different digital practices? Data reflexivity happens in the moment as we are experiencing and working with data yet emphasizes the need for contemplation and critique.

Data Strategies

Once someone can critique the implications of digital data, they are in a position to act. The fourth and fifth domains of the framework build a series of strategies and tactics for working with data. Here, we draw on the "four resources" model of literacy (Freebody and Luke 1990; Luke and Free-body 1999) to describe moments when people can act upon the structures and social relations associated with digital data. In terms of strategies, this involves "knowing about and acting on the different cultural and social functions that various texts perform" in ways that reaffirm the "constructed order" of a system (Luke and Freebody 1999, 5). More specifically then, Data Strategies might involve properly reviewing the terms of service agreements, adjusting privacy settings, implementing ad block technologies, or setting performance targets in order to influence the feedback of data. Regarding data breaches or an infringement of digital rights, the individual might take action through a local authority or government institution so they can investigate how this occurred and what needs to be done. An infringement of digital rights may be due to a platform changing its terms of service or a more stringent regulation introduced in the local jurisdiction. Regardless, the individual will need legal support to act. However, to do this, they need to be able to identify the infringement, know how their rights have been transgressed, and then which organization to contact for help.

Data Tactics

In contrast, many people's everyday lives involve working around digital structures by *not* relying on official strategies. Instead, people can also resort to political practices and forms of knowledge that subvert, usurp, and undermine norms and expected ways of doing things. The fifth domain of personal Data Tactics fits with several oppositional approaches toward digital media. Such tactics might involve acts of data disobedience intended to mitigate, evade, or perhaps sabotage dominant structures of data reuse and recirculation, as well as align with the idea of data as a site of resistance (as discussed in chapter 3). It might also involve the deliberate use of false information to disrupt the connection between the personal data generated and the individual (e.g., entering an erroneous birthdate or gender identity) or setting up an independently assessed virtual private network to protect privacy. This might also decrease the likelihood of a data breach or an infringement of digital rights.

Tactics could also involve more creative appropriations of digital data designed to achieve more niche or specialized insights and benefits—for example, altering one's appearance to counter surveillance and facial recognition technology or repurposing personal data to create visualizations and

Table 4.1
The critical data literacies framework

Domain	Description/key questions	Actions	Chapter discussed
Data Identification	What is digital data?	• Identification of data and its type (materialization)	5
Data Understandings	What are the origins, circulations, and uses of these different types of digital data?	• Identifying how and where digital data are generated and processed	5
		• Interpreting the information that is represented by processed data (data visualizations, charts, and graphs)	5
Data Reflexivity	What are the implications of these different types of digital data for self and others?	• Analyzing and evaluating the profiling and predictions that are made from processed digital data (e.g., sentiment analysis, natural language processing)	6
		• Understanding the implications of managing, controlling, and applying digital data (individual and collective critique)	6
Data Strategies	How can I manage and make use of these different types of digital data?	• Applying, managing, and controlling data	6
		• Building technical skills and interpretive competencies (reading the terms of service, adjusting privacy settings, blocking technologies, developing a shared language)	6
		• Applying the information that is represented by processed data (personal insights into digital self and performance)	6
Data Tactics	How can I do digital data differently?	• Employing tactics of resistance and obfuscation (tactics)	7
		• Repurposing data for personal and social reasons (creative applications)	7

representations for specific purposes. While these are somewhat uncommon practices, having the critical knowledge to understand why someone
might do this and the effect it would have are indicative of a more sophisticated and critical level of data literacies. In subsequent chapters, we conceptualize these uses of data as different ways of "writing" with data.

Conclusions

This chapter has considered the specific advantages of approaching digital
data through the lens of critical literacies. While literacies are often associated
with formal education, this approach is equally useful *beyond* the classroom
and can incorporate cognitive, affective, and embodied responses to data.
Unlike other responses to datafication, a critical literacies approach emphasizes the need to fit with people's existing levels of understanding and use
their experiences and beliefs as the starting point for thinking more deeply
about data. Most important, the critical data literacy framework just outlined
in this chapter offers the basis for a more *systematic* approach to supporting
people and communities to engage more critically with digital data and the
ongoing datafication of everyday life. The critical data literacies framework
therefore brings together both bottom-up and top-down responses to datafication and organizes these into domains leading to more critical and agentic
data practices.

This approach can be adapted to suit different ages and levels of
understanding—from elementary school children to adults of all ages. The
critical data literacies framework can also be adapted to suit the needs of
individuals and collectives. Over the next three chapters, then, we explore
what it means to use the critical data literacies framework *in practice*—what
are the possible ways that we can identify, understand, and act upon data?
To start this process, chapter 5 tackles the first domains of data identification
and data understanding. As the logic of the critical data studies framework
suggests, we need some basic knowledge of how data is generated, collected,
and processed before we can understand how data-driven decision-making
and automated systems function.

5   Making Sense of Digital Data: Understanding Data
    in Everyday Life

Introduction

This book has already identified a wide of range of ideas and assumptions about digital data. In popular discourse, data is still often referred to as big, objective, powerful, insightful, and so on. Platform companies, internet service providers, and IT industry actors are keen to present data as an essential part of digital life because it helps sustain a range of profitable activities, which we discuss later in this chapter. On the flipside, there is also a persistent sense among many people that data is creepy, disturbing, or scary. Even after twenty years of the smartphone, the idea that our digital devices are spying, following, and watching us persists, especially in our most intimate and vulnerable moments. Some of these understandings form a kind of folk wisdom of data, while other discourses and metaphors are part of organized marketing campaigns for tech companies or big business. Regardless of how they come to circulate in society, these discourses shape what we think data is, what it can do, and how we should be engaging with it.

Lots of these popular understandings of data do not hold up to close scrutiny. For example, take the common metaphor of data as the new oil. This was originally intended to convey an idea of data as a limitless natural resource that could power society and be a source of great profit. However, as with all fossil fuels, oil now has a lot of negative associations—not least due to its part in exacerbating climate change. This has seen recent attempts to promote the more environmentally friendly idea of "data as sunshine." As Google's chief financial officer Ruth Porat claims, "We keep using it, and it keeps regenerating!" (Ghosh and Kanter 2019). Other recent metaphors describe data as a stream, lake, or cloud. Drawing on such natural associations serves a dual purpose—encouraging the public to accept the idea that data is natural, while at the same time promoting to investors, Big Tech, and platform operators that data can be collected constantly at little or no cost and in ways that are not easily "monitored, measured or regulated" (Lupton 2013).

All these common understandings, metaphors, and beliefs offer shorthand ways of understanding complex ideas around digital data and enable everyday people to make sense of abstract concepts by connecting them to more familiar and tangible ones (Puschmann and Burgess 2014). As such, these metaphors and beliefs have come to have great power in recent years. For example, the idea of big data has reshaped formalized domains such as biology and economics, as well as reorganized the corporate landscape. It has also influenced what is taught in schools and universities—conveying a need to focus on data science and develop statistical and analytical skills in student populations that are likely to go on to work in data-related jobs (Halpern 2014).

Given the contradictory messages surrounding data, it is perhaps not surprising that people are often quite confused when thinking about it. Indeed, studies have found that people often have some awareness of the various ways their data is used but feel powerless to do anything about it, because they lack knowledge and understanding (Lupton and Michael 2017; Draper and Turow 2017). In our own work (Pangrazio and Selwyn 2018; Pangrazio and Cardozo-Gaibisso 2021), we have found that young people often have exaggerated expectations around how data might be used by a range of dodgy actors like hackers, pedophiles, and scammers while having far less concern for the more routine and regular ways that it is being processed and used by data brokers and other online services. Clearly, relying on folk wisdom or the discourses propagated by Big Tech is insufficient in making sense of data. So, while it is important to take these common metaphors and beliefs seriously, it is also important to think about how we might develop alternate meanings that are more useful, informative, and beneficial for people making use of digital technologies on a daily basis. We need more realistic understandings of what data is and how we can manage and protect how it is being used.

In this chapter, we expand on the first two domains of the critical data literacies framework—Data Identification and Data Understandings—that are concerned with developing a social "reading" of data. In the previous chapter, we introduced the overall critical data literacies framework and how it sets out the different stages involved in developing critical engagement with the digital data in our everyday lives. In this chapter, we focus more closely on locating and defining the text of data so that it can become the basis of critical education and inquiry. More specifically, we expand on a central feature of critical data studies—human subjects data (Dalton, Taylor, and Thatcher 2016). The idea of human subjects data (data that creates humans as subjects) helps us to identify how the data that is volunteered or extracted from people is constructed into texts that have the power to shape the way social phenomena are thought about and acted upon.

In short, this chapter takes a closer look at what is often described as datafication. This term was popularized by Mayer-Schoenberger and Cukier's (2013) early enthusiastic writing about big data and has since been taken up by many commentators as shorthand for the transformation of digital interactions into records that can be collected and commodified. Datafication refers to a few distinct stages in which digital data becomes useful: data generation, data collection, and data processing. In particular, this chapter focuses on these stages to unpack and understand how digital data comes to have meaning and power in the world. In many respects, critical data literacies seek to interrupt these processes so that data can be interpreted and used *beyond* the datafied systems they are intended for. But before doing any of this, we need to be able to identify how digital data is used in society and understand how it becomes a text that we can analyze and act upon. This constitutes the first stage of our framework, Data Identification—that is, how data is generated and collected.

Data Collection: Creating the Language of Data

Given the sheer number of digital entanglements that are now a commonplace feature across everyday life, it can be difficult to keep track of when data is being generated and the different forms it can take. In this section, we approach the collection of data from a social perspective that focuses on the nexus between text and reader. The aim is to bring greater awareness to how, when, and where data is being generated, as well as its many different forms. As discussed in previous chapters, many of the existent definitions of data originate from math, computer science, and other data traditions and are inherently operational and technical in focus. While these might all be helpful distinctions for data scientists and academic researchers, they tend to reflect technical characteristics in terms of how the data might be processed rather than the ways in which people might ordinarily encounter data in everyday life. In contrast, we explore five different types of data that are generated through everyday use of digital technology—alphanumeric data, image data, geolocational data, audio data, and metadata. The purpose of highlighting these data types is to bring greater awareness to nondata specialists about the types of data that are generated and collected.

Alphanumeric Data

Alphanumeric data refers to information that is communicated via numbers and letters. This could include a written post uploaded to social media or a link shared with another person. It could also include the huge swathes of data that are generated and collected from wearable devices and mobile sensors, which provide detailed numeric information on someone's heart rate, steps walked, or their sleeping and eating patterns. Alphanumeric data underpins most of our digital interactions and is therefore often taken as representative of human beliefs, understandings, and interactions. As such, alphanumeric data is thought to provide detailed insight into communication patterns and opinion, social interactions and culture, and human biology and lifestyle choices. This can, in turn, be used to predict behavior or incentivize particular activities, making it extremely valuable for marketers, pollsters, and companies. While it might seem a basic form, alphanumeric data is wrought with complexities that are reflected in how it is used. For example, while there is now a universally understood set of numbers, there are many different languages and systems of notation such as the twenty-six-symbol Latin alphabet, the twenty-eight letters of the cursive Arabic script (read from right to left), or the much more expansive Cyrillic script.

Visual Data

Many of the most popular online activities of the past twenty years have been predicated around visual data. Taking photographs, watching videos, and sharing selfies now dominate people's online activities simply because they are often considered more engaging and communicative than written text. Furthermore, smartphones with in-built cameras mean that it only takes a few clicks to share images with a global audience. Photos and videos are incredibly data-rich sources of information that can be processed for a range of purposes. Given this depth and detail of information, it is hardly surprising that digital platforms are designed to encourage a visual turn in our communication practices. Visual data is not just yielded from photos uploaded onto social media—even the photos on our phone that are not "shared" are constantly processed and analyzed. For example, searching the photos on a smartphone for dog, winter, or sunny will filter all the photos on your phone that "fit" that description. Also, visual data can contain biometric information (such as someone's facial features or voice), and many mobile phones have algorithms to store, analyze, and process these using facial processing and object detection software. In addition, video data can provide rich and detailed information about how people interact with the world in real time. Home security cameras, drones, and fleets of satellites are now taking high-resolution photos and videos that are uploaded to the cloud and analyzed. In the past, video analysis was limited to manual logging of video footage, but high-powered video analytics now automate this task, enabling much greater volume and detail of video data to be analyzed (Varah 2014).

Geolocation Data

Geolocation data refers to latitude and longitude position and can be collected in a number of ways—from our credit card transactions to the tags put into the photos that we take. Most mobile devices today collect geolocation data, but whether or not it is shared with the tech company (and other third parties) depends on the chosen privacy settings. There are two ways in which geolocation data can be collected: device-based data collection and server-based collection. As the name suggests, device-based data collection gathers GPS (global positioning system) data through any device that has mobile network coverage and location settings that are switched on. Installing a new app will often result in a request to "Share your location." While geolocation data may not be required for the app to function, it is a rich source of data and easily collected by apps on a mobile device. Conversely, server-based data collection is made possible through a device's internet protocol (IP) address—a unique identifier for a device on a local network or the internet—and is collected through Wi-Fi or Ethernet connections as soon as anyone visits a specific location. So, walking past a Starbucks will result in the store's Wi-Fi "pinging" your mobile phone and recognizing that you are nearby. This allows Starbucks to target you with a discount or special offer. With server-based collection, service providers can map an IP address of any internet-connected device to a real-world geographic location.

Geolocation data is highly personal, meaning that there is a large lucrative market for the buying and selling of location data from apps. Geolocation databases are provided or sold to third parties, including governments and institutions as well as data brokers. This data might be useful for councils wanting to work out where to place pedestrian crossings or future shop owners wanting to determine the best location for their store. Geolocation data can be processed to provide valuable business intelligence as well as personal information about where someone lives and works. This data can be used as a proxy for highlighting intimate information, such as someone's sleeping patterns, based on the use of smartphone inactivity to infer where someone's bedroom is and how long they were asleep for. All told, where people have been (including at what times of day and how frequently) can be used to infer a great deal of contextual information. Take, for example, the places that we habitually go to. This information can be used to ascertain our preferred supermarket of choice, the likelihood of having a gambling problem, medical conditions, sexual preferences, and other personal details that we may prefer others did not know.

Audio Data

Sound data or audio file data is a growing area of interest for data scientists and has a range of applications, including music classification, voice recognition, and digital signal processing that can be used across settings such as health care, sales, and customer support (Chauhan 2020). Audio data is composed of a mixture of wave frequencies at different intensities. It also has a temporal factor, where sound fragments have a particular duration, rather than just existing as a data point. This means sound data is more like video data than image data (Korstanje 2021). The unstructured or semistructured nature of audio data can make it difficult to process. For example, image data can be classified through matrices as it is based upon pixels. However, in raw form, audio data is essentially variations in air pressure that are picked up by the ear. The first step in collecting this data, then, is to digitize it. Sound can be digitized by turning air pressure into a voltage and then converting that voltage to a number. The amplitude and frequency of the sound wave are important, but most audio files contain multiple sound waves at a mix of frequencies and amplitudes (Korstanje 2021). Once compressed into a WAV or MP3 file, the data can be processed. Genre classification, for example, might include using the metadata associated with that file (e.g., author, publisher, lyrics). Voice recognition software might be used to infer age, gender, or make a personal ID match. At a more complex level, a spectrogram turns the sound file into images that can then be processed using neural networks, which we discuss later in this chapter.

Metadata

A final type of data that is worth being aware of is metadata. Metadata is data about data and is typically produced automatically by various technologies. For example, if an individual accesses Facebook from a friend's device, personal data will be generated through the individual actively logging on to the platform. While most metadata generation is automatic and invisible to users, it can also be intentionally gathered by platforms. Facebook attaches metadata to people's images so that they can be reidentified as coming from the source. The metadata provides information about what time the device was used and for how long the platform was accessed. For example, chapter 2 briefly outlined the EXIF data that is attached to any photograph—such as date stamps and time stamps, location data, what camera was used and with what settings, and so on.

Metadata provides a trace or outline of internet activities and is used to organize and categorize data. It is essential for transmission and communication, and for this reason, digital infrastructures cannot function without it (Mayernik and Acker 2018). As it is essential for assembling, organizing, and categorizing the data, it is also important in developing and augmenting meaning. Indeed, metadata is frequently used by data brokers to build personal profiles of people, even though most people remain unaware of this data. As Rob Kitchin (2014, 9) explains, metadata about content might refer to names and descriptions of particular fields such as columns on a spreadsheet to "help a user of a dataset to understand its composition and how it should be used and interpreted." The choice of what information is collected and when it is recorded is determined by platform operators (Mayernik and Acker 2018). Yet, as with many data-related phenomena, hard-and-fast definitions are not always helpful. Digital traces may serve as data in one context, but in another context, that same data operates as metadata as it provides insight into how the digital system or platform is operating. As Mayernik and Acker (2018, 178) put it, "One person's metadata are another person's data." All of this points to the fact that metadata is powerful and, like other forms of data, can be manipulated for particular purposes (Acker 2018).

Data Processing

Making sense of how these different forms of data is generated is therefore a key initial element of critical data literacy. Some of the data just outlined may be collected in analogue form, but digitization enables that data to be read and processed by algorithms in a standardized manner. Following on from this, however, is getting to grips with the next step in the datafication process—data processing. This stage of datafication involves the preparation and processing of data in order to turn it into something meaningful. Data processing draws on programming, mathematics, and subject matter expertise to deliver insights into people's backgrounds, behaviors, and the wider social world. One fundamental process here is bringing different bits of data together. Data scientists look for meaningful dependencies among different bits of information, as data on its own is rather limited. Data processing can therefore be highly complex, but it is possible to explain the basic steps to grasp how insights are gathered. As data-processing techniques become more complex—from data mining to machine learning and AI—it might be reasoned the role that humans play becomes less and less important. Needless to say, the humans who design the algorithms and created the models that drive these processes still have a huge impact.

There are two main reasons for wanting to process data. First, data can be processed to answer specific questions and address particular problems. Second, data can be used in a more open-ended manner to look for patterns, correlations, and anomalies that can generate new questions. Drawing on Minelli and colleagues (2013), we might say that data processing is used for four main purposes:

- **Description** (What and when did something happen? How often does it happen?)
- **Explanation** (Why did it happen? What is its impact?)
- **Prediction** (What is likely to happen next? What if we did this or that?)
- **Prescription** (What is the optimal answer or outcome? How is that achieved?)

Seen in these terms, it is easy to imagine ways in which various actors might want to process someone's personal data. For example, a bank might like to predict whether a customer is likely to default on their home loan, or a company might want to market to a particular group of customers based on their characteristics and behaviors. However, from the perspective of critical data literacies, the appropriateness of this processing depends on the quality of the data that is selected to be used, its suitability to addressing the problem, and what is done to the data along the way. As such, a few aspects of data processing require our careful consideration.

Data Preparation

Preparing data is crucial to data processing, and it is estimated to take up to 80 percent of the time involved in data analytics (D'Ignazio and Klein 2020). All data must be cleaned and wrangled into a format that enables it to be algorithmically processed. More specifically, this involves *selecting* the data to be included, *preprocessing* the data to remove bias errors, missing fields and noise, and then *structuring* the data for input to analysis. This work will often also involve *reducing* the number of dimensions within the data, and perhaps even *enriching* the data by combining it with other data sets (e.g., census data) to enable deeper insights (Kitchin 2014).

If we think back to the notion of data being "cooked," then all this preparation gives a sense of how data is manipulated and molded by humans. These steps can take place in any order and are repeated until the "right" data set is created. For example, alphanumeric data will often require several steps to clean it for processing. This will include removing HTML tags, punctuation, and "stop" words such as "this," "there," "that," and "is." It might also require stemming words or reducing adverbs and adjectives to their stem (e.g., truncating "tastefully" to "tasty") and then converting everything to lowercase (Lata 2018). Alphanumeric data is particularly complex to analyze because it is high-dimensional due to the number of unique words in any given document (Gentzkow, Kelly, and Taddy 2019). The goal, then, is to reduce language into a series of numbers that can be processed algorithmically. Even this initial process of swapping one set of symbols for another results in a massive change to what this data now "says."

As such, preparing data is often described in terms of cleaning, tidying, trimming, pruning, and transforming in order to turn great swathes of data into the most meaningful data sets that can be algorithmically processed. Important decisions are being made at every stage by data scientists in order to do this. For example, they need to select data that is representative, decide which other data sets to link it to, and how to wrangle the data into a form that can be processed by algorithms. Indeed, understanding the power of data means developing a knowledge of how the data is collected and collated, rather than just focusing on the algorithms that manipulate it (Feinberg 2022). The creation of data sets will typically involve removing the contextual information from the data. For this reason, D'Ignazio and Klein (2020, 132) argue data preparation can be a "destructive rather than a constructive act." Indeed, filtering out bits of information can drastically change the outcomes of data processing.

One key aspect of this processing work is labeling data. Labeling data refers to various processes including detecting, tagging, classifying, and moderating data samples that are then used to train algorithms and machine learning models. For example, compiling a training data set for facial recognition models requires labeling large collections of photographs of human faces with specific features such as eyes, nose, and mouth. If, in addition, the model seeks to detect emotion or sentiment, then different facial expressions will also need to be labeled. This is usually done by human raters—often low-paid online piece workers. However, emotions like joy, anger, and confusion are expressed in culturally specific ways, making this a fraught process. Training data *should* be an accurate approximation to the data that the fully developed system will operate on "in the wild"—providing what is referred to in data science as a ground truth for machine learning models.

Not surprisingly, one of the most common problems in algorithm design is that the training data does not turn out to match the data being operated on in the wild (Gillespie 2016). In one notorious case, Google and Facebook were censured for image recognition technologies that classified images of Black faces as gorillas or primates (Vincent 2018; Mac 2021). Similarly, reducing the gender spectrum down to a binary labeling of M/F is equally fraught—as is assuming that gender can be inferred from someone's facial appearance. Training data is crucial to establishing the effectiveness of any algorithm. As the examples illustrate, reducing complex social phenomena to discrete labels is not a straightforward exercise.

Data Processing—The Basics

Before any prepared data can be processed, a model must be created. As communication scholar Tarleton Gillespie (2016, 19) explains, a data model is the "formalization of a problem and its goal articulated in computational terms." Put simply, this can be illustrated by the noncomputational example of assembling a piece of furniture, like a wardrobe. The *problem* can be expressed as the fact there are clothes strewn all over the bedroom. The *goal* can be expressed as assembling a wardrobe to store the clothes. These two things together (i.e., problem + goal) constitute the model. However, assembling the wardrobe involves several sequential steps such as collecting the necessary parts for the wardrobe, accessing the required tools, working out the relationships among these objects, and then following a set of instructions outlining how to put the parts together.

If we apply this analogy to digital data, a model seeks to address a problem (or problem space, as data scientists sometimes call it) that often takes the form of reaching a decision of some sort. A good example might be helping banks decide whether to give a customer a loan. In this example, the problem arises from too many people defaulting on their loans and the bank losing money. As such, the goal is to prevent these people from receiving a loan in the first place and/or putting measures in place to protect the bank should any customers default. The data that might be thought relevant to addressing this problem could include the customer's credit rating, their history of loan repayments, employment status, and perhaps their ZIP code. A training data set with all these variables can be collated from data drawn from past customers where the question of whether or not they were able to make their loan repayments is known. The training data can be used to model the likelihood of loan repayment from prospective customers based on the data they include on their application form—that is, their credit rating, employment status, ZIP code, and so on. To do this, an algorithm can be designed to determine the relationships among these different bits of information and then predict the question of loan repayment.

An algorithm is any set of steps to do something in a specific way. Continuing the metaphor of data being cooked, one of the most common analogies for an algorithm is a recipe (i.e., set of instructions) that outlines the steps required in order to achieve a predictable outcome. For example, the steps required in the morning to get ready for work might be expressed as (1) get out of bed, (2) eat breakfast, (3) get dressed, and (4) leave the house. This can be described as the operational logic for getting ready for work. Other activities, such as baking a cake or building a wardrobe, will also have their own unique operational logic.

While these algorithms are quite simple, in computational models, the algorithm is usually highly complex and requires multiple steps. In a computational model, an algorithm is specified as a series of logic statements that allow it to be applied in all circumstances. To do this, an algorithm will execute a certain section of code only if certain conditions are met; otherwise, it will take an alternative route (Bucher 2018). This conditional logic is known in computer programming as the "if-then statement." The idea being if some condition is true, then do this, or else do that. For example, *if* the restaurant is open, *then* we will eat out. Otherwise, we can go home to cook dinner. As a simple algorithm, this might be expressed as *If* the restaurant is open, *Then* we go out, *Else* we cook dinner at home. In computational terms, the if-then statement is a series of "defined steps that if followed in the correct order will computationally process input data to produce a desired outcome" (Kitchin 2017, 16). These algorithmic processes can then be applied to analyzing data by hand. Indeed, the word "algorithm" is derived from the ninth-century Persian scholar Muhammad ibn Mūsā al-Khwārizmī, who studied mathematics, astronomy, and geography. Yet, algorithms gain power in an era of digital data because these steps can be executed in a fraction of the time it would take us to perform the same step; however, essentially *"they are still the same steps"* (Louridas 2020, 23).

Coming back to the example of the bank, data collected from millions of previous loan holders is used to train the algorithm so that it can be used to predict the likelihood of someone else defaulting on their loan. Given that the outcome of the training data is known, they can test the effectiveness of the model in making predictions. Once the model (training data + algorithm) is fine-tuned, it can be used on data relating to new customers to make predictions about their likelihood to repay their loans. In simplistic terms, the algorithm might filter applicants (i.e., *if* an applicant has a criminal record, *then* they will not be granted a loan), or it may categorize applications into groups (i.e., *if* an applicant has defaulted on their loan before, *then* they are subjected to particular penalties to protect the bank). Applicants would likely be filtered, categorized, or ranked to help the bank decide on whether they should be granted a loan and then the conditions of the loan. For example, the model may label a potential customer as a "risky borrower" and therefore subject them to higher interest rates. All of these decisions can be made almost instantaneously. Crucially, neither the prospective loanee nor the loan manager needs to be aware of the calculations and logics being applied—leading to what might be termed the "computer says no" phenomenon.

Machine Learning—Supervised and Unsupervised Models to Learn from Data

Many data-driven technologies are dependent on algorithms. A key element of critical data literacies is therefore recognizing when algorithms are being used, having an informed guess at which variables are included in this algorithm, and what basic logics might be at play. More complex forms of data processing fall under the label of artificial intelligence (AI). In simple terms, AI refers to computer systems that take data relating to their surroundings and past experiences in order to make decisions and predictions that would usually require human intelligence. These decisions and predictions allow tasks to be performed without explicit human instructions. In this sense, AI systems are developed to simulate specific forms of human logic and sense-making. This is achieved through the capacity of current digital technologies to process huge amounts of data relating to specific tasks that the human mind is simply not capable of processing in a similar time. In short, AI is a computerized process of making bounded decisions by automated means based on large-scale data analysis.

The most common form of data processing associated with AI is machine learning. Machine learning is used for a range of complex data-related activities, such as filtering spam and malware, speech recognition and voice synthesis, and scanning X-rays and blood tests for anomalies like cancer. A combination of methods, tools, and algorithms are used to train software systems to analyze, understand, and find hidden patterns in data and make predictions. The overriding goal in machine learning is to iteratively evolve an understanding of a data set—"to automatically learn to recognize complex patterns and construct models that explain and predict such patterns and optimize outcomes" (Kitchin 2014, 103). As with any type of data processing, the quality of data that is collected and used is therefore crucial to the outcome of any machine learning model. This is countered by the underlying imperative to collect as much data as possible related to the phenomena in question, thereby increasing the chance that it *might* provide a correlation or a pattern.

There are two broad approaches to machine learning modeling. In *supervised* learning, data is labeled by humans to create the training data set and guide the learning process. The prelabeled data makes it easier for the models created to make decisions based on the logic rules that the data scientist has defined. In this way, the model learns to match inputs to certain known outputs. However, computers can learn to recognize the data and label it without the need for human intervention—what is known as *unsupervised* machine learning. In unsupervised learning, the data in the data set is not labeled, and inferential methods are used to find patterns, relationships, and correlations. This approach is sometimes bolstered by people also inputting data into machine learning models, helping to reinforce or correct them. For example, ReCaptcha (a technology owned by Google) functions at one level to determine whether a website user is a robot or not. However, in demonstrating their humanness, each person using ReCaptcha is helping train object recognition models by indicating which parts of a photograph feature a motorbike, car, traffic lights, or similar feature of real-life environments.

Another technique to be aware of when trying to understand the logics behind data-driven technologies is data mining—a particular type of machine learning that extracts anomalies, patterns, and correlations from large data sets. For this reason, the term "data mining" is a misnomer as the data itself is not being extracted, but rather patterns and correlations within that data are being extracted. This technique is used by data scientists to identify notable data clusters, anomaly detection, deviations and outliers, dependencies, and other trends among different data objects. For example, this technique might identify a correlation among particular variables that otherwise do not appear relevant but enable the creation of a new proxy. For example, ZIP code data might prove to be a reasonably statistically significant proxy for socioeconomic status, regardless of clearly being based on a weak connection that does not always hold for every person living in that ZIP code area. However, while this weak association might be well known by the data scientist responsible for establishing this proxy, problems arise when proxies are later taken as ground truths in machine learning models (Crawford 2021).

Deep Learning—Unsupervised Learning

Much of the recent hype around AI relates to a specific advanced form of machine learning that remains rarely applied in practice but is also worth being aware of. Deep learning has generated much interest lately as it is seen as key to developing particularly powerful forms of AI. One of the central characteristics of deep learning is the application of machine learning techniques to artificial neural networks. These are networks modeled on the complex layered structure of biological brains. Deep learning involves sets of training data being continually disassembled and reassembled through the layers of an artificial neural network, with each network node assigning different weightings to a specific data point. Crucially, the excitement surrounding deep learning stems from the idea of systems being able to train themselves to refine the accuracy of these algorithms until they are capable of reaching accurate conclusions. This capacity to learn autonomously using the operating principles of neural networks is speculatively seen as heralding the future achievement of powerful levels of humanlike reasoning and language skills—what some commentators consider to be "the holy grail" of "generalized AI" (Gomes 2017).

The development of deep learning follows on from the growing availability of massive data sets over the past decade. An early proof of concept for deep learning came from a team of Google engineers led by Andrew Ng in 2012, involved in training huge neural networks on data from 10 million YouTube videos. This massive volume of available data is seen to have transformed the potential of machine learning. As Andrew Ng (2015) has since reflected, "The analogy to deep learning is that the rocket engine is the deep learning models and the fuel is the huge amounts of data we can feed to these algorithms."

Deep learning processes now underpin various types of AI applications. For example, deep learning has become a key component of work around the image-processing capabilities that underpin the operation of self-driving tractors and autonomous drone weaponry. Elsewhere, big data processing is used to identify people and locations at increased risk of crime (so-called predictive policing) and to configure forms of customized health care through the analysis of population-wide genomic data (so-called precision medicine). Many of these advances are driven by the expansion of types of digitized data. For example, the emerging field of affective computing seeks to detect and recognize human emotions from a range of data relating to facial detection, body gestures, galvanic skin response, and other physiological measurements. When this is combined at scale with geolocational data, a detailed picture of what populations are doing, where they are, and what they are thinking can be created. Needless to say, a whole host of marketers, pollsters, institutions, and companies would be interested in these insights.

Data Processing—Recurring Issues and Concerns

Returning to our overarching concern with identifying the text of digital data, these forms of algorithmic processing, machine learning, and deep learning are clearly all driving the construction of different data-related texts in highly complex ways. In this sense, the critical data literacies approach encourages us to make sense of data processing as a form of writing. A new language is created through the different types of data that are being collected through digital technologies, and new kinds of information and insights are being created through the processing of this language. For example, new representations of people and other social entities are being "written" through the production of data doubles and the identification of novel associations and patterns among different social phenomena. These new texts are created for different audiences and for different purposes. Just as writing is an arbitrary and abstract process, so too is data processing. At this point, therefore, it is important to take stock of some of the issues associated with data processing. So now that we have some sense of how digital data is processed (and in a literacies sense, how the text is written), what concerns and problems emerge?

Issues of Bias

One of the immediate issues raised by these forms of data processing is the issue of bias. This book has already raised all manner of examples of data-driven bias that we might now understand as related (at least in part) with these forms of data preparation and data processing. For example, concerns have been raised over the propensity of facial recognition technologies to fail to detect faces with nonwhite skin tones, the possibility of credit rating systems refusing to grant loans to people from particular suburbs and locations, and the algorithmic overinflation of calculated exam grades for students from fee-paying schools. These issues point to a fundamental mismatch between the ways in which computer scientists and social scientists approach the issue of bias. On one hand, many data scientists might contend that these problems can be fixed by better data practices and technical rigor and that algorithms and AI models are not biased in and of themselves. Instead, it might be reasoned that algorithms and AI models simply amplify bias that has crept inadvertently into the data sets that they are trained on and/or the data that they are fed. As such, it might appear that any data-driven bias is ultimately fixable with better data.

Nevertheless, as Deb Raji (2021) describes, this is not the case. Of course, it is right to acknowledge that the initial generation of data can reflect historical bias and that the data sets used to develop algorithmic models will often contain representation and measurement bias. However, as we have just described, every aspect of an algorithmic system is a result of programming and design decisions and can therefore contain additional biases. These include decisions about how tasks are conceived and codified, as well as how choices are modeled. Algorithmic models are also subject to what are termed aggregation biases and evaluation biases. All told, any outcome of an algorithmic model is shaped by subjective human judgments, interpretations, and discretionary decisions along the way. In this sense, the concerns raised so far in this book about the unfair outcomes of data-driven processes need to be seen in terms of biased data sets, biased models, *and* the biased contexts and uneven social relations within which any algorithmic system is used. This means that algorithmic bias is not simply a technical data problem, but a sociotechnical problem of humans and data . . . and therefore not something that can be easily fixed.

Much of the tension between computer scientists eager to fix their problematic data systems and critics concerned by the inherent harms reflects profound differences in terminology and perceptions of the object of concern. Raji (2021) reminds us that computer scientists, technologists, and data scientists often still take offense when confronted with talk of algorithmic bias because of differences in terminology. In technical terms, data scientists are often trained to think about bias in very precise terms of statistical bias— one of the issues that any data scientist will strive to minimize when developing accurate algorithms and machine learning models. As anthropologist Kate Crawford (2017) puts it, "We are speaking different languages when we talk about bias." To avoid such confusion, talk of data bias is perhaps better framed in terms of social bias and therefore linked to issues of fairness, harm, and discrimination. In computer science terms, these conversations are perhaps best understood as a problem with classification and the classifications that technology developers ascribe to people and their social contexts. In other words, addressing issues of statistical bias, underrepresentation, and variance in data sets are not the main problems to be confronted.

Issues of Causality

Another difference between data science and social perspectives is how statistical correlations among variables can slip into assumptions of social causes and effects. Just because a pattern or correlation is found in data does not mean that a meaningful relationship exists. Despite this, databases become proxies for a whole range of social phenomena and, once processed, can have real-world implications. For example, returning to one of the short stories from the prologue to this book, the number of links a college applicant clicks on a university website can now be used to determine their likelihood of course completion. Given the drive within higher education to collect as much data as possible, university administers are faced with the matter of what to do with the data. Thus, the use of data relating to website activity might be seen as a case of the data determining what is processed rather than the actual problem, issue, or question. Consequently, narratives are required to make sense of the relational juxtapositions that are created through databases (Crawford 2017). These narratives then shape public discourse and human understandings, which can ultimately limit social, educational, and economic opportunities for people.

Such issues relate to several broader critiques of data science. For example, in chapter 2, we highlighted how the amassing of big data runs an increased risk of apophenia—the tendency to perceive connections and relationships among different phenomenon when actually none exist. While most data scientists remain well aware of such limitations (and standard truisms such as "correlation does not equal causation"), in practice, digital data processing continues to be guided by a sense that the more data that can be collected and processed, the better. As such, concerns over the provenance and contextual origins of this data are sidelined.

Issues of Transparency

These two specific issues of bias and (non)causality reflect the wider concern of transparency of process. Here, it can be argued that a fundamental concern that needs to be raised in terms of most digital technologies is that data processing is "black-boxed" and hidden from view. While we have tried our best to define key aspects of data science and outline the different steps involved in processing data, there is much of this process that nonexperts stand little chance of being aware of, let alone understanding. Indeed, even those who create machine learning models tend to lose track of how their creations operate in the wild, as these models are constantly evolving in relation to the data. For this reason, it is nearly impossible to gauge the fairness with which people and things are processed in contemporary society because much of that process has been hidden or black-boxed (Pasquale 2015). Who decides what constitutes a training set? How are these decisions used?

This concern is arguably even more serious when data processing is auto-mated through machine learning and AI. Data can be bought and traded by myriad third parties, making it impossible to definitively identify how it will be processed and used. So, while this chapter has attempted to provide a sense of how data is generated, collected, and processed, these are, in a sense, approximations that will change and shift with each and every piece of data. As communications scholar Matthew Crain (2016, 6) explains, as soon as "information has been swept into the data broker marketplace, it becomes challenging and in many cases, impossible to trace any given datum to its original source." For this reason, identifying the new texts that are created through data is, at best, a speculative process. In this way, tradi-tional notions of critique that relied upon transparency and deconstruction have limited use when it comes to data.

That said, it is not a given that greater transparency necessarily leads to more sophisticated understandings of data. Ananny and Crawford (2018) remind us that transparency has limitations and does not necessarily lead to understanding, change, or liberation from oppressive systems. Indeed, seeing inside the systems of machine learning or AI does not necessarily mean that it will be any better understood. Even the engineers and data sci-entists who created these models do not always know how they will evolve when left unsupervised and may be unable to show the logic behind the systems' decision-making (Ananny and Crawford 2018). While we need an understanding of data-processing systems, we also need to consider how social systems apply these insights. Analysis should move between these different layers or levels so that we can both understand data processing as well as the bigger picture of how these technological and social systems intersect and to what effect. With this in mind, the focus for critical data literacies should be on looking *across* systems to understand the relations between humans and machines and how they are shaped in the interests of power. After all, technological systems are continuously evolving and innovating, meaning that aspiring to greater transparency will only be use-ful for the briefest period of time. Seeing and revealing does not necessarily lead to greater knowledge or control. Instead, Ananny and Crawford (2018) argue it might be more useful to reflect on *how* we know what we know about a system.

Conclusions

This chapter has expanded on the first two stages of the critical data literacies framework to provide a detailed account of how data is generated, collected, collated, and then processed. Of course, in making these critical observations, we do not want to be overly dismissive of any of these forms of data work. As with any critical approach, it is important to remember that data processing underpins all manner of socially beneficial—if not essential—processes. One only needs to think of how data processing is used to support radiologists in analyzing X-rays or even to enable intelligent personal assistants in the home. Underpinning our critical approach to data literacies is a hope that things can be better. As such, one important reason to be asking these questions is to reflect on what is being done well and explore how it can be applied to the more problematic aspects of datafication.

In this sense, it is important to begin to consider how these forms of data processing are applied in different contexts—as Alex Albright (2019) puts it, social settings and institutional systems that are "chock-full" of human judgments, human discretions, and human biases. Indeed, this chapter has outlined data preparation and data processing in largely context-free terms. While knowledge of these context-free uses certainly builds our understanding of the datafication process, it does not provide a tangible way of applying this knowledge to improve our own entanglements with data. Nonspecialists are more likely to see data used in more practical everyday applications, such as targeted advertising, automated prompts to walk 10,000 steps, or recommendations to "friend" someone on Facebook. Indeed, as we have discussed in previous chapters, data is used across most domains in society—home, work, education, and leisure. Given the myriad possibilities for how data can be used, the next chapter considers tangible instances of four real-world uses of data: (1) selling, (2) safety and security, (3) convenience and personalization, and (4) governance and optimization.

In particular, the next chapter uses these examples of how data is used *in context* to expand on the third and fourth stages of the critical data literacies framework—Data Reflexivity and Data Strategies. Within the overall critical data literacies framework, these domains relate to key moments at which the individual can intercede in the datafication process. Applying the arguments developed in this chapter, we argue it is possible to work out and enact strategies to use data in ways that suit the needs of the people rather than the companies, institutions, or organizations in their lives. Put simply, one of the goals of the critical data literacies approach is to find ways to support people to *do data*, rather than having data *done to them*. As such, we need to shift the focus of our subsequent conversations around how to reinsert the human back into the datafication process. More specifically, the next chapter is about learning to take control over who has access to personal data and how it is being used. Certainly, data protection and privacy are both important parts of this—what we might liken to choosing *who* may write with your data. Nevertheless, to be literate with data also means using it to construct our own meanings and write our own stories. Taking back control of digital data therefore forms the focus of our next set of discussions.

6 Managing, Accessing, and Protecting Data: Strategies for Living in a Datafied Society

Introduction

One of the central ideas underpinning critical data literacies is that developing a good understanding of how digital data is being generated, processed, and used by others can therefore provide a strong basis for then being able to take practical steps to do more with data ourselves and ensure we are not being disadvantaged. The next two chapters turn attention toward the "writing" phase of data literacies, by considering how people can access, manage, and protect their data in ways that better fit their *own* needs. This is not as straightforward as it sounds. Any response needs to fit the different contexts in which we generate and encounter data. The levels of agency and control that anyone has will differ depending on what context they are in. For example, what someone can do with personal data generated by their workplace technology use will be very different from dealing with personal data arising from their online shopping. A key part of putting the critical data literacies framework into action therefore involves tackling some important political questions regarding data provenance and ownership.

One recurring theme throughout our discussions so far is the difficulty of working out exactly who has control over the data that is generated by and/or about each of us. With many software applications and platforms, for example, ownership of digital data is often attributed to the company or institution that captured and collected the data, rather than the person who generated it. This becomes a significant limitation to individuals accessing their own data and can understandably push some people into a default position of wanting to "keep their data private." However, many others now accept that living in a datafied society means that *some* sharing of personal data is unavoidable and, often, beneficial.

This chapter identifies and explores the trade-offs and tensions that emerge when it comes to thinking about data access and control. This raises questions of balancing data privacy with data visibility and the compromises that come with digital convenience. From a critical data literacies approach, then, these issues can be thought of in terms of *who* is allowed to write with data. Keeping personal data private might be thought of as preventing *others* from "writing" with our data, while the process of an individual accessing and using their *own* data might be seen as similar to assuming the role of author. We argue these issues are perhaps better seen as taking collective control and agency of our digital identities in the age of data. Indeed, while critique is often considered to be an individual practice, the chapter concludes with the need to collectively negotiate the issues of data management, access, and control.

The Need to See Data in Context

One of the key themes from chapter 5 was the dangers of seeing data in wholly decontextualized terms. Of course, to be operational in the world of data science, data must be decontextualized. Strings of numbers are wrangled into spreadsheets and mathematical models, which are then processed and analyzed to produce new insights and understandings. At either end of this process, the people who use these technologies are involved. At the front end, people *generate* data during their day-to-day lives in the form of clicks, posts, and likes. At a later point, they *interpret* processed data in the form of metrics, dashboards, and graphs. However, these processes of data generation and data interpretation only really make sense when put in terms of their context and situation. For example, a runner who uses an app to track their speed and distance but who has just returned to running after an injury will know why they have recorded slower times. Context helps provide the full story of social phenomena in a way that data—on its own—cannot. In contrast to this, most of the descriptions in chapter 5 of how data is generated, collected, and processed made little reference to the context in which this data was being extracted and processed and largely free of involvement by the people for whom the data purports to represent.

In chapter 6, we reinsert the human back into the datafication process and explore strategies that people can use to manage, access, and protect data. Adopting a literacies approach to data therefore requires reflexivity—the third stage of our critical data literacies framework—to bring consciousness and thought to when and how data might be processed and used. While there are myriad uses of data in society today, this chapter explores these data strategies through four different contexts that have come to define datafied society:

- the use of digital data to sell goods and services (more accurately, to encourage people to buy goods and services),
- the use of data to keep things safe and secure,
- the use of data to customize and personalize, and
- the use of data to govern and optimize.

Each of these different contexts is considered in terms of the fourth domain of the critical data literacies framework—that is, what *data strategies* people can use to disrupt these data flows so they have a greater say in who can access their data and how it is be used. Data strategies are essentially normative practices that can be enacted within a device or system, such as adjusting security settings within the platform or reading the terms and conditions attached to a particular platform. These can be contrasted with data tactics, which refer to more oppositional approaches toward digital media that include subversion and resistance, which we discuss in chapter 7.

As the following examples will illustrate, data strategies are by no means failsafe ways to manage and control your data. As we explain in the latter parts of the chapter, there are always limitations to what can be achieved given the proprietorial nature of the digital systems and environments in which much of this data is generated. So, for our first context, let us consider what data strategies and actions might relate to the growing use of data to sell goods and services—what can be more specifically described as the data economy's reliance on making money from advertising and marketing.

Seeing Data in Context: Data-Driven Advertising

One of the most common reasons for personal data to be generated is so that it can be used to sell new products, services, and ideas to prospective consumers. As noted earlier, geolocational data can be processed to target people at specific times and locations to let them know about sales or offers. Alphanumeric and visual data can be mined from social media platforms to infer the emotional response that someone might have toward a particular topic or brand. These "insights" can then be used by companies to determine who to target through their marketing campaigns. Advertisements and other prompts within social media platforms further reinforce and promote engagement. Joseph Turow (2011) describes this as the "long click." The long click involves several steps, including tracking internet users across websites through third-party cookies, reinforcing responses to clicks and convincing them to use their frequent-shopper card, debit card, or credit card to generate even more data. Insights from this endless cycle of tracking and tracing can be used to sell various items, services, and concepts and is therefore considered highly valuable information for an array of companies and third parties.

To apply the critical data literacies framework in this context, we need to begin by identifying how and when data is used in daily life to sell things. In chapter 4, we outlined three distinct points when data might be identified—that is, when people voluntarily *give* information to systems, as well as when devices and systems *extract* information and processed data that is *presented back* to people. The most difficult of these to identify is extracted data, as we are often unaware of this information being generated and collected amid the busyness of everyday life. Indeed, it is often easier to *identify* data when it is used to sell things back to us. The first and perhaps most obvious instance of this is when we see an advertisement that feels eerily prescient to the point of appearing as though someone might have been eavesdropping in on private conversations.

Of course, targeted advertising does not require covert spying or eavesdropping. If enough data points are gathered, then it raises the likelihood that you may be interested in *one* of the things that are shown to you during your time online (especially given how adept most of us have become at tuning out when presented with obviously mistargeted adverts). A study by Mozilla, for example, suggested that a relatively small list of someone's favorite websites (perhaps as few as fifty) can enable advertisers to create a unique profile for them (Cimpanu 2020). To give a simple example, someone who has recently searched for swimsuits and visited an airline price comparison website might reasonably be presumed to be interested in holidays, and therefore advertising for global hotel chains is likely to get their attention. Coupling this inference with any socioeconomic data that a third party may also have about them (such as their ZIP code or the car they drive) might help refine the targeting of an advertisement either for budget or luxury accommodation.

Of course, data is not just used to sell goods, services, and holidays; it is also used to sell ideas and people. Dark advertising or dark posts were initially conceived by Facebook engineers to show up as sponsored content in users' feeds (McManus 2016). Although Facebook has tried to rebrand these as unpublished posts, the main selling point of this advertising is that these messages are difficult for any other person or company apart from the targeted individual to see (hence the "dark" description). This type of messaging enables publishers to micro-target people without broadcasting the same messages to a wider audience. Each social media platform has its own form of dark posts—for example, advertisers can target Facebook users who might have viewed a particular website or live in a particular location. Mark Andrejevic and colleagues (2021) demonstrated how Australian political parties were able to target voters through dark ads in the runup to the 2019 federal election to drive home specific aspects of their election campaign. For example, this messaging was able to target users who had an interest in particular brands of car—drawing on Facebook's insights into online activity, which enabled them to infer which type of car a person was likely to own (or at least aspire to own). The dark ad that appeared in the user's feed was then able to resonate more strongly with each individual, highlighting political issues that would likely be of personal interest, such as the threat of one political party's intention to tax large SUVs or small electric vehicles (depending on the person viewing the advert).

Seen in terms of the critical data literacies stage of reflexivity, this example raises the obvious question of "why am I seeing this advertisement?" It may be that several days earlier, you searched online for a new Toyota SUV, posted on a four-wheel driving forum, or did not immediately click past an advertisement for new car tires. Any of these actions could generate data to infer your interest in a particular type of vehicle—all forms of information that are voluntarily *given* to systems. Being conscious of this supposedly volunteered information is difficult given the large amounts of time that we are online and the masses of information that we are continually contributing, but it is increasingly important as it is shaping private and public life (Shepard 2022). Being data literate means making connections between the information that is given to the system and the targeted advertisement that is subsequently seen—whether that be to sell you a product, service, political party, or idea.

In this case of micro-targeting, it is possible that the targeted individual is the only person to see that specific version of the dark ad, as even official regulators are not privy to the ads people are exposed to. It is perhaps unsurprising, then, that these data-driven profiles appeal to publishers trying to promote content that may be considered unsavory or controversial for mainstream audiences. As such, micro-targeting is an increasingly popular method for scammers and peddlers of "fake" news. This has also been illustrated in several high-profile cases of ethically questionable practices involving some of the major technology providers. One of these involved leaked documents from Facebook showing that the company shares information with advertisers relating to the inferred emotional state of its teenage users, such as when they might feel insecure, nervous, worthless, and anxious. This can help advertisers pinpoint specific times in the week when these individuals might respond best to a confidence boost (Levin 2017). This form of micro-targeting raises concerns over coercion of vulnerable groups, psychological manipulation, and discrimination on the basis of age, race, and class (Andrejevic et al. 2021b).

Moving to the next stage of the framework, we need to build *understandings* of how personal data is processed to sell things. Here we can apply what we know about data processing explored in chapter 5. One well-known instance of data-driven selling was the Cambridge Analytica scandal of 2018. This involved the Cambridge Analytica data analytics company harvesting millions of Facebook user profiles to drive a remarkably effective online campaign to sell Donald Trump as president and demean his much more politically experienced opponent, Hilary Clinton. This advertising campaign saw data scientists build a model that enabled them to accurately predict the kind of voter who could be swayed to vote for Trump. Despite the abundance of already existing Facebook data, Trump's team achieved a more accurate level of profiling by augmenting these insights with patterns identified from a 120-page online survey that a sample of Facebook users was paid to complete. The survey enabled the data scientists to find clusters of traits (e.g., if someone is loud, then they can be assumed to also be gregarious) and then develop a profile of individuals that could be targeted as "swing voters." In particular, the data scientists used the "Ocean" model of profiling to create a measure of each individual user's openness to experience, conscientiousness, extroversion, agreeableness, and neuroticism.

Crucially, the key element of this survey was requiring survey takers to grant the company access to their Facebook account through an app (Rosenberg and Dance 2018). This allowed the data scientists to correlate survey insights with a whole host of personal information, including real name, contact details, and location. So, while the survey could provide the target variable (the profiles of the people they needed to target with the campaign), the Facebook data could provide a powerful feature set that could be correlated with those profiles. Crucially, the Facebook app granted access to survey takers' Facebook accounts, as well as the Facebook profiles of their friends— giving the Trump team insights into the personal backgrounds of almost 87 million US Facebook users (Rosenberg and Dance 2018). In this way, Cambridge Analytica was able to create an ensemble model of many millions of data points. Different machine learning models were created from the data, enabling the data scientists to work backward through Facebook likes to accurately predict the personality types of each Facebook user and therefore determine which people to target. While these machine learning models took some fine-tuning (it was reported that over 250 algorithms were developed), the process of data mining and targeted advertising was deemed particularly successful. Indeed, many commentators suggest Trump's 2016 election victory was due to the targeting of these swing voters who eventually got him across the line.

While this was a particular type of targeted advertising, it serves as a real-life illustration to help us understand the basic steps in this process. This might be described as follows: model created>training set compiled>algorithm designed to work on the training set to predict the known outcome>algorithm released onto data in the wild. So, given these sorts of understandings, what actions can a critically literate person take to better manage and protect their data from being used in these ways? Here, we can turn to the "four resources" model of literacy (Freebody and Luke 1990; Luke and Freebody 1999) to identify the points at which someone might get involved with the structures and social relations that shape how their personal data is generated, processed, and used. In literacy terms, this might be described as "knowing about and acting on the different cultural and social functions that various texts perform" in ways that reaffirm the "constructed order" of a system (Luke and Freebody 1999, 5). In terms of the critical data literacies framework, however, this can be described as *data strategies*.

In terms of data strategies, then, a critically literate person might start quite simply by reading the terms of service agreements of the digital platforms that they are involved with and then adjusting their privacy settings accordingly. It might also involve adjusting geolocation settings. This does not necessarily mean switching these settings off permanently. Instead, being data literate means understanding the implications of changing any setting, as well as having the technical skills to do so. Data strategies might also mean thinking carefully about agreeing to complete online surveys—particularly if they ask you to sign in using your Facebook account or provide your email address. It is important to be critically reflexive—why am I being asked to do this? Who might be interested in the information I give and how might it be used?

A further set of data strategies relating to targeting and selling might involve implementing ad block software that prevents ads, videos, or other displays from being shown on a webpage. People might opt to change their browser settings, so not to allow third-party cookies, or choose to use web browsers such as Brave, which automatically blocks online advertisements and website trackers. As explained in chapter 5, third-party cookies are created by websites other than the one being used and therefore enable a host of third parties to track people across the internet. Popular web browsers (such as Safari and Google Chrome) are under increasing pressure to disable third-party cookies—a shift expected to radically alter the online advertising business model. All told, these data strategies provide people with choice when it comes to who (or what) has access to their information and how it can be used. After all, some people might still consider targeted advertising to serve a purpose—not only for consumers looking for a bargain but also as a means of allowing digital platforms and products to be provided free of change . . . if, of course, one is willing to pay with their data.

Seeing Data in Context: Data as a Means of Safety and Security

A second notable context of data use is for safety and security purposes across a variety of domains—such as home, school, and workplace, as well as at state and national levels. The use of data for safety and security purposes is often justified through a sense of obligation and duty—for example, keeping one's family, neighbors, coworkers, and fellow citizens safe. For example, during the COVID-19 pandemic, a host of apps were mandated by governments to help limit the spread of infection—alerting people when they might have visited a high-risk site or come into contact with an infected individual. Of course, the effectiveness and use of these apps were soon questioned, as was the storage and security of the data being generated. Nevertheless, data is now used routinely across many areas in personal and public life to enable access and control, as well as to keep people, places, and objects safe and secure.

Using data to track people online is often referred to as dataveillance. As Jose van Dijck (2014, 205) explains, dataveillance differs from surveillance in that it is not monitoring for any explicit purpose but rather "entails the continuous tracking of (meta)data for unstated pre-set purposes." Not only are dataveillance technologies used by law enforcement, but they are now an increasingly popular way for parents and guardians to keep track of what their children are doing online. Parental control apps are marketed as a way of "keeping children safe" from inappropriate content and interactions and are downloaded onto a child's mobile phone, laptop, or tablet to enable dataveillance by parents. Research by the Australian eSafety Commission (Office of the eSafety Commissioner 2018) found 4 percent of parents of preschoolers to be using parental control apps, with this proportion increasing to 7 percent of parents with elementary school-age children and 8 percent of parents with teenagers. In the United States, 16 percent of parents use geolocation tracking to monitor their children's internet use (Anderson 2016), while in the United Kingdom, an Ofcom Report from 2020/2021 found 29 percent of parents to be using content-filtering features of parental control software. These forms of personal and intimate dataveillance of others is known as "other tracking" (Gabriels 2016), with global trends suggesting that these figures are set to continue to rise throughout the 2020s.

This particular context of data use raises several points on which we need to reflect—not least, how data is being used in this process of keeping things safe and secure. If we take the example of parental monitoring apps, then we can see how data in the form of real names and email addresses is *given* to any system when signing up, while these monitoring apps must also have access to all the other apps and platforms that parents want monitored. In order to carry out such detailed monitoring, parental control apps therefore *extract* large amounts of information without the parent or child knowing. Being critically data literate involves recognizing the difference between when data is being *given* and when it is being *extracted* and therefore making decisions about who should have access to personal data and how it should be used. However, over 80 percent of parental control apps also request access to location, contacts, and storage permissions, with many of these permissions not necessary for the app to function (Feal et al. 2020). In fact, most parental control apps request what is sometimes termed "dangerous permissions"—that is, permission to access information that could affect the family's privacy as well as the device's normal operation by making it less secure and vulnerable to attack. For example, Boomerang, a popular parental control app, is reported to request over 90 permissions, 16 of which might be considered "dangerous" (Feal et al. 2020).

A key part of critical data literacies is therefore making sense of how this happens. Here, then, we are reminded of what sociologists Dave Beer and Roger Burrows (2013) call the "social life of data," which refers to the fact that digital data is used and reused across different contexts and for different purposes by a diverse range of actors. In addition, even data that might appear private can be retrieved via other hidden technologies. At face value, data from the child's device is collected and processed by the company that makes the parental control app. This is then sent to the parent, who has a corresponding app that feeds back summary data of what websites their children have been using and for how long. However, many parental control apps also allow "data-hungry" software development kits (SDKs) to also piggyback on the original app—thereby circulating the data well beyond the parent and app provider.

In this instance, it would be very useful for parents to be aware of SDKs and how they operate. Third-party SDKs are developed by companies *separate* from the original app and therefore have different protocols around data sharing and privacy. Many are able to extract personally identifiable information, such as name, location, and contacts from children and parents. The Google Play Store does not require developers to disclose whether they have embedded third-party SDKs in their product, meaning that parents cannot make informed decisions about how their data will be used when they consent to the terms of service. Consequently, it was reckoned in 2020 that the 165 most popular parental control apps in the Google Play Store had extensive security and privacy vulnerabilities (Ali et al. 2020). Similarly, another US study focusing on whether parental control apps complied with the Children's Online Privacy Protection Act (COPPA) to protect the personal data of children under thirteen years, found that roughly 57 percent of these apps were in violation of the law through their use of SDKs (Reyes et al. 2018).

The case of parental control apps highlights the fact that while the marketing for these technologies centers on issues of care and safety, many companies are failing to fully protect and care for their clients' personal data, which is shared with an array of third parties and data brokers. Many areas of technology development are similarly prone to "function creep"—that is, the "gradual expansion of the functionality of some system or technology beyond what it was originally created for" (Koops 2021, 29). Indeed, data-related function creep seems commonplace with technologies that are ostensibly designed to keep us safe and secure.

This wider circulation of intimate data was illustrated in a recent case of a US text-based counseling service—offering a confidential means for potentially suicidal teens to seek guidance through text-based messaging (see McNeil 2022). Drawing on over $20 million of startup funding raised from tech-related philanthropic sources (including Melinda Gates and Steve Ballmer), Crisis Text Line was subsequently found to be harvesting text data from its teen callers with a view to developing other products—despite initial claims to "NEVER share data" of the teens contacting the service. Some of the service's leaders reasoned that it would be unethical *not* to use this data to gain insights into teen suicide behavior. Less nobly, the data was seemingly used to drive the development of a spinoff service described as "a Grammarly for emotion"—helping other online customer service teams respond to texts in a caring, empathetic, warm manner. This clash between the ambitions of tech developers and innovators and the complex nature of something like suicide counseling typifies the dangers of what McNeil (2022) terms "the Silicon Valleyfication of Everything":

> Crisis Text Line put its market proposition above the needs of its vulnerable users: its dehumanizing data collection practices were part of a series of callous acts. Suicide prevention doesn't look like the "speed of a private tech company" or "awesome" machine learning. It requires safety and care with no strings attached. This care includes generosity and expansion of public resources like access to housing, food, healthcare, and other basic needs; it can't be measured in KPIs. The very purpose Crisis Text Line claimed to serve is incompatible with the Silicon Valley way of doing business.

So how might critical data literacies help people redress such imbalances? When it comes to safety and security, the strategies for protecting our data are pretty straightforward—we either consent to use these technologies or not. However, to be fully informed of *how* these technologies make use of our data and *who* is using it requires a slightly different set of investigative strategies. The first step is to adopt a critical disposition toward granting "permissions" when using monitoring apps and to carefully consult the terms of service of other technologies to which you are being asked to grant permission. A helpful tool here is the Blacklight online resources mentioned in chapter 4, or the Terms of Service; Didn't Read (TS;DR) site, which summarizes the terms of service and privacy policies of major internet sites. Created by a community of programmers and designers, TS; DR gives major websites a grade and outlines points of concern to make it easier for the general public to give full consent.

In addition, other tools can reveal some of the more hidden technologies and processes involved in using data for safety and security purposes. For example, trails and traces can be examined by using tools such as Chrome's browser add-on Thunderbeam-Lightbeam. Originally developed by Mozilla, Thunderbeam-Lightbeam for Chrome is a browser extension that visualizes the third parties that are tracking your internet activities as an interactive map. At a more complex level, IX Maps enables people to see how their personal data circulates across the internet as well as the points at which security agencies such as the National Security Agency might intercept it.

Seeing Data in Context: Data as a Form of Personalization and Convenience

A third illustrative context is the processing of data to personalize online experiences, customize digital content, and supposedly make our interactions with digital services more convenient. As discussed throughout this book, personal data can be used to infer much about people's likes and dislikes, their interests, and where they work and live. This information can be used to help filter digital content to provide more personalized, streamlined experiences when online. It can also be used to make digitally mediated interactions more convenient and frictionless. Familiar examples of this might include autocomplete options and other automations designed to save time and effort.

Personalization of digital content on platforms is seen as important by software designers and developers because it increases people's attention and engagement. Google, for example, provides tailored results for search queries based on someone's browsing histories and other relevant personal data. Educational platforms strive for personalized learning to complement students' learning preferences or focus on knowledge areas that might improve with some extra attention. Indeed, the field of learning analytics attempts to develop data-driven tools that measure, collect, and analyze student data to improve learning. By processing personal data, platforms ensure that each person's experience is different even though they are engaging in the same activity. This is particularly apparent when it comes to social media platforms where the unique nature of each person's social networks means what they see in their feeds is also unique. Media researcher Taina Bucher (2012, 16) argues that this algorithmic filtering erodes the notion of an online "public," as content is "filtered in terms of the identity of specific users." Whether the platform is used for socializing, working, dating, or entertainment, the processing of data to personalize and customize experiences has become essential to the platform's success.

These processes are illustrated in YouTube's video recommendation system—deemed one of the most effective systems for personalizing digital content. In 2018, it was reported that more than 70 percent of time spent on the platform involved watching videos recommended by YouTube's recommender algorithms (Solsman 2018). The YouTube recommendation system has changed over the years, most notably with the introduction of the autoplay feature in 2015. Nevertheless, it retains core features—in particular, a commitment to not necessarily recommend the most similar videos but instead ensure diversity and novelty in what the audience is being prompted to watch.

YouTube's recommender systems rely on input data—notably content data from each viewer's video streams. Of particular value is user activity data, which includes favoriting, liking, and how long a video was watched for. While explicit acts of favoriting and liking might be reliable, other sources of input data are not always accurate. For example, just because someone watched a video in its entirety does not mean they actually liked it or want to see more of the same content. After all, they may have just left the room when the video started to play, which is why the video was watched in its entirety. Wherever possible, YouTube attempts to cross-check and compare input data from an array of sources in order to address any deficiencies. So, for example, the platform will log user inactivity and send a message to ask if viewers are still watching.

The next step In the video recommendation system involves identifying and mapping similar videos through processing techniques such as association rule mining and co-visitation counts. Association rules seek to discover interesting relationships and patterns among variables and are based on the if-then logic discussed in detail in chapter 5. Machine learning models are created to find the most frequent patterns among which videos have been watched together, develop association rules, and then use these rules to recommend content that the viewer is likely to be interested in (the familiar online refrain of "people who liked that, also liked this"). Co-visitation counts refer to how many times a pair of videos were co-watched in the same session within a given time period. This culminates in an allocated relatedness score of the video to the original seed video (Davidson et al. 2010). Other factors also taken into consideration include the global popularity of videos. Ultimately, what is arrived at is a set of videos related to the seed video. Significantly, YouTube does not rely on just one algorithm (what people often imagine to be *the* YouTube algorithm) but instead a system of algorithms working to create the best viewing experience (Bucher 2018)— hence the description of the YouTube video recommendation *system*.

This complex system is far more complicated than a simple correlation ("people who liked that, also liked this"). Instead, to generate "candidate" videos, the set of related videos is combined with the personal activity of the user and ranked. Several factors are considered here, including

- video quality—a measure derived from view count, ratings, and quality;
- user specificity—a measure referring to the viewer's interests and tastes and derived from the qualities of the seed video and watch times of videos; and
- diversification—a process where videos that are *too similar* are removed.

Following these logics, videos that are closely matched with a user's tastes and preferences will be boosted in the ranking, while those that are similar to the seed video are removed.

While every recommendation system is different (and no doubt YouTube's is constantly evolving) developing a relatively sophisticated understanding of how data-driven personalization works can help us to devise strategies to manage our engagements with recommender systems and other personalized services. In particular, critical data literacies draw attentions to the role of *social practices* in shaping how these systems function. For example, YouTube's video recommendation system has evolved over time, in part, due to how people have engaged with it. While these changes do not happen immediately or obviously, the power that consumers have to "speak back" to these systems is often underappreciated. If, for example, a mass of YouTube viewers collectively shifted their practices, they might well destabilize existent models and force search engines, recommendation systems, and social media platforms to change.

Critical reflexivity is key here. In many ways, we already formulate our own folk theories when using digital technologies, but these are often tacit and not something that people talk about. By making folk theories more explicit, users can engage with these systems more purposefully. People are an essential part of the data assemblage, and received wisdoms about how digital technologies work "provide users with resources to carry out a specific set of strategies of action through which they enact different modalities of power and resistance in relation to recommendation algorithms" (Siles et al. 2020, 11).

So, what might these strategies look like? In a basic sense is the ability to identify native advertisements or sponsored content that appears in our search results and choosing *not* to click on it. Being data literate also means having some awareness of these interconnections and the fact that activity on one platform can influence other digital experiences. For example, Google collects personal data from a whole host of sources, including someone's browsing history, Gmail and YouTube activity, location history, Google searches, and online purchases. Furthermore, if we visit a website that uses advertising services like AdSense, including analytics tools like Google Analytics or embedded video content from YouTube, "your web browser automatically sends certain information to Google" (Google 2021).

Another set of strategies relates to awareness of different systems' metrics and analytics, and understanding and manipulating these as appropriate (McCosker 2017). Data literacy strategies could therefore focus on specific aspects of the platform such as identity, activity, interactivity, and visibility and how these can be collectively or individually negotiated. Indeed, teenage social media users regularly draw on strategic knowledge to help actively shape the content that appears on their newsfeeds. Studies have found teens to make use of multiple accounts to segment interests and exert control over the algorithm. In another case, TikTok users have been found to collectively develop understanding of the platform algorithms by sharing ideas and insights in the comments section to develop a kind of "algorithmic folklore" (Akinrinade and Mukugosi 2020). In this way, everyday understandings and "stories about algorithms" (Schellewald 2022) are drawn upon to help users make sense of algorithms. From the point of view of content creators, successful YouTubers are well versed in giving their videos particular titles and use strategies like uploading multiple niche videos to make their channel recognizable to algorithms (Brown 2021).

Seeing Data in Context: Data-Driven Self-Tracking and Discipline

A final illustrative context is the use of data to improve and better one's health, fitness, and other aspects of well-being. Data from self-tracking devices, for example, is processed to help individuals regulate and monitor bodily processes and then set goals to optimize health and well-being. In some cases, self-tracking has a specific life-saving benefit, such as a diabetic monitoring their blood sugar levels or a heart patient monitoring heart rate and blood pressure. However, in many other cases, self-tracking is used to set smaller self-improvement goals and motivation. These forms of lifestyle self-tracking can take many forms—from smartwatches and Fitbits to blood pressure regulators and heart monitors.

Self-tracking devices enable people to monitor, analyze, and interpret a range of personal data relating to their health, physical, fitness, or even financial status. These can involve quite demanding practices. Deborah Lupton's (2020) work on self-tracking has highlighted the ways in which managing and interpreting the data generated can be both empowering and overwhelming. It is important to note that "self" tracking is not always voluntarily taken up. Employers can demand that workers self-track for wellness purposes and to boost productivity and work harder. Health and life insurance companies can incentivize customers to use self-tracking to help them calculate individualized premiums (Lupton 2020). These coerced forms of self-tracking raise several different issues, such as questions of who has access to this data and the purposes for which it is being used.

Also significant is the fact that some self-tracking devices are designed to use gamification logics to encourage users to optimize their performance, health, and well-being in comparison to preset goals or perhaps other people's data (Lyall 2021; Lindner 2020). For example, a self-tracking device may log someone's performance or patterns over a month and then feedback analytics that show how much they are running or walking compared to the previous month. This is intended to encourage us to run or walk more each day, while also binding people to these technologies and ensuring the continual flow of data into the data broker economy. On one hand, this cycle of self-monitoring and self-motivation may help people to feel greater levels of control, particularly during times of change or chaos (Lupton 2020). However, it may also lead to new forms of governance of the body, which can then slip into a state of self-disciplining, where the individual begins to trust the data generated by the device more than what they are feeling or experiencing. In this way, wearables and other mobile sensors constitute a significant form of datafication, where the body is a site of data generation and action.

While many people might welcome this use of data to internalize the discipline required to improve their health or fitness, from a critical data perspective, we also need to consider other implications. Who or what else benefits from constant self-tracking? If self-tracking devices are sharing personal data with data brokers, then this clearly benefits the company responsible for designing and selling the product. To what extent do interpretations of data through self-tracking devices change the way people think about and reflect on themselves, others, and their everyday lives?

One strategy for reflecting on the ways in which self-tracking data plays a role in our lives is through what Deb Lupton calls "data sense." Data sense is a way of thinking with (and through) these self-tracking devices and emphasizes the "role of fleshly and affective bodily affordances in people's responses to data" (Lupton 2020, 76). This focuses attention on the ways in which people respond to these forms of self-tracking data through their body, senses, and emotions. These responses to data are highly personal and intimately linked with sensory experience. However, affect and embodiment are also important aspects of critical data literacies, as they also shape data understandings, beliefs, and practices. Just as social literacies begin with the everyday experiences of data as affective and embodied, it is helpful to take a similar starting point when it comes to critical data literacies.

The example of self-tracking highlights the importance of the firsthand experiences people have with data, making this the foundation from which we can act, interpret, and build understanding of datafied systems. Nevertheless, it is important to retain an emphasis on reflexivity and critique, particularly when it comes to data understandings and data strategies. Clearly, then, several questions need to be asked about the political economy of self-tracking technologies as the terms, conditions, and business models of these products and services are related to maximizing the extent to which people engage with and adapt them. It is therefore interesting to think of strategies that people might deploy to create a critical distance from these highly personal and intimate forms of data, as well as disrupt the bonds of dependency that these technologies are designed to foster. For example, people might experiment with activities and provocations that decontextualize everyday use, such as suspending use for a period of time or swapping devices with a trusted other, so they can reassess, reflect on, and renew their engagement with it.

Conclusions

These four different contexts of data illustrate the varying nature and character that personal data can take. Self-tracking one's fitness is very different from having one's fondness for chocolate inferred from a set of geolocation data points. However, they are both gleaned from personal data. This chapter is predicated on the idea that data must be analyzed in context and as a kind of text or cultural expression "subject to interpretive examination" (Loukissas 2019, 7). In this chapter, we have expanded on the *data understandings* developed in chapter 5 to show how they can be applied in practice as data strategies. The aim of such strategies is to bring a sense of humanness back into datafication processes and to show what can (and cannot) be achieved by exploring and implementing ways of engaging with digital technologies on their own terms. These data strategies can take many forms—from using privacy settings and properly engaging with the terms of service to collectively developing folk pedagogies. Whatever the strategy, it is important that we keep experimenting and exploring ways to negotiate datafication and not just accept the default settings or dominant narratives of data. When engaging with any digital technology, there is always plenty of room for what Ruha Benjamin (2019) terms "informed refusal."

At the same time, however, it is important to note that strategies tend to remain within the status quo of the IT industry, data economy, and other vested interests, rather than challenging it. As Thomas Lemke (2019) reasons, strategies can be seen as generalizing and bolstering "the coherence of power relations." In other words, while useful to the individuals who are implementing them, these strategies inevitably serve to reinforce the general dominance of macro-level actors (such as tech firms) over those at the micro level. Such strategies might be presented as assisting people to renegotiate the terms on which they engage with digital data, but this does not necessarily equate to any meaningful sense of empowerment. Indeed, it could be argued that genuinely transformative change calls for collective action, which relies upon organization, communication, coordination, and a commitment to considering how our digital practices might impact others. The next chapter, therefore, looks at data tactics that subvert and resist the dominance of Big Tech. While the ideas in this chapter might help us to take control of who (or what) has access to our personal data, the tactics in the next chapter contain a more direct promise to support people to "write" with their digital data.

7 Reappropriating and Resisting Digital Data: Collective Tactics and Activism

Introduction

This chapter continues to expand a key underpinning theme of this book—that of "doing data differently." One of the driving rationales behind the development of critical data literacies is the idea of *acting* on our enhanced awareness and understandings of what digital data is and the roles that digital data plays in everyday life. Chapter 6 considered a series of *data strategies* that might go some way to redressing the impositions and disadvantages associated with living under datafied conditions. These are all actions that people are ostensibly free to pursue while using digital technologies in order to assert their rights (although, of course, in reality, software developers and technology firms assume that few people will actually bother to do so). It takes time and commitment to read terms of service agreements, adjust privacy settings, implement ad blocker technologies, and otherwise work to exert some control over the data that is associated with using technology. Nevertheless, as illustrated throughout chapter 6, there is much benefit in knowing your rights and then sometimes being able to go on to actually exercise these rights.

This chapter looks beyond these responses of being a circumspect but dutiful user of data-driven technologies. As Ruha Benjamin (2019, 14) reminds us, engaging with digital data on equal terms needs to be conceived in collective terms of being citizens rather than users—as she puts it, "Users get used." Engaging with digital data on its own terms (or, more accurately, on the terms laid down by data producers and other beneficiaries of the data economy) will only get us so far. Indeed, many of the strategies outlined in chapter 6 might be argued to not progress substantively beyond ideas of data security or cybersafety, in which the default position is to be risk averse and always try to keep personal data private. As such, the actions outlined in chapter 6 might not mount to a significant change in the dominant interests and power structures inherent in the contemporary data economy.

In contrast, then, this chapter considers the fifth domain of the critical data literacies framework—what we have termed data "tactics." This idea of tactics is an altogether more challenging and political response to the dominant interests of the data economy—raising the idea of working around digital structures by *not* relying solely on official strategies. Instead, we might also consider developing alternate ways of producing, processing, and making use of data. We might also consider engaging in resistant ways of subverting, disrupting, and opposing the dominant forms of data generation, processing, and use outlined so far in this book. All told, there are a number of more subversive and resistant ways in which we might be able to "do data differently." This chapter provides an overview of some more radical approaches and how they offer different perspectives on what is possible when people have a strong critical awareness of digital data and are prepared to act on it.

Recognizing Data as Something That People Can Contest

One of the key take-home messages of this chapter (and the whole book) is that individuals, groups, and communities can have influence over how data relating to themselves and their lives is extracted and used. This is not an easy thing to grasp amid the constant digital churn of our day-to-day digital lives. A Pew Research poll of over 4,200 US adults in 2019 found just over 62 percent considered it *not* possible to go through their day-to-day activities without companies collecting personal data about them. This poll also found 63 percent of respondents resigned to the government doing the same thing. At first glance, then, this threatens to render the tactics domain of our critical data literacies framework redundant. Perhaps digital data is *not* something that people see as a problematic issue in their lives after all? Perhaps this is *not* an issue where most people are prepared to change their minds? It is therefore worth reflecting a little on this apparent conundrum. How might we explain—and perhaps then overcome—people's apparent indifference to actively engaging with the ways in which data is done to them?

This apparent widespread indifference, disinterest, and/or inertia to change data practices has been justified in a number of different ways. First are accusations of widespread data apathy—raising the idea that the majority of the public do *not* want to change very much at all and mostly do not care about the issues raised throughout this book so far. After all, even people who are well aware of what companies such as Facebook, Spotify, and Amazon do with their personal data continue to willingly (even enthusiastically) click on these platforms on a daily basis. Others have framed this apparent apathy in more disenfranchised terms—such as the idea of digital resignation to having one's personal data extracted and then subjected to targeted advertising and other marketing. This explanation was first floated by media and communication researchers Nora Draper and Joseph Turow (2017, 65) as the "condition created when people desire to control the information and data digital entities such as online marketers have about them, but feel unable to exercise that control."

This notion of resignation at least offers a more nuanced reading than the idea of great swathes of the public seemingly being apathetic, passive, and uninterested. Draper and Turow (2017) contend it is not necessarily a case of people not caring. Rather, it is people feel unable to act and instead perceive that they have limited social leverage in relation to negotiating how they engage with data infrastructures. In short, the explanation here is that people soon reach the conclusion that there is little or no "possibility of circumvention or resistance to mass data collection" (Hintz et al. 2019, 117).

This idea of resignation at least implies that people have made an initial assessment of their situation, yet it perhaps downplays the spirit in which people engage with these platforms and systems. Indeed, it might be more appropriate to describe people as more compelled than resigned to be going along with the data demands of these systems. Data assemblages exist at a scale that defies attempts by individuals to challenge or manipulate the required terms of service. It is not that people decide to give up on the possibility of doing things differently but that there is absolutely no other reasonable alternative. This is the case, for example, with social media platforms that are often used by many of one's friends, families, and work colleagues. Not choosing to use this social platform will effectively result in missing out on the bulk of social interactions between friends and family. For most people, this is not a realistic option.

Alternatively, then, Hintz and colleagues raise the idea of surveillance realism. This does not infer that people have become realistic about the most sensible or valid course of action. Rather, it infers that people have "come to see surveillance as a 'realism' in the sense of being an inevitable social order" (Hintz et al. 2019, 120). In this sense, digital data and data infrastructures can be perceived as ubiquitous and so deeply embedded in everyday social, political, and cultural participation that it makes little sense to attempt imagining how they might be challenged in practical terms. This idea of realism is a more useful concept to link to our critical data literacies framework. It certainly highlights the fact that continuing to use platforms and systems regardless of the personal data consequences is not simply a choice or decision on the part of the individual. Neither can people be criticized as passive agents who simply fail to act. Rather—as we have noted across previous chapters— these responses are manufactured into the design, development, and marketing of digital infrastructures. As Arne Hintz and colleagues (2019, 119) put it, acquiescence to mass data collection has been "actively manufactured" into the design of digital platforms—privacy agreements between users and platforms are virtually impossible for everyday people to read, and some services are inaccessible if personal data is not shared. This means people have little choice but to comply with the data collection practices of the platform.

Another similar idea describes this realism hardening over time into some form of data normalization. As Lovink and Rossiter (2015) argue, one of the defining features of our current digital culture is the normalizing of data infrastructures so they appear beyond question or challenge. Commentators who have theorized what is sometimes termed the "postdigital" condition (such as David Berry, Hito Steyerl, and Florian Cramer) all suggest that digital technology has moved on from being a noticeably disruptive force in everyday life to now being a thoroughly unremarkable presence. For example, the internet is no longer an interface that one can "log on" and "log off" from but is now simply an environment in which we exist (Steyerl 2013). Similarly, the extraction of personal data is simply a continuous background feature of our day-to-day lives. Like a fish that does not notice the water that it swims in, it might simply be that we no longer notice what is going on with personal data in the course of our digital lives.

Thinking Differently about Acting Differently

At first glance, these different interpretations might appear to offer little or no hope for thinking otherwise. Yet, each of these descriptions offers various ways forward. For example, the idea of individuals feeling resigned raises the prospect of supporting *collective* consciousness around digital data and its discontents—supporting people to see that their private troubles are actually public issues. Key here is the importance of presenting alternate responses to personal data as a collective (rather than individual) responsibility. The idea of surveillance realism at least suggests a recognition of an unfair status quo and therefore the possibility of subsequent resistance. The idea of normalization raises the prospect of unnormalizing and defamiliarization—in other words, efforts to make the digital visible again (Cramer 2015). From this perspective, technological infrastructures should not be allowed to just recede into the background unquestioned but can be examined, critiqued, and perhaps resisted. None of these developments are guaranteed to result in change but at least speak back to the idea that most people are simply apathetic or resigned to data.

All told, these prognoses give impetus to the idea of stimulating what might be termed as people's data imaginations. In a basic sense, this refers to people's ability to think otherwise about how they might be engaging with digital data—reimagining ways of working with data and thinking what might be done differently. As implied in previous chapters, this is more difficult than it sounds. While someone might feel competent in engaging with digital data along the set lines in which they are accustomed, it is often difficult to "know what you don't know"—particularly when it comes to digital data practices that software developers and technology companies try their hardest to keep out of sight. That said, people's familiar data practices and approaches should not be dismissed out of hand. One of the underpinning reasons to develop the idea of critical data literacies is to support people to begin to think differently and *defiantly* about digital data. This is where the notion of a data imagination comes to the fore.

In a basic sense, the term "imagination" can be seen to refer to the capacity to move beyond what we already know, to see things from other points of view, and to extend our experiences and thoughts in ways that might result in new insights, ideas, and aspirations. Seen in this way, "imagination decomposes what already is, replacing it with what could be" (Hunter 2013, 114). There are various types of imagination—strategic, emotional, creative, and even critical imaginations. In terms of critical data literacies, our evocation of a data imagination draws inspiration from sociologist C. Wright Mills's (1959/2000) notion of "the sociological imagination." Here, Mills talks of the need to view any facet of society in terms of individual, structural, *and* historical issues. This therefore points us firmly toward seeing digital data not just in terms of one's own personal experiences but also in terms of shared issues and social structures that might be common to everyone in similar situations, contexts, and cultures. This frames the need for innovative, creative, unexpected, playful, and contrarian responses to the apparent no-hope dead end of the datafied society. People need to be exposed to different forms of digital data, different ways of organizing and engaging with digital data, and even different ways of talking about the roles that digital data play in influencing everyday life.

Supporting people to imagine the use of digital data along these extended and expanded lines might sound difficult, yet these ideas certainly align with some of the underpinning critical data approaches mentioned earlier in this book. For example, researchers working in the field of critical data studies are explicitly concerned with ideas of exposing and reimagining data infrastructures—laying bare the different components of the data assemblage and encouraging people in marginalized positions to disrupt and reimagine. Amid this interest in supporting citizen agency with regard to data, sociologist Helen Kennedy and colleagues point to the desirability of supporting people to become conscious or resisting agents. This area of work also encourages the idea of data being repurposed to enhance collective agency—that is, "feeding such data back to users, enabling them to orient themselves in the world" (Kennedy et al. 2015, 1).

Similarly, as was discussed in chapter 3, the idea of data feminism places great emphasis on collective approaches to developing alternate data conditions. One idea here is scaling up resistant data practices through co-liberation—a key strategy in data feminism and other data justice approaches. As D'Ignazio and Klein explain, co-liberation is a commitment to freeing the people rather than freeing the data, encouraging the development of data process and practices that are of mutual benefit for dominant *and* minoritized groups. This reframes the idea of "doing data differently" as a collective process in "developing community solidarity around local knowledge, and build[ing] new relationships across lines of social difference" (D'Ignazio and Klein 2020, 148). Finally, the idea of data justice also foregrounds the need to move beyond the idea of data rights (the power to better engage with data) to ambitions of data freedoms—that is, the power to choose how to engage with data (Taylor 2017). Key here is the idea of collective political responses and direct collective actions—not least the act of opting out and other forms of protest, confrontation, disobedience, and disruption.

So, reimagined along these lines, what *data tactics* might we envisage for the fifth stage of our critical data literacies framework? We can now go on to consider two distinct approaches to doing data differently. First is the idea of repurposing data for personal and social reasons—these are collective appropriations of digital data, designed to achieve more niche or specialized insights and outcomes. Second is the idea of employing tactics of resistance and obfuscation. This fits with a number of oppositional approaches toward digital media over the past thirty years—not least the 1990s' idea of tactical media (Garcia and Lovink 1997), alongside more recent calls for data obfuscation. As Brunton and Nissenbaum (2015) explain, these are tactics of data disobedience intended to mitigate, evade, or perhaps sabotage dominant structures of data reuse and recirculation.

While both these approaches are quite uncommon, having the critical knowledge to understand why one might choose to do this and what effect this might have is indicative of a more sophisticated form of data literacies. In this sense, the following alternative ways of dealing with data can be thought of as new ways of "writing" with data.

Repurposing Data for Alternate Social Reasons

First are a range of data practices that coalesce around ideas of good data, democratic data, and the general idea of people coming together to make shared, collective use of data for socially beneficial purposes (however these benefits might be collectively defined). As we detailed in chapter 3, this involves reimagining data production, processing, and use in ways that are democratic and rooted in population-based relations rather than along primarily individualized lines. This shows how we might move beyond concerns around issues of data protection and individual consent—all of which perpetuate a proprietary sense of data as being the property and responsibility of an individual. Instead, these alternate models are based around the idea of data being shared and used by groups of people who are all involved in decision-making and governance of the data (Ho and Chuang 2019).

Democratic Forms of Data Stewardship and Data Sharing
One key theme here is developing alternates to the commercial data brokers and other third-party actors that drive the data economy—what could be described as "democratic institutions of data governance" (Viljoen 2020). One neat example of this is the rise of data cooperatives as a democratic

form of data stewardship and data sharing. As we described in chapter 3, data cooperatives involve pooling together people's data, which can then be used for socially just purposes that are collectively decided upon. While only a few data cooperatives have been established to date, they offer an intriguing proof of concept into how personal data can be used for communal good.

Many of the most successful data cooperatives have been focused on the communal sharing of health-related data. For example, the Salus data cooperative has operated from its base in Barcelona since 2017. This is a nonprofit cooperative that collates the health and lifestyle-related data from its members. Salus has citizen-driven collaborative governance that allows cooperative members to collectively govern how their health data and medical records are used. One of the key aims of the cooperative is to decide when it is possible to share data sets with public research organizations looking to focus on medical and health care issues. As the cooperative publicity puts it, "Let's share and govern our data together. . . . Let's put our data at the service of the common good and our own well-being."

Similarly, the Swiss-based HealthBank data cooperative touts itself as a data exchange platform. The aim here is to allow members to collate all sorts of personal health-related data that is available online—from fitness trackers and smart medical devices that people might use at home to their official medical records and data generated from hospital medical devices such as the data from X-ray machines and magnetic resonance imaging (MRI) scanners. In one sense, HealthBank acts as a brokering service to provide each member with access to all their data, which they can authorize HealthBank to share with other institutions and organizations they choose—from their family doctor to relatives or friends. HealthBank can then offer opportunities for members to pool their data and make it available to medical researchers who can purchase anonymized data sets on aspects of health information that they are researching. These payments are passed on to cooperative members.

Perhaps the most interesting example of these models is the MIDATA cooperative (also based in Switzerland). This platform supports the establishment of data cooperatives in different regions and countries. Each local cooperative allows its members to collate and store their health and medical data on the MIDATA platform—including data from mHealth applications on smartphones and other mobile devices to official medical records and genomic data. Cooperative members can opt to give their own doctors and physicians access to this data, while also collectively deciding when and where to selectively provide data in response to requests from medical researchers and clinical studies. Data is often donated to nonprofit research institutes and sometimes sold to commercial researchers. In addition, members might decide to participate in app-based research projects where they provide new data to researchers. This has seen MIDATA being involved in citizen science research projects focused on multiple sclerosis, pollen allergies, and even in the development of a rapid response to the COVID-19 pandemic outbreak, where cooperative members provided ongoing data on their health status and possible symptoms during the initial spread of the virus. Crucially, the MIDATA cooperatives operate on a nonprofit basis—akin to blood donation or citizen science programs. Any profits from the sale of data to commercial researchers are donated back to public research.

Data Activism

Alongside these cooperative approaches is what we described in chapter 3 as the collective use of data for data activism. This involves the reappropriation of existing data sets and/or the collective generation of new data. The overarching aim here is to use data to contend and dispute official accounts, draw attention to underpublicized issues, and mobilize public opinion. This data activism can include coordinated programs of citizen recording and crowdsourcing new data sets. Here, local community members collaborate to measure and record evidence of issues otherwise not being recognized and documented by authorities. Favored data activist techniques include scraping data from public websites, crowdsourcing data from citizen reporters, and generating new data from surveys, sensors, or similar tools.

The range of issues that can be addressed through these data tactics is diverse—all reflecting the needs and concerns of local communities rather than official actors. One increasingly common topic for such action in the United States is citizen recording of racially motivated police brutality—a prolonged process of "sifting through government documents such as police reports, court transcripts, and legal forms and adding this information to a database of officer-involved homicides in the community" (Crooks and Currie 2021). This has been a strand of work coordinated by the Data 4 Black Lives collective, bringing activists, organizers, and mathematicians together to use data science techniques such as data visualization and statistical modeling to address justice issues for Black communities. Elsewhere, crowdsourcing techniques have been used to gather evidence for otherwise underreported crimes. For example, in response to a lack of national reporting, María Salguero took on the task of recording and publicizing each incident of femicide in Mexico that was reported by local news media—mapping each death by location, nature of death, age of victim, and relationship with the person who murdered them. This El Mapa de los Feminicidios en México information network has worked to keep the issue of femicide in the media attention and increase public pressure on Mexico's legislators to act.

The initial phases of the COVID-19 pandemic during 2020 and 2021 promoted various instances of data activism around the world in contexts where official recording and reporting of infection and death rates were being suppressed. For example, the "Lapor Covid-19" (Report Covid-19) volunteer group in Jakarta collated and publicized a pandemic severity index—offering a platform for citizens to independently record COVID-19 cases and therefore provide a check on government accountability. This service was also a popular means for citizens to report official violations of health protocols by government officials and other agencies. Similarly, in the United States, Data 4 Black Lives also produced and maintained a COVID-19 Disparities Tracker, which collated and publicized race data relating to infection and death rates across US cities, counties, and states—offering analyses that were often not being reported through official channels.

Perhaps the most coordinated example of data activism is the DataKind network. This is a global network with local chapters in Singapore, India, the United Kingdom, and the United States. Each local chapter supports data scientists, policymakers, and civic society actors to come together to co-design the development of data science interventions to address social and humanitarian issues. Describing itself as providing pro bono data science innovation, DataKind collectives have been involved in the development of various data-driven tools and programs that mirror commercial approaches but are focused on noncommercial issues. Projects include the development of data-driven decision-making tools that bring together various disparate and disconnected official data sets to help US care workers determine their clients' eligibility for around a dozen different social services. Similarly, DataKind's UK chapter developed a predictive machine learning model to identify clients at most risk of becoming overdependent on food bank services—thereby allowing social workers to make early decisions to prioritize additional support and engagement with social services.

Running throughout these different examples is a desire to make quick use of data to provoke tangible social change. These forms of data activism aim to produce what Gabrys et al. (2016) term "good enough data." These are data practices conducted by ordinary people, aimed at creating new data stories that might be used as part of official authorities' decision-making. While perhaps not as comprehensive or fine-grained as the official data that it seeks to challenge, these forms of alt-data can be surprisingly effective. Gutierrez (2018) argues that citizen-generated alt-data will often lead to the development of alternative data stories from the bottom up that are otherwise absent in official accounts. Indeed, as Ghosh and Faxon (2023) put it, these collective data exercises can easily be criticized from a technical point of view—lacking accuracy, validity, and complete data coverage. Yet the value of these forms of data generation lies in supporting participatory action and raising collective consciousness around issues. As we have stressed throughout this book, context is important in making sense of data, so there are good reasons why getting citizen-collected data may be superior to supposedly high-quality officially generated data (Ghosh and Faxon 2023).

This ethos is certainly evident in some other instances of data activism that take a defiant sousveillance approach—offering data-driven ways of combatting official data-based monitoring, judgment, and decision-making. One such example is the Augrented platform that operates in New York and San Francisco. Augrented uses data to allow people looking to rent an apartment to judge the state of the property, the provenance of the landlord, and the overall risks inherent in taking tenancy of a particular property. This platform was established in direct response to the powerful tenant profiling services that now exist for landlords—giving landlords data-driven scores and profiles on prospective tenants based on their previous renting histories, reliability of making payments, and so on. Some of these tenant-profiling services are notably invasive and discriminatory—scraping people's social media histories, credit histories, and criminal records in order to reckon the likelihood of them missing a future payment, damaging property, or requiring eviction. In opposition to this profiling, Augrented turns the tables on landlords and rental agencies—offering prospective tenants detailed data profiles on landlords' property portfolios, history of forced evictions, references from previous tenants, and so on. The service covers data on over 160,000 properties and calculates Renter Risk Ratings based on analysis of official data sets ranging from city building inspections to rodent inspections, earthquake protections, and 311 complaints to the city authorities about the property and/or the landlord.

Tactics of Resistance and Obfuscation

These latter examples clearly resonate with broader examples of citizen resistance and empowerment. One useful frame of reference is philosopher Michel de Certeau's writing on resistance, subversion, and reappropriation in everyday life. In particular, de Certeau's (1984) *The Practice of Everyday Life* continues to offer useful insights into how people work with (and against) the "formal structure of practice" in their everyday actions. Of particular significance is de Certeau's well-known distinction between strategies and tactics. Here, strategies are described as the ways in which powerful actors and dominant institutions get to define official practices and knowledges by encouraging people to engage with structures in ways that reaffirm the constructed order of the city. This description certainly resonates with the data strategies outlined in chapter 6—engaging with the terms of service, setting parameters, consenting to permissions being granted through platforms, and so on. All these strategies are predicted upon individuals becoming more vigilant of risks implicit in engaging with digital devices and platforms.

In contrast, many people's everyday lives involve working around official structures by *not* relying on these official strategies and resorting instead to political practices and forms of knowledge that subvert, usurp, and undermine official norms and ways of doing—what de Certeau termed "tactics." The notion of data tactics, however, fits with several oppositional approaches toward digital media that have taken various forms during the past thirty years. For example, oppositional behavior, subversion, and resistance have long underpinned philosophies of the computer hacking movement (Ross 1991) as well as the rise of tactical media during the 1990s and 2000s. Most recently have been calls for data disobedience (Brunton and Nissenbaum 2015)—intended to mitigate, evade, or perhaps sabotage dominant structures of data reuse and recirculation. All these different approaches are therefore helpful to critical data literacies, providing another angle on how we might engage in doing data differently.

Technical Tactics of Data Obfuscation, Jamming, and Spoofing

First are various tactics relating to what Finn Brunton and Helen Nissenbaum (2015, 1) term "data obfuscation"—"the deliberate use of ambiguous, confusing, or misleading information to interfere with surveillance and data collection projects." This is not to be confused with the data masking techniques used by data professionals. Instead, these are guerrilla tactics deployed by nonexperts—all loosely based around the idea of fighting data with (more) data. Brunton and Nissenbaum highlight a range of obfuscatory actions that can be taken—many of which involve the use of platforms, services, and software to help individuals to "hide in the crowd of signals" through data-related disappearance and time wasting, as well as prankish disobedience and minor acts of protest. In practice, such actions can take various technological forms—such as creating noise via Twitter bots, anonymizing geolocational data with cache cloaks, and flooding online platforms with inaccurate data. All of these tactics are justified as addressing the information asymmetry or epistemic asymmetry in which data are collected about us and used in ways that we do not understand.

Some of these actions involve considerable amounts of effort, time, and ingenuity. As such, these acts of resistance are as much symbolic as they are practical—designed to catch the attention of online audiences and demonstrate that dominant forms of the data economy can be resisted. For example, the mass adoption of the Zoom video meeting software during the COVID-19 pandemic lockdowns prompted groups of activists, researchers, creative technologists, and artists to collaborate on various forms of Zoom obfuscation and subversion under the banner of "Zoom Obscura." Their interventions ranged from simple analogue interventions such as placing watermarked stickers on webcams to code-based interventions. These included AI tools that inserted "deep fake" doppelgangers of the person speaking into video feeds, therefore allowing other participants to recognize the individual but hiding them from computer-based facial recognition software. Another tool added masking emoticons to people's faces to allow them to express emotions without yielding more personally sensitive video data.

Some of these symbolic data tactics are more deliberately low tech. For example, in 2020, the artist Simon Weckert demonstrated how Google Maps could quickly be manipulated by dragging a small cart loaded with ninety-nine smartphones along different relatively quiet streets. Presuming the various smartphone GPS signals to be emanating from ninety-nine different cars, the Google Map algorithm quickly redesignated the road as a "red" traffic jam. In the same year, news media gleefully picked up on a teenager's presentation at a US hacker conference detailing how groups of online teens around the world were teaming up to set up multiple Instagram accounts and all post deliberately obtuse content from multiple different devices and different locations at the same time. These mass-posted accounts were intended to effectively confuse Instagram's attempts to make sense of the metadata from posted content and render the tracking and targeting data meaningless. As one report put it, the teens were "giving Instagram quite the confusing cocktail of data" (Ng 2020).

While these activities and interventions all require considerable time, effort, and some technical know-how, a range of easily accessible digital applications and software tools can also be used to obfuscate and generally avoid data tracking while online—sometimes referred to as privacy by design. This includes the use of geo-spoofing tools such as a VPN (Virtual Private Network) to conceal the geolocation of a digital device. In addition, several privacy-enhancing software applications have been developed over the past decade—often by activists and researchers keen to encourage critical engagement with digital tools. These include web browser extensions that block access to advertising while also simulating clicks on any advert that is encountered—thereby providing erroneous data to tracking software and other attempts at data profiling. Other software is available that isolates any use of Facebook from other internet use, thereby preventing these social media platforms using third-party cookies to track general internet use.

Protesting

Another set of low-tech tactics that is becoming more prominent involves old-fashioned political protesting. The past few years have seen a growing trend for groups protesting data-based surveillance and data-driven decision-making. This has included protests by Uber drivers protesting unwarranted algorithmic deactivation, Uber Eats delivery riders protesting against algorithmic income reduction, and even medical tattoo artists protesting against the blocking of nipple images by social media content moderation. Such protests invariably garner media attention and play a useful role in increasing public awareness of data economy and data-related issues. As Chris Gilliard (2021) notes, in recent years, we have seen more resistant responses to data collection. What is particularly significant here is that these are conversations being had by groups of people who up until recently had not thought they had a reason to become involved with or even know about data. Now we are seeing "widespread acknowledgment of how these systems are impacting people's lives and an understanding that they have very little say and even knowledge of it" (Gilliard 2021, 265).

One of the most celebrated protests took place during the summer of 2020 in the United Kingdom. Like most countries, the initial phases of the COVID-19 pandemic threw the usual cycle of UK school examinations and assessments into turmoil. This prompted an announcement by the UK government that it would calculate a whole cohort of students' end-of-school qualification (A-level) results by algorithms based on historical school performance data (rather than using teacher-assessed grades supplied by schools). This resulted in millions of students in the class of 2020 getting their grades lowered. Crucially, these calculations disproportionately affected students from disadvantaged backgrounds and poorer government schools. In contrast, students from private fee-paying schools fared much better—for example, it was reported that not one grade from Eton would be algorithmically lowered.

This led to widescale condemnation and anti-algorithm protests—as commentators noted, this was one of the first times that the UK public had taken to the streets to protest against algorithmic injustice. After a few days, the government was forced in an embarrassing reversal, conceding that grading should revert to calculations based on teacher-based assessments. The UK prime minster of the time later dismissed the controversy in a notably uninformed manner as the result of a mutant algorithm. By contrast, UK teenagers could see that the issues at hand were far more complex and took a coordinated protest to bring this to the attention of the public. In recent history, protest about algorithms had tended to focus on data protection and privacy. However, as political geographer Louise Amoore (2020) noted, with the UK exam controversy, the students were not only protesting the exam grade algorithm but also how this data was being used to actively change their future opportunities. As she explained, these students were well aware of the fact that "the potential pathways open to young people were reduced, limiting their life chances according to an oblique prediction" (Amoore 2020).

Considering what has been covered in this book so far, this was perhaps not a surprising turn of events. High-profile writers such as Virginia Eubanks, Cathy O'Neil, and Safiya Noble have long been highlighting the tendency for data-driven systems to reinforce disadvantage and oppression in most public services—from housing to the criminal justice system. As such, there was little reason to expect the UK school system and UK data science to be any different. Nevertheless, the success of these protests in agitating national government change is seen as heralding increasingly frequent anti-algorithm political protests in the near future. As Amoore (2020) concluded, "The A-level scandal made algorithms an object of direct resistance and exposed what many already know to be the case: that this type of decision-making involves far more than a series of computational steps."

Fashion and Art as Sites of Data Disruption

Alongside these direct actions are instances of creative data resistance that are designed to provoke public discussion rather than be wholly effective countermeasures. These examples often emerge from the worlds of fashion and art—drawing on the traditions within these fields of producing work intended to challenge perceptions, provide social commentary, and disrupt conventional societal norms. For example, various forms of adversarial fashion have been designed over the past decade or so in response to various data-related incursions into everyday life. Many of these relate to confusing object recognition and facial analysis systems, alongside shielding smartphones and other devices from being tracked by geolocation services. Prominent designs include jackets covered in fake license plate images, nonfunctioning QR codes, the blurry eigenface images that facial recognition systems rely on, and other forms of junk data. A few of these ideas have crossed over into commercial production—what might be termed an online marketplace for the obfuscation industry. It is possible to purchase a lengthy wish list of products—including RF-shielded Faraday bags, nonidentifiable prosthetic masks, patterned glasses, angular asymmetrical stealth makeup, and hair accessories.

Alongside these fashion designs are more speculative artist-led projects designed to highlight issues of dataveillance and data tracking. In contrast to examples highlighted in earlier sections, these are not serious widescale attempts to disrupt data systems. Instead, these are minor acts of intervention aiming to draw attention to critical issues around data and digitizations by forcing temporary computation breakdowns and glitches. The writer-artist Zach Blas, for example, has developed various projects aiming to raise conversations around glitching data visibility and data opacity. Their work includes various facial weaponization objects—including face cages and "collective masks" modeled from the aggregated facial data of different people that would exceed the measuring capacity of biometric technologies. Elsewhere, the artist Adam Harvey developed a range of asymmetrical geometric makeup patterns during the 2010s with the evocative title "CV dazzle" (computer vision dazzle). This was designed to disrupt the capacity of computer-driven cameras to extract face data—initially inspired by Harvey's attempts to thwart Facebook's auto-tagging feature for recognizing people in photographs posted to the social network. The project name paid homage to the dazzle camouflage painted onto allied warships during World War I. This has subsequently inspired Dazzlewalk groups to be set up in London, with groups all wearing CV Dazzle and conducting guided tours of local data surveillance cameras and other sites of public surveillance.

Another much-reported critical art intervention was developed by the artist Trevor Paglan in conjunction with the AI critic Kate Crawford. The pair's ImageNet Roulette installation and exhibition was designed to draw attention to the workings of the ImageNet data set—a data set of over 14 million images organized into 20,000 categories, which continues to be one of the key training data sets for the development of object and facial recognition software. Part of ImageNet Roulette was a feature that allowed any internet user to upload photos of their own face to demonstrate how a facial recognition system trained on the ImageNet data set might miscategorize facial images in ways that were often humorously wrong but also demeaning, derogatory, or discriminatory. This constituted what Laura Bridges (2021) describes as the public shaming of one of the most influential data sets used in the development of computer vision, object recognition, and facial analysis AI. Eventually, the adverse publicity led to ImageNet agreeing to delete 1.5 million images that had previously been labeled in the data set's "person" category.

The Difficulties of Putting These Tactics into Action

All these approaches and actions provide glimpses into alternate ways that digital data might be approached, (re)appropriated, and resisted. While none of these examples have entered into widespread use, they do offer an idea of "how things might be otherwise" and some hope that we do not need to feel resigned to a lifetime of data domination and disempowerment. Engaging with data in this manner is a crucial component of critical data literacies. As Ananny and Crawford (2018) reason, people's critical understandings of the machinations of the data economy are most likely to result from active engagement with the actual systems. This is not something that one can fully understand from reading abstract accounts of how algorithms operate or how Facebook is designed to generate user profiles. That said, any excitement over these alternate tactics and approaches needs to be tempered by reflection on their limitations and the tensions that their implementation throws up. Indeed, these alternate tactics and approaches are not easily taken up and pursued. These gaps between what we might like to do differently with data and what we end up doing (and not doing) need to be acknowledged and reflected upon as part of critical data literacies. So how should we make sense of this disarticulation between critical data awareness and our actual data agency?

First is the point that even people who have developed a refined and sophisticated critical understanding of data are likely to lack time, energy, resources, and motivation to act differently. All of the collective reworkings of data described in this chapter require considerable organization and devotion to initiate and maintain. Similarly, even the simplest tactics of resistance and obfuscation require sustained effort, additional work, and a capacity to put up with the inconvenience of not going along with the expected options. While we might not be wholly happy with third-party use of personal data, many of us might not consider this to be the most pressing problem in our lives—particularly in comparison to other world problems. Even if we are personally enthused by the activist rhetoric of obfuscation and cryptography practices, or the obvious collective power of cooperatives and activism, it is important to retain a sense of perspective. For many people, data is simply not enough of a big deal to merit this degree of attention.

Second—and following on from this initial observation—is the point that many of the Big Tech interests underpinning the data economy make it incredibly difficult to engage in the sorts of actions outlined in this chapter. As we saw in chapter 6, big platforms such as Facebook, TikTok, and Google are designed to make it difficult to *not* engage in a typical manner, to opt out and/or deviate from the default. Moreover, these companies spend a lot of money on public relations and brand reputation to manage potentially problematic issues. As highlighted in a spate of recent whistle-blowers from within Big Tech companies, corporations are keen to promote positive messages, while suppressing their own internal research findings about the harms of their products. Moreover, these companies are quick to deter and ban any groups looking to highlight problematic issues and encourage alternate forms of engagement. This has been the case with Facebook's blocking of university researchers attempting to document and disrupt the algorithmic promotion of fake news and misinformation—with the company claiming that such investigations constitute a violation of its terms of service (Ortutay 2021). In short, these are multibillion-dollar corporations that do not take kindly to efforts to resist and disrupt their core profit-making business.

Alongside these practical challenges, it is also worth problematizing the seemingly progressive position of pursuing data for social good. As apparent in many of the data cooperative and data activist examples highlighted earlier in the chapter, this promotes the idea that data science, while never capable of providing perfect solutions, can nevertheless be harnessed to improve current circumstances. On one hand, it is laudable that progressively minded data scientists are willing to engage in more nuanced thinking and engagement with social issues. After all, an ambition to "do good" brings a human focus to what might otherwise be largely technical concerns. Nevertheless, such efforts still perpetuate an optimism that data can be used to address (and perhaps solve) complex social problems. This can result in dangerous oversimplifications of issues that are politically complex and might lack clear consensus over what is desirable. As such, data scientists run the risk of blithely wading into hotly contested political territory and acting in a contestable (perhaps regressive) manner. As mathematician Ben Green (2021) notes,

> By framing their notions of "good" in such vague and undefined terms, data scientists get to have their cake and eat it too: they can receive praise and publications based on broad claims about solving social challenges while avoiding any actual engagement with social and political impacts.

Moreover, it is important to remain mindful of the compromises implicit in reshaping data practices along lines of social justice, fairness, and so on. These are not win/win changes. Instead, adjustments that might be good for some people who were previously marginalized in established data processes might not be good for others. For example, moves toward increased sharing and openness of data sets will lead to losses in terms of data protection or data privacy. Similarly, adopting particular definitions of "fairness" (e.g., redesigning a predictive model in order to reduce the discriminatory impact of that model toward minority groups) is likely to come with a trade-off of reduced predictive accuracy. While a college lecturer might be happy to be able to check out her prospective landlord, she might be less happy to see her own perceived shortcomings profiled in aggregated data from disgruntled students on a RateMyTeacher-style site. No use of data in society—however well intentioned, resistant, and progressive—is wholly straightforward and beneficial to all. To reiterate a point raised in chapter 1, while we should not see data as wholly bad, it is sensible to see data as problematic—regardless of the causes that stand to benefit from its use.

Finally, are the practical problems that often beset collective and communal actions. All the tactics and approaches outlined in this chapter require a collective consciousness—in contrast to the dominant framing of digital data in terms of individualized rights, responsibilities, benefits, and problems. This need to approach digital data in a collective manner is an implicit value throughout all of the good data and data activist approaches outlined in this chapter. Similarly, the idea of resisting data along collective lines is also implicit in many of the data tactics detailed before. Indeed, de Certeau (1984, xi) was keen to stress that an emphasis on tactics "does not imply a return to individuality." As such, it would seem sensible to presume that tactical engagement with social media might be more effective if carried out by groups and collectives rather than individuals. As illustrated in the idea of a collective Dazzlewalk complete with CV Dazzle makeup, around a city, these actions are more powerful when carried out by a mass of people.

It seems reasonable to conclude that many of the issues that arise from personal data need to be situated as collective and/or community issues and therefore resisted through collective tactics and actions. However, this is all a lot harder than it sounds—in short, collective consciousness and community forming are never easy. As has been long noted in discussions of organized resistance, community activism, collective action, and other forms of social movement, the dynamics of coming together around a common cause is difficult to sustain over the extended period of time required to initiate effective change. It is also difficult to translate the shared normative orientation of a few concerned activists over to a mass consciousness (James and Van Seters 2014). This is not to argue that the ideas raised in the stage of the critical data literacies framework should be given up on and not pursued. However, we should not assume that making any progress will be easy to achieve.

Conclusions

This chapter highlights some potential opportunities for change that are implicit to critical data literacies—in other words, ways in which the framework *might* be used to produce positive (rather than just protective) data outcomes. However, it has also pointed to the practical limitations and likely tensions of any such efforts. This is not to suggest that we give up completely on the idea of working to foster increased data agency, data imaginations, and alternate forms of doing data. Yet, it is important to approach any such efforts with a sense of realism and the enormity of the task at hand. Any efforts to implement these principles need to start by recognizing the complex, challenging nature of doing data differently and not be content simply with reiterating "romantic and impractical calls for [data] self-governance" (Obar 2015, 2).

That said, thinking through these possible tactical approaches and agendas does raise some exciting ideas about how things might be different in the near future. Above all, this chapter highlights the power of conceiving people's data agency on a collective rather than individual scale. It also continues our emphasis on understanding the ways in which data practices are enmeshed (for better and worse) within the broader contexts of people's everyday lives and digital practices. These previous discussions also raise the tricky question of whether we want to be pushing for either mending or ending the dominant processes and practices of datafication. While some readers might be fully enthused by the prospect of waging war on the data economy through protest, obfuscation, and other forms of antagonism, many others might feel uneasy at the prospect of working toward the absolute cessation of datafication. Yet, the examples cited in this chapter also raise the question of perhaps simply reinforcing existing problems and the status quo. For instance, while we might want to be collectively developing new forms of data use, this still results in giving data-driven systems and platforms "more data, more attention, more human devotion to tweaking its algorithmic core" (Pasquale 2020, 75). Indeed, in many respects, striving for better forms of data-driven technologies throughout our everyday lives actually provides support for the generation and processing of more data.

All these questions, ideas, and challenges are taken into the concluding chapter. Here we turn our attention to thinking about possible data futures and how we might develop critical data literacies over the next ten years and beyond. What data-related trends and technologies might increase in significance throughout the next ten years and beyond? What individualized and collective data literacies might be necessary, alongside organized and institutional responses to datafication? What are the key developments and approaches that need to be urgently addressed to shape our future data societies in ways that genuinely support democracy and human flourishing?

8 Data Futures

Introduction

One of the challenges of writing a book about any aspect of digital technology is ensuring what we write now is still relevant and useful when it might be read ten years later. In this sense, we are confident that most of the issues and arguments raised in this book will be relevant for some time to come. Regardless of whether you are reading this in 2023 or 2033, the core concepts and concerns around the ongoing integration of digital data into everyday life will remain important. Nevertheless, this is a fast-changing area of discussion and debate. The datafication of society is evolving rapidly in terms of the technologies, processing capacities, computational techniques, and what data will be used to do. As such, it is well worth considering what might lie ahead. What current niche data practices might suddenly blow up and become part of mainstream society? What currently unforeseen developments are possible? Any form of literacy requires constant updating, so remaining critically data literate will inevitably be an ongoing effort.

This concluding chapter considers what possible data futures we might anticipate in the next few years and decades and how this might inform us about our current engagements with data. Thinking about futures is an essential aspect of developing critical data literacies and can help test and refine the core issues and concerns that we have developed throughout this book. This is a neat way of anticipating future forms of some of the key issues that have already been foregrounded in this book. How should we reimagine our current ideas of data regulation or data ethics? What new thinking about issues such as data resistance or data sovereignty is required? How might we have to act now to ensure that data plays a part in genuinely supporting democracy and human flourishing? Anticipating possible data futures is not simply a speculative exercise in letting our imaginations run wild. This is a key part in preparing ourselves for the datafied world(s) to come.

Thinking about Data Futures: From Corporate Hype to Academic Anticipation

Over the past few years, many different groups of critically minded people have been thinking carefully about futures (rather than histories) as a means of making sense of twenty-first-century society, especially in terms of the challenges that are arising from developments in AI, biotechnology, and climate change. These are often described as unprecedented challenges, leading to renewed interest in asking questions of the future—what was once largely dismissed as the disreputable and spurious pursuit of futurology. Grappling with questions about the future has gained considerable credibility over the past few decades as an essential element of social theorizing and thinking. Influential organizations such as the UN and OECD have set up "Futures" programs. Universities have established "Futures Institutes." As the sociologist John Urry (2016, 187) put it a few years ago, "In order to operate in the world . . . we must peer into the future—there is no choice."

Commonsense Expectations and Predictions of the Future of Datafication

Of course, despite this newfound political interest and academic credibility, most talk around data-related futures remains relatively simplistic and optimistic and based on the idea that we are already set on a path of ever-increasing datafication. In short, many people are happy to expect that the future can be seen in linear terms of more of the same—or, more accurately, *even* more of the same. In this sense, conceiving the future of digital data in extrapolated terms of what we already know could be seen as making good common sense. After all, looking at what is *currently* deemed as cutting-edge technology R&D can often give a good sense of which areas of emerging technology development are likely to thrive over the next few decades. At the time of writing, it might seem a fairly safe bet to expect that the next few decades will see continued innovation in areas such as artificial intelligence, automated decision-making, big data analytics, edge computing, platformed personalization, smart sensors, and the internet of things. It might also seem reasonable to expect continued work in neuroscience and pharmaceutical technology to eventually lead to significant breakthroughs in cognitive analytics and emotion detection. Elsewhere, we are already seeing initial work on the development of DNA-based data storage allowing the storage of huge volumes of digital data at a molecular level.

All these areas of current cutting-edge developments might be seen as giving us a fairly good sense of future mainstream technologies. Indeed, when discussing the topic of digital futures, it is common to hear people take solace in the William Gibson quotation that "the future is already here—it's just not evenly distributed." Yet, even if these areas of technology development in big data, neuroscience, and DNA storage *do* continue as broadly expected, this tells us little about the societal impacts that such advancements might have. As such, it makes sense to be wary of anyone who is too confident in their claims about the ongoing datafication of society. Indeed, the most bold and assured visions of digitally driven futures tend to be made by people with something to sell. A big pharma company has a vested interest in pushing visions of data-driven precision medicine. Given the many vested interests in our current car culture, many people are eager to foresee a future where fully autonomous vehicles operate in complete safety and comfort.

Of course, not all discussions and debates around future data developments are quite so self-interested, yet even what might seem to be objective attempts at mapping empirical trends tend to result in highly speculative and desocialized accounts. Preferred techniques for such forms of future telling often include forecasting, statistical predictions, and other methods of accurate speculation. Here, for example, we find numerous corporate pronouncements of expected expansions of the data industry and data markets—involving breathless accounts of hundreds of zettabytes of data being produced each year, with confident predictions that "the amount of data created over the next three years will be more than the data created over the past 30 years" (Press 2020).

Again, such projections and forecasts are justified as likely extensions of recent technological progress. For example, most experts concur that significant increases in data production will result from the increased numbers of sensors that are already beginning to be embedded in everyday devices and settings as part of the internet of things—especially in terms of sensors generating data from live video and audio streams. For example, at the beginning of the 2020s, the consultancy firm Gartner (2021) felt confident enough to estimate that 75 percent of workplace conversations would be recorded and analyzed by 2025. Some predictions of global growth are based on the planned datafication of low-income countries over the next decade or so—especially expansions into regions with previously low levels of internet connectivity. Other expected trends include the increased use of "synthetic" data (i.e., data modeled on "real-life" data) to provide sufficient volumes of data to train deep learning AI models. All told, there are various rationales from the world of technology and business to presume that our data futures are already set in predictable directions.

From a Predictable Future to Possible Futures

While not wholly spurious, even these seemingly plausible statistical projections remain speculative and lacking in social context. To be blunt, these are future visions that are led by the IT industry and other business interests and are therefore liable to deprioritize the social impact and potentially lack consideration and concern. Of course, imagining the future in optimistic predictable terms of continued linear progress is a key trope in the continuation of capitalism. As Lisa Suckert (2021, 1167) reminds us, "It is indeed hard to imagine an economic regime that is more oriented towards the future than capitalism. . . . Any kind of entrepreneurship or investment depends on the propensity to imagine better days ahead."

As such, it is sensible for us *not* to simply go along with such expectations of continued expansion and growth. That said, from a critical data literacies perspective, taking a detached interest in such predictions can provide useful insights into how data companies and technology firms justify their actions. As engineer Mads Borup and colleagues (2006) contend, engaging with industry and commercial visions of the future can be a fundamentally generative way to understand how these corporate actors use ideas of the future to "guide activities, provide structure and legitimation, attract interest and foster investment" (Borup et al. 2006, 285–286). Indeed, there is a growing critical literature addressing the sociotechnical imaginaries being advanced by governments, corporations, and other stakeholders in the data society and data economy (e.g., Sadowski and Bendor 2019; Means 2018). These are interesting ways of shining a critical light on what big companies see themselves as doing and how they justify their actions.

Nevertheless, we need to remain mindful of what science, technology, and society scholar Lee Vinsel (2021) curtly terms "lend[ing] credibility to industry bullshit." The dangers of taking corporate expectations of data futures *too* seriously risks reproducing (and even increasing) hyperbole and lending credibility to industry promotional claims that overstate the abilities of tech firms and/or the capabilities of their emerging products. As well as compounding unrealistic expectations, spending excessive time and energy focusing on these future predictions distracts attention away from current existing concerns—especially the actual risks and harms arising from current existing technologies (Nordmann 2007). In light of the various critical data approaches that we have turned to throughout this book, there is little excuse for engaging with the topic of data futures without giving due attention to matters of injustice, inequality, power, and resistance.

So, how else might we engage more carefully (and more usefully) with the question of data futures? As has just been argued, mainstream visions of the future not only suffer from a lack of social awareness but also fail to approach the datafication of society in sufficiently problematic terms. More specifically, these current data futures are based on the fundamental expectation of the continuation of current conditions *and* the presumption that these conditions are largely beneficial. Regardless of their motivations, all these forecasts and predictions tend to presume that the assemblage that underpins our current data society, data economy, and data politics will continue. In short, it is presumed that the status quo will remain largely intact.

Approaching the future of data and society through this lens of what seems probable, likely, and familiar might seem sensible in comparison to the wild futurology speculations from the 1970s and 1980s about killer robots and colonizing Mars. Yet, from a critical data literacies perspective, approaching data futures in terms of the probable, likely, and familiar are decidedly limited starting points. Above all, talking about the future in terms of likely trends and projected figures forecloses alternative ways of doing things that might prove necessary in the face of the unprecedented challenges mentioned earlier.

Instead, one of the key aspects of the recent resurgence of futures thinking is a deliberate emphasis on paying close attention to what is unforeseeable alongside what is foreseeable. This is the reason that people now talk increasingly about "futures" in a plural sense—stressing the idea of "futures" (plural) indicates that there is no *one* linear future that can be predicted and forecasted. Instead, it makes far more sense to prepare ourselves for a range of possible different futures that may (or may not) occur. The emphasis here is on preparedness rather than prediction—acknowledging that many future risks are literally unknowable. As John Urry (2016, 1) puts it, "Futures are unpredictable, uncertain and often unknowable."

Anticipating Data Futures: Three Possible Scenarios

In the remainder of this chapter, we take this spirit of hopeful (re)imagining in the face of unknown and unforeseeable futures and apply it to what is known as anticipatory approaches in futures studies (see Poli 2017). The idea of taking an anticipatory approach starts from the premise that it makes little sense to deal with the idea of unknowable futures by blindly attempting to second-guess what is most likely to happen. Instead, unknowable futures are best engaged with by imagining how we might *like* to be living. This notion of "we" does not involve a self-centered set of preferences but involves recentering the perspectives of previously marginalized interests and nonpowerful groups (Facer 2019). In other words, this fits neatly with what has been described throughout this book in terms of data justice, data feminism, and other critical data approaches.

In light of these critical data concerns, a host of challenging questions might now be asked of datafication into the 2030s and beyond. For example, how might alternate approaches to living with data be established that do not presume the continuation of dominant Big Tech products and the "Silicon Valleyification of everything"? What might follow in the wake of Facebook, TikTok, and the current dominant genre of social media platforms? What are the data implications of ongoing environmental crises, geopolitical upheavals, and other instabilities? What regulations and laws will be passed to counter the increasing power of Big Tech and define our digital rights? Crucially, the focus here is on using these speculations to inform anticipatory behaviors—that is, changes in our present behaviors rooted in these imagined and desired futures (Poli 2017).

So, how might we anticipate desirable forms of data and society in light of essentially unknowable futures? In this spirit, we now go on to outline three brief scenarios that illustrate the scope of what different critical data futures might look like. Scenario building belongs to a group of "foresight" (as distinct from "forecast") approaches that lend themselves to developing understandings of possible futures of data and society. Here, the construction of these scenarios aims to produce vignettes that highlight different ways that our data societies might develop and then identify key factors that would be capable of driving change in different directions.

While concerned with broadly the same types of data and data technologies, the three different scenarios that you are about to read highlight the contested nature of what might be considered plausible data futures. Clearly, how these scenarios might be elaborated depends on whatever different forms of society, shared values, and political philosophies we see as preferable. Contrasting iterations of these basic scenarios might be developed that highlight different relationships between government and commercial actors, as well as different cultural understandings about community, family, work, and other institutions. We also consider how critical data literacies might figure in these scenarios and societies with links back to key ideas in the book. When reading each of these scenarios, it is important to remember that these are not accurate predictions of what is likely to happen. Instead, these are provocations around what we might like to be (or, at least, need to be) doing.

Scenario 1. Resisting a Rampant Data Economy

Our first scenario anticipates the continued expansion of the data capitalist logics described throughout this book—that is, the acceleration and intensification of dynamics of data extraction and exploitation. So, what might societies predicated around the "datafication of everything" look like? Here, we might imagine the rearrangement of public services around the logics of platform rentierism—for example, health care provision where patients do not visit a local doctor but are triaged through the proprietary platform provider that happens to be in partnership with their local municipality. This data is then shared with public health agencies as well as sold onto various commercial third parties. Elsewhere, we might also imagine the addition of data-generating capabilities to public assets to grow their economic value—such as smart libraries or datafied parks. Of course, some public spaces and services might simply prove unprofitable to extract data from and therefore cease to be maintained. Hard-to-quantify aspects of everyday life might be usurped by crude proxies and profiles—reduced to a set of more easily generated data points that stand in for their more complex precedents.

This scenario also anticipates how people might experience these data-driven intensifications and how critical data literacies might help negotiate the opportunities and challenges that emerge. This might include feeling compelled to adjust one's patterns of living and working in ways that "fit" with these data regimes—in other words, people having to behave in ways that are easily datafiable and algorithmically visible. Typical strategies may include adjustments such as speaking in easily parsed dialects and tones, contorting one's face into decodable expressions, and generally behaving in standardized, extractable ways. Developing this knowledge of how datafied systems work and what is required to be recognizable (or invisible) to them is therefore one way of being critically data literate. Navigating such challenges is key. For example, if a family would like to take their children to a park or a library, knowing it is owned by Google, then reading the terms of service for entry and making an informed decision about the privacy implications would outline the practical steps for enacting critical data literacies in everyday life. Once the family identifies, understands, and critically reflects on how data about the family is being generated, processed, and used, they may decide to go to an alternate non-Google park. The additional travel time might be balanced out by the less onerous data impositions.

It is also important to consider what forms of social knowledge will be privileged and valued under these conditions. For example, people's social status might be grounded in predicted behaviors and probabilistic risks, rather than past accomplishments and actual achievements. On the flipside, new forms of coded inequality might emerge in the form of data-driven racism, classism, ableism, and so on. Of course, such data futures might understandably appear decidedly undesirable to many social scientists. As such, it is worth considering how these conditions might be negotiated and resisted by those *not* directly profiting or benefiting from the extraction of data. This could draw on data tactics like data obfuscation and data disobedience—with people disrupting dominant regimes of data collection and analysis in ways that damage data capitalism. Such actions might range from minor acts of infrastructural interference to mass acts of data refusal and data contamination. We might also agitate for organized resistance on the part of tech workers and other sympathetic data industry "insiders." Tech-savvy citizens might work on the development and open distribution of counter-datafication tools—such as encryption tools, geo-spoofing software, VPNs, and other off-grid technologies. Most provocatively, we might see minoritized groups establishing alliances with the interests and orientations of other resistant groups such as anarchists and cryptographers to develop creative forms of "black ops" (McGlotten 2016).

We might also see people starting to use data-sharing apps that claim to give people additional value (perhaps in the form of bespoke data-driven insights or even financial rewards in exchange for their data). At the same time, we might anticipate future forms of adversarial reapplications of data—collective uses of data that promote dissatisfactions with dominant datafication regimes, provoke citizen resistance, and inspire people to engage with alternate forms of data use. This might mean digital data being reappropriated to publicize the differences, contradictions, and absurdities of the data-driven organization of society (see Hoeyer 2023)—provoking people's passions and directing public anger against datafied society and data capitalism. In the words of Crooks and Currie (2021), digital data might provide a means of affective stimulation to "enflame political differences and mobilize communities to begin to act" against the data economy.

Scenario 2. Toward a Communitarian Cooperative Culture of "Data for Good"

Our second scenario imagines the full take-up and pursuit of the various forms of good data outlined in chapter 3. This includes the idea of democratic data processes and practices and seeing data in terms of whole communities and populations, rather than individualized benefit and profit. So, what might societies predicated around the idea of good datafication look like? Here, we might imagine a society based around alternative forms of data governance that are communally rather than commercially driven. For example, we might imagine a scenario where all forms of data are automatically transferred to public ownership and used for public purposes—what was described in chapter 3 as the idea of data as a public infrastructure. This might see most commercial providers and IT companies give up on the idea of trying to profit from extracting user data. Instead, data might be more like water—something that is generally free to be used for public good, although (as is the case with bottled water) some firms might attempt to sell "premium" versions to niche markets.

So what might data as a public utility look like? We might anticipate cities collating data to allow community groups to democratically address pressing social challenges—such as how best to reduce air pollution or traffic flow or where to direct public services. This might involve the creation of local data hubs that allow local residents, community groups, and civil society to generate bottom-up citizen data and then collaborate with municipal data scientists to make data-based decisions—from determining bus routes and timetables, establishing the allocation of public resources, identifying emerging social needs, and ensuring that cities are run along fair and just lines.

These examples all involve the support and steering of official public authorities and municipalities. Alternatively, good data futures might also involve the popular requisition and deployment of data from the bottom up by ad hoc collectives of local people and interest groups. This might see people banding together to collate their data relating to a local matter or controversy in order to mobilize public action and lobby those in power. Governance over how data is controlled, owned, and used might sit with the local communities and contexts to which the data relates. For example, we might see the establishment of a worldwide Indigenous data network, promoting the principle that First Nations' peoples take a lead in self-determining how data relating to themselves and their contexts is generated, collated, processed, and used. Any company or organization wanting to use data relating to a particular land or peoples will have to negotiate with the traditional custodians about how they do so. In all these instances, data is positioned as a source of public value. This marks a sharp turn away from the commercial idea of data being individually owned and instead something that belongs to the community or collective.

This scenario relies on widespread critical data literacies across the community, with all members of society having the skills and understandings to navigate the data infrastructures described. This relies on all individuals being able to see and realize the potential of data as a common good, which will benefit not only small pockets of the economy but also society at large. In this scenario, critical data literacies might well be a key part of the formal school curriculum, in a similar manner to civics or geography, so that students learn about datafication issues as well as learning how to vote or care for their environment. Such critical data education should start early and be embedded into students' digital practices to maximize the relevance to their everyday lives. With an informed society, Big Tech firms would not only be held to account but would also be expected to cooperate with communities and civil society. Removing the commercial imperative for data might mean data processing is less opaque. For example, Big Tech firms may be forced to participate in public repositories where the most significant algorithms in society (i.e., search, newsfeed, or video recommender systems) are made publicly available and new updates and changes are documented for public scrutiny.

This scenario certainly implies a strong public understanding of data and its collective applications—communities that understand their rights and responsibilities when it comes to the collective uses of data. In this sense, we might see a closer alignment of critical data literacies and ideas of Indigenous data sovereignty. For example, Māori statistician and advocate Darin Bishop (2016, 296–297) outlines a number of principles that are fundamental to Māori data sovereignty, including

- the data for Māori are readily accessible;
- that it is possible to disaggregate the data for Māori by key variables such as age, sex, and location;
- the information is meaningful to stakeholders, particularly Māori;
- the units of measurement include both Māori individual and Māori collective identities;
- the relevant definitions, classifications, and methodologies have been developed for Māori;
- the system recognizes the distinct Māori institutions that exist within Māori society;
- the system recognizes the social, economic, environmental, and cultural areas of Māori development; and
- appropriate benchmarks and comparators have been developed for Māori within the system.

Such principles can be applied on a community-wide scale and move beyond concerns over how data is accessed and processed, while also encompassing broader questions about power in society. If, for example, there is more equitable distribution of power and representation from marginalized groups, then it is reasonable to assume that more equitable data processing and uses would follow. As sociologist Maggie Walter (2016, 80) writes, "A seemingly unbroken circle, dominant social norms, values and racial understandings determine statistical construction and interpretations, which then shape perceptions of data needs and purpose." Rather than data being used to complete this circle, it could instead be used to *break it* and ensure a different set of values and beliefs underpins how, why, and where data is used.

Scenario 3. Rethinking Datafication in an Era of Climate Crisis

Our third scenario considers possible data futures in light of the multiple, interconnected crises associated with ongoing environmental instabilities. This encompasses a range of issues: from the part that data extraction plays in the depletion of nonrenewable natural resources to the deleterious human and ecological consequences of anthropogenic climate change. These constitute pressing areas of uncertainty over the next few decades and clearly need to feature in any talk of data in future society. So, what possible data futures might unfold in an era of climate catastrophe and ecological instability? What might it mean to take seriously the relationship between data and fossil fuels and the ecological impact of computational capitalism?

These questions anticipate a state of digital post-abundance, with a planet that can no longer sustain the energy demands of unlimited cloud storage and data processing, the energy demands and natural resource depletion implicit in the production of digital hardware, and the damaging effects of e-waste and digital disposal. In short, this is a scenario predicated around the challenge of what to do once the world passes the point of peak tech. As media studies scholar Sy Taffel (2021, 4) argues, this anticipates the "need to abandon the fantasy that data extraction is a weightless endeavor that can grow infinitely." In blunt terms, then, how might we anticipate data futures that are not built upon continuous and plentiful extraction of data?

Here, it is possible to imagine scenarios where data capitalism is forced to reconsider how economic value might be most efficiently generated by an ever-dwindling number of digital assemblages. This might involve tech firms and data brokers concentrating on only the most profitable forms of data extraction and processing—with profitable individuals and organizations recompensed for the continued datafication of their everyday activities, while the majority of others are cast aside and rendered unquantifiable. This might see a reordering of society around a hierarchy of data classes based around the economic value that can be generated from their datafication. At the same time, only the most potentially profitable data gets archived and stored. Digital data itself becomes a rare precious resource.

Alternatively, we might imagine an era of digital degrowth based around logics of data justice and good data—where the value of data is framed in terms of social benefit and public good. This might necessitate the immediate cessation of resource-intensive data practices that lead only to economic profit rather than social good. For example, there would be no sense in supporting continued cryptocurrency mining or continuing to extract data simply to target advertising toward consumers to purchase nonessential products. Instead, we might choose to redistribute any available digital and data resources in ways that deliberately advantage the global poor and those displaced by climate migration. We might prioritize what data-processing capacity remains for climate and ecological modeling and other data applications that might help communities cope with ongoing environmental degradation. We might choose to prioritize data for purposes of public health. Alternatively, we might imagine autonomous local collectives working outside of state and market systems to generate their own data that relates directly to the immediate effects of flooding, drought, winds, and other unpredictable and highly localized conditions. Sy Taffel (2021, 12) speculates, "This growth should be achieved alongside substantial reductions in current digital activities that serve little or no social or ecological purpose." What constitutes social benefit will be contentious and should involve public scrutiny and debate, involving marginalized groups. Importantly, this should involve a reevaluation of practices based upon use values, rather than the current hegemonic practice, which involves leaving it to the market-based exchange value (Taffel 2021).

While reducing the datafication of societies and focusing what little resources we have on tackling pressing climate-related issues might appear sensible, it might also lead to problems regarding whole-community engagement with critical data literacies. For example, with data as a precious commodity, fewer people would have the resources and networks to access data literacy programs. By contrast, others in society would be relying heavily on their skills and expertise with a diminishing ability and motivation to scrutinize the ethics of their practices. Their data literacies would most likely be instrumental in approach with less consideration for the more socially just and collective approach to data literacies discussed throughout this book. This could lead to a society of "data haves" and "data have-nots," or a skilled minority with the ability to do data to others, while most others can only have data done to them. This could further fracture society along a familiar set of social and economic lines.

Thinking Further about Data Futures

Depending on your viewpoint, each of these scenarios might seem convincing or not. However, this is not an exercise in trying to second-guess the most plausible or accurate scenario. Given the essentially unknowable nature of how the next few decades will unfold, it makes sense to engage with *all* these possible futures, as well as many others. How we choose to anticipate data futures depends upon how unknowable we acknowledge these futures to be. In these times of global economic and political instability, ongoing climate change, and potential future pandemics, it seems sensible to adopt a starting point that the future is not guaranteed to unfold in broadly similar ways to what has come before. As such, any data future that we wish to anticipate from a critical data literacies viewpoint should not be seen as straightforward extrapolations of present predicaments.

Instead, all these different scenarios just presented remind us that datafication might well unfold in ways that are essentially uncertain, multifactorial, and nonlinear in nature. The futures of data and society are embedded within various complex predicaments and challenges—a fact that should prompt us to think about "futures [as] made up of unstable, complex and interdependent adaptive systems" (Urry 2016, 188). Of course, the main aim when addressing any possible data futures is to make better sense of how we might act in the present. In this sense, the three scenarios just presented are perhaps most useful as a source of ideas for interpreting current unfolding data-related social and technical change. As education researcher Keri Facer (2020) puts it, ideas of "the future" are primarily ideas that should be used in the present—prompts to see new possibilities, ask different questions, and establish new practices. Or, put another way, "the future illuminates the potential of the present" (Barbrook 2007, 8).

So, how can thinking about future forms of data and society inspire us to move on from old ideas and assumptions? Here, Keri Facer reasons that we need to "think about how different ideas of the future create new possibilities and resources to stimulate, challenge and inform what we are doing in the present" (Facer 2020). In this sense, one of the primary benefits of continuing to engage with the idea of critical data futures is the ways in which we are pushed into reimagining what data and datafication might be under different circumstances and conditions. Most usefully, spending time thinking about possible data futures pushes us to consider what present actions are required in order to fulfill these visions. While we should not take them completely seriously, as Nordmann (2007, 42–43) puts it, we should take "such scenarios seriously enough to generate insights from them and to discover values" that help us reflect upon current societal arrangements.

Engaging with the three futures scenarios just presented (and the role of critical data literacies in these) therefore raises values of what might constitute fair use of data, approaching the harms of data along relational lines, and so on. Engaging with these futures scenarios also raises logics of cooperativism, sustainable approaches, and political activism. Engaging with these futures scenarios draws attention to reconfigurations of regulation, governance, resistances, and responsibilities that perhaps need to be foregrounded in terms of current debates around the ongoing datafication and data-led shaping of society. Above all, these scenarios bring a welcome focus on people (in particular, people's interests, relations, and diverse life circumstances), reminding us that any discussion of data futures needs to be framed along human-centered lines. As Genevieve Bell (2021) contends,

> In this moment, we need to be reminded that stories of the future . . . are never just about technology; they are about people and they are about the places those people find themselves, the places they might call home and the systems that bind them all together.

In all these ways, then, continued consideration of possible data futures offers a neat way for critical data literacies to keep an eye on "how might things be otherwise." Of course, there are limits to doing this. For example, we should not lose sight of the lessons that can be learned from data histories. Indeed, many of the future scenarios just outlined are rooted in predigital histories and continuities—not least ideas of cooperativism, activism, community organization, and citizen resistance. Just as we might be quick to criticize big data advocates as presenting their field as "perpetually new, ahistorical and revolutionary" (Dalton, Taylor, and Thatcher 2016, 3), we should not fall into a similar trap when outlining alternate possibilities. In addition, we should not lapse into lazily imagining overly generic scenarios and lose sight of the importance of local context, local conditions, and how data are shaped by the places they are produced in.

These warnings notwithstanding, engaging critically with the idea of data futures provides a ready means to put the ideas of data and datafication under pressure. In this spirit, we need to continue to develop what Evelyn Ruppert (2018) terms "counter-imaginaries of datafication"—fighting currently prevalent corporate ideas of what is thinkable about data and society—not least dominant understandings of what practices are preferable and which actors we might want to be performing them. Key here is the need to diversify the voices, values, and viewpoints that are represented in this future building. As Laura Forlano (2021) reasons, "Merely stating that the future will be better or different does not make it so." Social change requires a deep understanding of the power and politics tangled up in these futures, as well as different understandings of temporality and the ways in which the future is defined. We need to move beyond the status quo to consider pluriversal futures, Black futures, feminist futures, queer futures, trans futures, crip futures, and so on (Forlano 2021).

At the same time, we need to work to convert these pluriversal futures into a workable present. As Kazansky and Milan (2021) suggest, this includes moving our thinking from currently speculative responses to more formative plans and then on to stabilized sets of tools and tactics. We also need to pay full attention to any accompanying ontological and epistemological changes that might be necessary in our social institutions and society at large. Above all, we need to retain hope that the dominant forms of datafication currently found in our digital societies are *not* a done deal. Instead, we need to remain inspired by our collective capacities to anticipate better data futures to come.

Critical Data Literacies: Concluding Thoughts

We conclude this book by refocusing our thoughts back to the present. Chapter 1 commenced by pitching the idea of critical data literacies as a means of better understanding, analyzing, and changing our relationships with digital data. Making good on this promise has pointed to a number of different but interrelated aspects of what it might mean to be critically data literate. First is an awareness of the full range of what data involves—from the material infrastructures to the policies that regulate data privacy. Throughout this book, we have seen how the implications of data reach into most (if not all) social, economic, and political dimensions of society. This relates back to the idea of seeing data as assemblage. In other words, data is most comprehensively understood in terms of the coming together of different people, places, processes, and practices. As we have seen across these eight chapters, it helps to be aware of the various materialities and infrastructures associated with data, including the way it impacts our built environment and how we interpret and respond to data analytics.

Second is the importance of seeing and engaging with digital data in context, meaning critical data literacies should confront the entanglements of digital data with organizational and institutional processes. For example, datafication has become a crucial part of contemporary education provision, with the infrastructures, devices, and processes shaping how school and university are experienced by teachers and students. In this way, school data literacies might be quite different from the data literacies needed for working in a hospital, or in politics, or journalism. Here, different systems of thought and forms of knowledge that emerge from professions and industries shape how data is done by people within these different contexts as part of their everyday working lives.

Third is developing good understandings of the multibillion-dollar data broker industry where digital data is sold in order to make predictions about future behaviors. The fact that this is personal data means it can be accumulated to build profiles of individuals that can be sold to companies for marketing purposes. Indeed, personal data is a large class of sensitive information. As we discussed in chapter 1, Facebook alone collects over 50,000 unique attributes associated with its platform users and their contacts. These cover all manner of characteristics and dispositions that can be used to reckon the likelihood of people's interests, behaviors, and actions. The overriding goal here is to segment individuals into populations with the purpose of selling them something—be that an item or idea. We explored the uses of data in detail in chapter 6, in terms of advertising being a key driver behind the rise of digital data in society.

Fourth is how the nebulous nature of what constitutes digital data and the lack of transparency about how it is processed presents challenges in developing understandings. It is unrealistic to expect a critically literate nonexpert to attain specialist levels of data science knowledge and expertise. Nevertheless, we outlined the basics of data processing in chapter 5, introducing key steps such as data preparation, algorithmic processing, and machine learning models. While this technical awareness is certainly helpful, we highlighted that it is just as important to look *across* these systems and processes to identify and critique their social and political implications. We drew attention to the fact that the inferences drawn from data processing are often imprecise and that there might in fact be some comfort in the fact that these systems do not know us as well as some software developers and data scientists might like to think. However, when this data is used decisively—that is, to make decisions about our future opportunities and life chances—and is based on problematic assumptions or imprecise data, then social issues are intensified.

Fifth is considering the many social justice issues associated with data-driven decision-making, governance, and the changing nature of power in civil society. In chapter 5 we discussed the problems associated with steps in data processing, such as proxies. For example, based on problematic societal assumptions relating to race, class, and gender, these proxies often work to ensure the dominant social order is not only maintained but also intensified. In a similar way, the ground truths that become the basis for machine learning models mean some realities are elevated at the expense of others—often replicating the assumptions and experiences of the individuals responsible for developing these systems and institutions they work for. In many ways, then, the basis of critical data literacies is an appreciation of the breadth of what data is.

Much of this involves an enhanced awareness and understanding of the complex technical features and processes involved. Sixth, then, is the challenge of developing useful forms of critical data literacies across general population and publics. In this sense, we have taken care to stress that everybody does not need to be subjected to a sustained program of advanced data literacy. Better still would be to pursue some form of enhanced public understanding of data. In establishing such a program, it will be important to take heed of lessons learned from previous iterations of public understanding of science. In particular is the need to avoid any unhelpful deficit model of public understanding, where public responses and values are seen to stem from a lack of specialist technical knowledge that is currently held only in specialist data science communities. Following Collins and Pinch (2014), there is no sense in attempting to increase public understanding of the esoteric technicalities of data science (in effect, bringing nonexperts up to the expertise levels of a professional data scientist). Instead, there is merit in working to increase public understandings of the broad *processes* of digital data and data science.

In addition, another important focus for any public education efforts should be on developing mutual understandings between data specialists and laypeople of issues relating to the ongoing datafication of society. Indeed, data specialists have much to learn about the societal contexts within which their work is applied. In this sense, it is perhaps more useful to begin to develop ways of stimulating and supporting the mutual development of professional and public "interpretations" of data (Wynne 2014). This would involve different "publics" of data (from general publics, to policymakers, to data scientists) working together to increase the awareness as well as the capacity to mobilize that critical awareness into change.

Crucial here is the idea of boosting collective understandings of what it means to be critical about data. Here, much of our discussions have been given over to ways of revealing and analyzing the political economy of data-driven technologies that might appear at first glance to be ostensibly "free," yet involve the commodification of personal data. This requires us to remain skeptical about any claims relating to the personal benefits and convenience of living a data-driven life. This requires us to remain suspicious of claims around the power of the data gaze. Instead, this requires people working to document, understand, and explain the social and political processes that underpin the ways in which digital data impacts their everyday lives. Thus, much of what we have described in critical terms throughout this book might be seen as illusion destroying—uncovering implicit and/or misleading assumptions and working *against* the power relations that constitute digital data as integral to the ongoing reproduction of economic growth, capitalist interests, and all the injustices and harms that follow.

A key final piece of this puzzle is a willingness to not give up completely on the possible utility and value of digital data if approached along different lines. As such, critical data literacies encourage continued constructive (rather than destructive) critical engagement with data. As with critical approaches to technology in general, our critical data literacies framework is not concerned simply with debunking and deconstructing aspects of digital data that we cannot bring ourselves to believe in. Instead, critical data literacies emphasize the need to develop new ways of engaging with data—thinking about new data processes and practices that we do consider worth building, as well as pointing out existing aspects of datafication that are worth protecting and caring for. This sensibility therefore pushes us beyond unmasking the wrongs of digital data and developing the skills and processes to *interrupt* the wrongs of digital data.

Conclusions

This book has made the case for seeing data and datafication through the lens of a literacies approach. Literacies are ever-changing and evolving—they are not something that is attained and then forgotten about. As such, everyone needs to be invested in maintaining and developing understandings of digital technologies and how they are generating, collecting, and using our data. Everyone needs to be attuned to how it feels to live within datafied systems and the ways in which our everyday experiences are changing as a consequence. As has been highlighted throughout this book, critical data literacies begin with the affective and embodied experiences of data, as well broader political and economic outcomes. We should be asking ourselves critical questions about what is gained and what is lost, who benefits and who loses, and what and how the technology makes us feel, to ensure we do not lose sight of how our everyday life is being shaped and changed by data.

It is only from these personalized and embodied experiences of data that cognitive and critical understandings will have meaning. And perhaps more important, it is only from the personal and embodied experiences that meaningful data strategies and tactics can be devised and sustained. Based on a sense of agency and purpose, critical data literacies should be seen as a creative process. They can help us to develop our data imaginations—that is, thinking beyond the expected ways of doing data to identify new and creative ways we can use data to enrich our everyday lives.

This book has posed a lot of questions, but hopefully, it has also developed a starting point from which to begin tackling these questions together and for ourselves. If we think about what literacies have achieved in terms of helping people from all walks of life better understand the world and their place in it, then a focus on critical data literacies should bring hope when engaging with a world increasingly reliant upon digital data. This hope can take many forms. Hope might mean ending the algorithmic bias that has come to characterize these systems. Hope might mean mending the newsfeeds that only expose us to particular views and ideas. Hope can also mean finding new ways to use data that will enable our communities to thrive and flourish.

Just as authors, screenwriters, and game developers have created works to entertain and draw our attention to different issues and perspectives, a critically data-literate population might approach data in the same way. What might upcoming generations of data writers, artists, and activists of the future create? What issues and topics will they draw our attention to? Whose perspectives may be opened up and what kind of insights will this reveal? How will data be used to inform and entertain? Above all, critical data literacies encourage us to think about data as an aspect of society that deserves (if not demands) attention and expertise far beyond the field of data science. Our societies need people from all backgrounds and academic disciplines to engage with digital data in meaningful ways so they too can not only shape how datafication takes place but also use creative and critical methods to explore the potentialities it holds. Understanding statistics and data processing is just the beginning. Critical data literacies signal a new era in our engagement with the digital technologies of the future.

Glossary

AI: Artificial intelligence (AI) refers to computer systems programmed to respond to new inputs on the basis of pre-existing data. These systems are usually focused on a specific task and are trained on pre-existing data that relates to that task. For example, a chatbot designed to produce written text will have been trained on large amounts of pre-existing written text. By extrapolating the associations and patterns evident in existing data, these systems are used to produce outputs, make decisions and suggest predictions that would usually require some degree of human intelligence. These decisions and predictions allow tasks to be performed without explicit human instructions.

Algorithm: An algorithm is a finite sequence of specific steps—instructing computers on what to do with data in order to perform a calculation or solve a problem. In this sense, an algorithm can be understood like a set of mathematical formulas that are used to transform "input" data into a set of different "outputs."

Alphanumeric data: Information that is communicated via letters and numbers.

Bias: There are various forms of statistical bias that data scientists see as compromising the accuracy of data (the difference between measurements made on an object and the true value of the object). These include systematic errors in the generation of data that can lead to representation and measurement bias. In addition, data-driven models are also subject to what are termed aggregation biases and evaluation biases. One key challenge for all data scientists is reducing (and ideally eliminating) these statistical biases from any data process or systems. In contrast, social scientists also draw attention to the many social biases associated with the development and implementation of data-driven systems. From this perspective, data bias is not simply a technical data problem but a sociotechnical problem of humans and data . . . and therefore not something that can be easily "fixed."

Big data: A popular term during the 2010s referring to the huge volumes of data being generated from people's ever-increasing use of technology. From a technical point of view, advances in data storage and parallel computational power allowed data scientists to tackle massive unstructured data sets that previously would have been too large to make sense of.

Big Tech: The large multinational tech corporations that provide the infrastructural core (Van Dijck et al. 2018) of our digital societies now significantly influence our societies, economies, cultures, and politics. The term "Big Tech" remains useful shorthand for talking about corporations such as Alphabet (Google), Meta, (Facebook), Apple and Microsoft—all exerting a powerful influence on twenty-first-century society in a similar manner to Big Oil, Big Banking, Big Tobacco, and other twentieth-century power blocs.

Biometric data: Data that can be generated from the human body—either physical appearance (such as facial features), physiological functions (such as heartbeat), or behavior (such as gait). These body measurements and calculations can be used to identify people (such as in the case of iris recognition technology) or infer characteristics about their background and behaviors (such as facial processing to infer age, gender, or emotional state).

Critical data studies: A recent field of study bringing together social scientists and others working in the humanities, law, politics, and arts with an interest in the ways that digital technologies are shaping societies. Above all, critical data studies are primarily interested in the computational processes that lie behind the digitization of data and the outcomes arising from this digital data, rather than simply the creation of the data itself.

Dark advertising/micro-targeting: Online advertising that uses personal data profiles to target specific advertisements to small segments of the online audience, without others being aware of the advertisement. This allows advertisers to produce different advertisements for the same product that might appeal to certain opinions, preferences, and prejudices. Common examples include using data profiling to target advertisements based on people's inferred political preferences, sports teams, or ethnic background.

Data: The plural of the Latin word "datum." In modern terms, data has become understood to refer to the process of observing, measuring, collecting, and reporting information about things. As Rob Kitchin (2021, 26) notes, "Data are generally considered to be pre-factual and pre-analytical in nature; that which exists prior to argument or interpretation." This aligns with popular distinctions that continue in some areas of information science and knowledge management between data, information, knowledge, and wisdom. In other words, a piece of data can only become information with context and meaning-making.

Data activism: The use of data for activist purposes—using data to highlight difference, raising (rather than resolving) questions, and stimulating grassroots political involvement and engagement through the development of alternative data sets that add extra context and/or challenge official data.

Data assemblage: A heuristic from the field of critical data studies that highlights the various technological, political, social, and economic apparatuses that underpin the generation, circulation, and deployment of data. Any data assemblage (such as a social media platform or a national census) involves the bringing together of various people, places, processes, and practices, as well as systems of thought, forms of knowledge, and underpinning materiality and infrastructures.

Data broker: Companies that specialize in the collection and trading of personal data. Data brokers are involved in the direct extraction of information from consumers, as well as purchasing information from companies and government agencies, and "scraping" information from public records. This information is then sold to third parties (such as advertisers and marketers).

Data cleansing: One of the main preparatory elements of any data analysis—methodically checking data sets for errors, gaps, and inconsistencies and making amendments and adjustments that allow the data to be used. Often, data analysts will opt to perform data cleansing automatically through data-wrangling tools or computer scripts that can standardize or transform large volumes of data. Regardless of its standardized nature, data cleansing is a subjective process—involving making choices over what data to correct (and how it might be corrected) and what data is discarded or ignored.

Data double: Digital identities that are created by someone or something else often through automated personal data collection. They are different to the profiles you create about yourself and are often composed of information that is collected without you knowing.

Data economy: The economic system that has grown up around the internet and other digital systems, where data is generated, collated, and sold for profit by data brokers to other third parties. Value is derived from data in various ways—to improve software and systems, to support government and business planning, to make large-scale predictions about markets, and to target online advertising, as well as other forms of insight and analysis.

Data feminism: Approaches that apply Black feminist notions of intersectionality to understanding how different people experience different forms of benefit/harm from data regimes depending on their background and circumstances. Data feminism therefore shifts conversations away from "getting rid of" data injustices and instead works to rebalance them. The data feminist approach raises a number of important issues—such as embracing data as a means of highlighting pluralism and foregrounding conflicting viewpoints and multiple perspectives.

Data for good: The idea that digital data can be deployed in ways that have clear social purpose—in areas such as education, heath, humanitarian aid, community development, and other areas of societal benefit. "Data for good" has become a popular trope among technology developers, business leaders, policymakers, and civil society. Running throughout all these cases is the underpinning inference that "good" ends can arise from deliberately designed programs of data use and/or technology business processes.

Data gaze: The belief that massive amounts of data now being digitally generated throughout society can potentially drive new forms of knowing and action—what Dave Beer (2019, 22) has described as "speedy, accessible, revealing, panoramic, prophetic and smart" perceptions and insights (Beer 2019, 22).

Data Identification: The first domain of the critical data literacies framework, Data Identification refers to an awareness of the various ways we encounter data in everyday life, from data that is given to digital systems to data that is *extracted* without our knowledge. It also means recognizing data dashboards and analytics as a form of *processed* data.

Data infrastructure: The material things, institutions, people, and computer code that enable the generation, collation, processing, and circulation of digital data. Rather than being ephemeral, digital data is dependent on vast infrastructures. Alongside people working as coders, developers, content moderators, data labelers, and other forms of manual automation are physical networks of cables, pipelines, undersea trenches, and data warehouses spread around the world.

Data justice: A strand of thinking within critical data studies that highlights the relationships between datafication and social justice. Key here is the idea that data-driven social justice issues are primarily structural in nature and form. As such, any moves toward data justice require collective responses that involve a wide range of peoples, groups, and interests who can work together to articulate the challenges that datafication pose to them and also what local responses might be appropriate.

Data lake: A recent trend in business to establish vast repositories that can store all the data that can be possibly generated and collated within an organization, with the expectation that it might prove useful in the future. The idea of the data lake therefore reflects a trend for the speculative accumulation of data with no immediate analytic purpose in mind.

Data obfuscation: The resistant tactic of producing ambiguous, false, or misleading information in order to avoid detection by data-driven software and systems.

Data profiling: The use of personal data to create profiles about people in order to bring insights into their tastes, interests, and purchasing habits. Data profiling involves accumulating a lot of different data relating to an individual and then attempting to make connections and relations between these different data points and the data profiles of other people. Profiles provide representation of individuals for companies, organizations, and institutions to connect with.

Data Reflexivity: The third domain of the critical data literacies framework refers to thinking about how digital data is being used and analyzing the implications of data processing.

Data Strategies: The fourth domain of the critical data literacies framework refers to normative practices to manage and protect data. This might include things like reviewing the terms of service agreements, adjusting privacy settings, implementing ad block technologies, or setting performance targets in order to influence the feedback of data.

Data Tactics: The fifth domain of the critical data literacies framework refers to practices and forms of knowledge that subvert, usurp, and undermine norms and expected ways of doing things. These tactics might include countering surveillance and facial recognition technology or repurposing data in creative and unanticipated ways.

Data Understandings: The second domain of the critical data literacies framework, data understandings refers to the ways in which data is processed and used. This involves making sense of visual representations of data, such as dashboards, graphs, and metrics, as well as understanding the source data underlying these representations. It might also involve knowing the basics of data science, such as what an algorithm is and how data sets are constituted. As data infrastructures are complex and opaque, it can be difficult to analyze exactly how data is being captured and processed.

Data visualizations: Data is increasingly communicated and made sense of in the form of computer-generated charts, maps, graphs, infographics, dashboards, and other visual forms. Visualizations are an important way in which people engage with data, leading to concerns with how visualizations can provide a misleading sense of data objectivity or accuracy, as well as how popular visualization software acts as an important mediator of data in everyday life.

Datafication: The process of turning vast amounts of activity and human behavior into data points that can be tracked, collected, and analyzed.

Dataveillance: Data-driven surveillance—that is, the act of using data and metadata to continuously track people online, usually for unspecified purposes.

Digital: In a basic sense, "digital" refers to discontinuous data, based on the two distinct states of off or on (or 0 and 1) with no value in between. Digital technologies are only capable of distinguishing between these two values of 0 and 1 but use binary codes to combine these zeros and ones into large numbers and other practical forms of information.

Digital data: The generation, collation, processing, analysis, and circulation of data by computers and other digital technologies. Over the past forty years or so, the application of data in digital form has vastly expanded and extended what can be done with data, as well as led to additional forms of data that are generated through the use of digital technologies.

Geolocational data: Data that is continually generated by internet-connected devices (such as smartphones, laptops) relating to the latitudinal and longitudinal location of the device. Any device or process that uses geolocation data is essentially collecting it—ranging from our credit card transactions to the tags put into the photos that we take. Location data can be processed to provide valuable business intelligence as well as personal information about where someone lives, works, or even their sleeping patterns. Given this, there is now a large market for the buying and selling of location data from apps.

Indigenous data sovereignty: The idea of data sovereignty is growing in popularity as a way of holding digital data accountable to the governance structures, cultural interests, and knowledge structures relating to the communities and cultures where it originates (and to which the data relates to). In particular, the idea of Indigenous data sovereignty promotes alternate forms of data processes and practices that are rooted in Indigenous beliefs and value systems, epistemological approaches, and ontological assumptions.

Internet of Things: A term referring to the rapid increase in internet-connected sensors now being embedded in everyday devices and environments—especially in terms of sensors generating data from live video and audio streams. This proliferation of continuous recording and connectivity is leading to significant increases in data production in both public and private settings.

Interoperability: The use and usefulness of data depends upon how easily it can be shared across devices and digital systems. While discrete data packets can be easily circulated within a digital system, different devices, platforms, and systems must be able to connect with each other in order for that data to be shared. This ability for different systems to 'talk' with each other is known as interoperability.

Literacies: Literacies refer not only to how we might make sense of symbolic languages to read, write, and speak but also how this process is involved in identity building, critical thought, knowledge, and understanding.

Metadata: Metadata is data about data and is typically produced automatically by various technologies. For example, a range of metadata is attached to any digital photograph that is taken—such as date stamps and time stamps, location data, what camera was used and with what settings, and so on.

New literacies: The idea of seeing literacies as a part of everyday life (not just something that is learned in school). This idea of social literacies acknowledges the forms of understanding and knowledge required to navigate experiences in informal settings such as home, community, and leisure. Seen along these lines, then, there is not just one literacy that is acquired through formal instruction but rather a variety of languages, texts, and ways of expressing meaning that contribute to literacies.

Personal data: Any information that relates to an identified or identifiable person.

Personalization: Using data to customize products and services around the needs, interests, and circumstances of individuals. For example, data-driven personalized learning systems have been developed to adapt students' engagement with learning content according to their specific needs, capabilities, and past performance.

Platform: A contested term but generally refers to an online space where exchange takes place between producers of products, services and information, and users and customers. While a platform is composed of a set of stable components, it is designed to support variety and evolvability by constraining links between components. Tarleton Gillespie (2010) argues that computational definitions of platform are too narrow. In his political discussion of platforms, he demonstrates how the term is adopted discursively by intermediaries for particular purposes.

Platformization: Refers to the rise of digital platforms across cultural and economic sectors and spheres of life, thereby reorganizing practices and imaginations around these platforms (see Poell, Nieborg, and Van Dijck 2019).

Proxy: Many forms of data are not direct measurements of something but abstractions and representations. Proxies are measurements that can stand in for things that cannot be measured or are difficult to measure—for example, using unemployment rates as a proxy for the overall state of the economy or the newspaper that someone subscribes to as a proxy for their social class. As such, this form of data is highly inferential and should not be taken as an accurate or direct measure.

Raw data (cooked data): The popular idea that something has to be done to data before it can be of use to either humans or machines—hence the need for data processing. In data science terms, data is assumed to be raw in the sense that it has no meaning until it is interpreted by a data- processing system. This logic might be extended to presume that data has no meaning in everyday life until it is processed by humans. In contrast, social scientists argue that data is always cooked from its inception, rather than ever existing in a precooked raw state. Seen in this light, any data point results from someone making a choice about what needs to be measured and how it should be measured. By making such choices, they are also inadvertently deciding what does *not* get measured.

Self-tracking (quantified self): Personal data that is collected from *people's bodies* via wearable self-tracking devices such as fitness trackers, smartwatches, activity trackers, virtual reality headsets, and eSport equipment. These technologies collect masses of personal data that bring insight to various bodily features and functions, including motion, speed, heart rate, gait, proximity, and sleep and excretion patterns. Many self-tracking devices now use gamification to encourage users to compete with themselves and others to optimize performance, health, and well-being—thus binding people to these technologies and ensuring the continuous and ongoing generation of digital data.

Sociomaterial: A social science approach that understands a phenomenon such as digital data as a vast network of technologies, physical objects, people, language, and spatial arrangements—all interacting with each other. This approach draws attention to the people, things, and physical infrastructures that enable the generation, processing, and use of digital data. In this sense, digital data is seen in social and material terms, rather than an abstract computational entity.

Techlash: The shift in public opinion from the "techno-optimism" of the 1990s and 2000s to growing concerns during the 2010s about privacy, surveillance, the right to be forgotten, and the threats of online misinformation and other forms of digital malevolence. The term "techlash" was first coined by the *Economist* magazine in 2013—prompted by growing public suspicion of government data surveillance and the increased influence of Big Tech companies.

Terms of service: The legal agreements between a service provider and a person who wants to use that service.

Trace data: The masses of data traces generated through everyday uses of personal devices, software, systems, and other technologies—often unbeknown to the people using the technology. For example, a smartphone will generate a constant trail of geolocation and altitude data—sometimes also referred to as a data exhaust or data trail.

References

Abrams, M. 2014. The origins of personal data and its implications for governance. *SSRN.* https://papers.ssrn.com/sol3/papers.cfm?abstract_id=2510927

Acker, A. 2018. *Data craft: The manipulation of social media metadata.* New York: Data & Society. https://datasociety.net/library/data-craft/

Akinrinade, I., and J. Mukogosi 2020. Strategic knowledge: Teens use "algorithmic folklore" to crack TikTok's black box. *Points: Data & Society.* https://points.datasociety.net/strategic-knowledge-6bbddb3f0259

Albright, A. 2019. *If you give a judge a risk score: Evidence from Kentucky bail decisions.* Harvard John M. Olin Fellow's Discussion Paper. http://www.law.harvard.edu/programs/olin_center/Prizes/2019-1.pdf

Albury, K., Burgess, J., Light, B., Race, K., and Wilken, R. (2017). Data cultures of mobile dating and hook-up apps: Emerging issues for critical social science research. *Big Data & Society* 4 (2), 2053951717720950.

Ali, S., M. Elgharabawy, Q. Duchaussoy, M. Mannan, and A. Youssef. 2020. Betrayed by the guardian: Security and privacy risks of parental control solutions. Paper presented at the ACSAC 2020, Austin, TX.

Amin, A., and N. Thrift. 2005. What's left? Just the future. *Antipode* 37 (2): 220–238.

Amoore, L. 2020. Why 'ditch the algorithm' is the future of political protest. *The Guardian*, August 19. www.theguardian.com/commentisfree/2020/aug/19/ditch-the-algorithm-generation-students-a-levels-politics

Ananny, M., and K. Crawford. 2018. Seeing without knowing: Limitations of the transparency ideal and its application to algorithmic accountability. *New Media & Society* 20 (3): 973–989.

Anderson, M. 2016. *Parents, teens and digital monitoring.* Pew Research Centre. https://www.pewresearch.org/internet/2016/01/07/parents-teens-and-digital-monitoring/

Andrejevic, M. 2014. The big data divide. *International Journal of Communication* 8:1673–1689.

Andrejevic, M., A. K. Obeid, D. Angus, and J. Burgess. 2021. Facebook ads have enabled discrimination based on gender, race and age. We need to know how "dark ads" affect Australians. *The Conversation.* https://theconversation.com/facebook-ads -have-enabled-discrimination-based-on-gender-race-and-age-we-need-to-know-how -dark-ads-affect-australians-168938

Angwin, J., S. Mattu, and T. Parris Jr. 2016. Facebook doesn't tell users everything it really knows about them. *ProPublica.* https://www.propublica.org/article/facebook -doesnt-tell-users-everything-it-really-knows-about-them

Apple, M. 2010. Len Barton, critical education and the problem of "decentred unities." *International Studies in Sociology of Education* 20 (2): 93–107.

Barbrook, R. 2007. *Imaginary futures.* London: Pluto Press.

Barrowman, N. 2018. Why data is never raw. *The New Atlantis* 56:129–135.

Bates, J., Y. Lin, and P. Goodale. 2016. Data journeys: Capturing the socio-material constitution of data objects and flows. *Big Data & Society,* July–December, 1–12.

Beer, D. 2019. *The data gaze.* Thousand Oaks, CA: Sage.

Beer, D., and R. Burrows. 2013. Popular culture, digital archives and the new social life of data. *Theory, Culture & Society* 30 (4): 47–71.

Bell, G. 2021. Touching the future: Stories of systems, serendipity and grace. *Griffith Review* 71:251–262. https://www.griffithreview.com/articles/touching-the-future/

Benjamin, R. 2019. *Race after technology.* Cambridge: Polity.

Bishop, D. 2016. Indigenous peoples and the official statistics system in Aotearoa/ New Zealand. In *Indigenous data sovereignty: Toward an agenda,* ed. T. Kukutai and J. Taylor, 291–306. Canberra: Australian National University Press.

Borup, M., N. Brown, K. Konrad, and H. Van Lente. 2006. The sociology of expectations in science and technology. *Technology Analysis & Strategic Management* 18 (3–4): 285–298.

Bouk, D. 2017. The history and political economy of personal data over the last two centuries in three acts. *Osiris* 32:85–106.

Bowker, G. 1994. *Science on the run: Information management and industrial geophysics at Schlumberger, 1920–1940.* Cambridge, MA: MIT Press.

Bowker, G. 2005. *Memory practices in the sciences.* Cambridge, MA: MIT Press.

Bowker, G. 2013. Data flakes: An afterword to "Raw data is an oxymoron." In *Raw data is an oxymoron,* ed. L. Gitelman, 167–173. Cambridge, MA: MIT Press.

Boyd, D., and K. Crawford. 2012. Critical questions for big data. *Information, Communication & Society* 15 (5): 662–679.

Brand, J., and I. Sander. 2020. *Critical data literacy tools for advancing data justice: A guidebook.* https://datajusticelab.org/2020/06/12/djl-publishes-guidebook-on-data-literacy-tools/

Bridges, L. E. 2021. Digital failure: Unbecoming the "good" data subject through entropic, fugitive, and queer data. *Big Data & Society* 8 (1): 1–17. https://doi.org/10.1177/2053951720977882

Brown, A. 2021. Making the YouTube algorithm less elusive with the help of Gregory Chase. *Forbes.* https://www.forbes.com/sites/anniebrown/2021/07/13/making-the-youtube-algorithm-less-elusive-with-the-help-of-gregory-chase-a-creator-with-10m-subscribers/?sh=2d0671e7d681

Brunton, F., and H. Nissenbaum. 2015. *Obfuscation: A user's guide for privacy and protest.* Cambridge, MA: MIT Press.

Bucher, T. 2012. A technicity of attention: How software "makes sense." *Culture Machine* 13:1–23.

Bucher, T. 2018. *If . . . then: Algorithmic power and politics.* Oxford: Oxford University Press.

Bucher, T. 2021. *Facebook.* Cambridge: Polity Press.

Buckingham, D. 2003. *Media education: Literacy, learning and contemporary culture.* Cambridge, MA: Polity Press.

Buckland, M. 2015. Document theory: An introduction. In *Records, archives and memory: Selected papers from the Conference and School on Records, Archives and Memory Studies,* ed. Mirna Willer, Anne J. Gilliland, and Marijana Tomić, 223–237. Zadar: University of Zadar. https//:chrome-extension://efaidnbmnnnibpcajpcglclefindmkaj/https://people.ischool.berkeley.edu/~buckland/zadardoctheory.pdf

Burgess, J., K. Albury, A. McCosker, and R. Wilken. 2022. *Everyday data cultures.* Cambridge: Polity.

Burkhardt, M., D. Van Geenen, C. Gerlitz, S. Hind, T. Kaerlein, D. Lämmerhirt, and A. Volmar. 2022. *Interrogating datafication: Towards a praxeology of data.* Bielefeld: Transcript Verlag.

Carr, N. 2019. Thieves of experience: How Google and Facebook corrupted capitalism. *LA Review of Books,* January 15. https://lareviewofbooks.org/article/thieves-of-experience-how-google-and-facebook-corrupted-capitalism/

Chauhan, N. S. 2020. Audio data analysis using deep learning with Python (part 1). *Audio, Data Processing, Deep Learning, Python.* https://www.kdnuggets.com/2020/02/audio-data-analysis-deep-learning-python-part-1.html

Cheney-Lippold, J. 2017. *We are data: Algorithms and the making of our digital selves.* New York: New York University Press.

Christl, W. 2017. Corporate surveillance in everyday life: How companies collect, combine, analyze, trade and use personal data on billions. *Cracked Labs Report.* https://crackedlabs.org/dl/CrackedLabs_Christl_CorporateSurveillance.pdf

Chun, W. 2021. *Correlation, neighborhoods, and the new politics of recognition.* Cambridge, MA: MIT Press.

Cimpanu, C. 2020. Mozilla research: Browsing histories are unique enough to reliably identify users. *ZDNet.* https://www.zdnet.com/article/mozilla-research-browsing-histories-are-unique-enough-to-reliably-identify-users/

Collins, H. 2014. Are we all scientific experts now? *Polity Communication & Society* 9 (5): 553–571. http://dx.doi.org/10.1080/01596306.2014.942836

Collins, H., and T. Pinch. 2014. *The golem at large: What you should know about technology.* Cambridge: Cambridge University Press.

Constanza-Chock, S. 2020. *Design justice: Community-led practices to build the worlds we need.* Cambridge, MA: MIT Press.

Couldry, N. 2020. Recovering critique in an age of datafication. *New Media & Society* 22 (7): 1135–1151.

Couldry, N., and U. A. Mejias. 2019. *The costs of connection: How data is colonizing human life and appropriating it for capital.* Stanford, CA: Stanford University Press.

Crain, M. 2016. The limits of transparency: Data brokers and commodification. *New Media & Society* 20 (1): 1–17. https://doi.org/10.1177/1461444816657096

Cramer, F. 2015. What is "post-digital"? In *Postdigital aesthetics*, ed. David M. Berry and Michael Dieter, 12–26. London: Palgrave Macmillan.

Crawford, K. 2017. The trouble with bias. Paper presented at the Conference on Neural Information Processing Systems, Long Beach, CA.

Crawford, K. 2021. *Atlas of AI: Power, politics, and the planetary costs of artificial intelligence.* New Haven, CT: Yale University Press.

Crooks, R., & Currie, M. 2021. Numbers will not save us: Agonistic data practices. *The Information Society* 37 (4): 201–213.

Dalton, C. M., L. Taylor, and J. Thatcher. 2016. Critical data studies: A dialog on data and space. *Big Data & Society* 3 (1): 2053951716648346. https://doi.org/10.1177/2053951716648346

Daly, A., S. K. Devitt, and M. Mann. 2019. *Good data.* Amsterdam: Institute of Network Cultures.

Dastin, J. 2018. Amazon scraps secret AI recruiting tool that showed bias against women. *Reuters*. https://www.reuters.com/article/us-amazon-com-jobs-automation -insight-idUSKCN1MK08G

Davidson, J., Liebold, B., Liu, J., Nandy, P., & van Vleet, T. 2010. The YouTube video recommendation system. Paper presented at the Recommender Systems Conference 2010, Barcelona, Spain.

De Certeau, M. 1984. *The practice of everyday life*. Berkeley: University of California Press.

Dencik, L., A. Hintz, J. Redden, and E. Trere. 2022. *Data justice*. Thousand Oaks, CA: Sage.

Dhar, V. 2013. Data science and prediction. *Communications of the ACM* 56 (12): 64–73. https://doi.org/10.1145/2500499

D'Ignazio, C., and L. Klein. 2020. *Data feminism.* Cambridge, MA: MIT Press.

DiSalvo, C. 2019. Software. In *Digital STS: A field guide for science and technology studies*, ed. J. Vertesi and D. Ribes, 365–368. Princeton, NJ: Princeton University Press.

Dourish, P. 2017. *The stuff of bits: An essay on the materialities of information*. Cambridge, MA: MIT Press.

Dourish, P., and M. Mazmanian. 2011. Media as material: Information representations as material foundations for organizational practice. Paper presented at the Third International Symposium on Process Organization Studies, Corfu, Greece.

Draper, N., and J. Turow. 2017. Toward a sociology of digital resignation. Paper presented at the Data Power, Ottawa, Canada.

Dreyfus, H., and P. Rabinow. 1982. *The subject and power*. Chicago: University of Chicago Press.

Emejulu, A., and C. McGregor. 2019. Towards a radical digital citizenship in digital education. *Critical Studies in Education* 60 (1): 131–147.

Emerson, L. 2016. Media genealogy: As if, or, using media archaeology to reimagine past, present, and future: An interview with Lori Emerson. *International Journal of Communication* 10:14.

Eubanks, V. 2017. *Automating inequality: How high-tech tools profile, police, and punish the poor*. New York: St Martin's Press.

Facer, K. 2019. The university as engine for anticipation. In *Handbook of anticipation*, ed. R. Poli, 1439–1457. New York: Springer.

Facer, K. 2020. Eleven things I've learned from educational futures work that might be helpful for COVID-19. https://kerifacer.wordpress.com/2020/03/31/11-things-ive -learned-from-educational-futures-work-that-might-be-helpful-for-covid-19/

Farrell, M. 2020. The prodigal techbro. *The Conversationalist*, March 5.

Feal, Á., P. Calciati, N. Vallina-Rodriguez, C. Troncoso, and A. Gorla. 2020. Angel or devil? A privacy study of mobile parental control apps. *Proceedings on Privacy Enhancing Technologies* 2020 (2): 314–335.

Feinberg, M. 2022. *Everyday adventures with unruly data*. Cambridge, MA: MIT Press.

Fenwick, T. 2010. Re-thinking the "thing": Sociomaterial approaches to understanding and researching learning in work. *Journal of Workplace Learning* 22 (1/2): 104–116.

Forlano, L. 2019. Materiality. In *Digital STS: A field guide for science and technology studies*, ed. J. Vertesi and D. Ribes, 11–17. Princeton NJ, Princeton University Press.

Forlano, L. 2021. The future is not a solution. *Public Books*. https://www.publicbooks .org/the-future-is-not-a-solution/

Freebody, P., and A. Luke. 1990. Literacies programs: Debates and demands in cultural contexts. *Prospect: Australian Journal of TESOL* 5 (3): 7–16.

Freire, P. 1970/2006. *Pedagogy of the oppressed*. Repr., New York: Continuum.

Gabriels, K. 2016. 'I keep a close watch on this child of mine': a moral critique of other-tracking apps. *Ethics and Information Technology* 18:175–184.

Gabrys, J., H. Pritchard, and B. Barratt. 2016. Just good enough data: Figuring data citizenships through air pollution sensing and data stories. *Big Data & Society* 3 (2). https://doi.org/10.1177/2053951716679677

Gandy, O. 1993. *The panoptic sort*. Oxford: Oxford University Press.

Garcia, D., and G. Lovink. 1997. The ABC of tactical media. *Nettime*. http://www .nettime.org/Lists-Archives/nettime-l-9705/msg00096.html

Gartner. 2021. Top ten strategic predictions for 2021. www.gartner.com/smarterwithg artner/gartner-top-10-strategic-predictions-for-2021-and-beyond/

Gee, J. 2000. The new literacy studies: From 'socially situated' to the work of the social. In *Situated literacies: Reading and writing in context*, ed. D. Barton, 180–197. London: Routledge.

Gentzkow, M., B. Kelly, and M. Taddy. 2019. Text as data. *Journal of Economic Literature* 57 (3): 535–574.

Ghosh, R., and H. O. Faxon. 2023. Smart corruption: Satirical strategies for gaming accountability. *Big Data & Society* 10 (1). https://doi.org/10.1177/20539517231164119

Ghosh, S., and J. Kanter. 2019. Google says data is more like sunlight than oil, one day after being fined $57 million over its privacy and consent practices. *Business Insider*. https://www.businessinsider.in/tech/google-says-data-is-more-like-sunlight

-than-oil-just-1-day-after-being-fined-57-million-over-its-privacy-and-consent
-practices/articleshow/67640224.cms

Gieseking, J. J. 2018. Size matters to lesbians, too: Queer feminist interventions into the scale of big data. *The Professional Geographer* 70 (1): 150–156.

Gillborn, D., P. Warmington, and S. Demack. 2018. QuantCrit: Education, policy, 'Big Data' and principles for a critical race theory of statistics. *Race Ethnicity and Education* 21 (2): 158–179.

Gillespie, T. 2010. The politics of 'platforms'. *New Media & Society* 12 (3): 347–364.

Gillespie, T. 2016. Algorithm. In *Digital keywords: A vocabulary of information, society and culture*, ed. B. Peters. 18–30. Princeton, NJ: Princeton University Press.

Gilliard, C. 2021. 'Smart' educational technology. *Surveillance & Society* 19 (2): 262–271.

Golumbia, D. 2018. We don't know what "personal data" means. *Uncomputing.* https://www.uncomputing.org/?p=1983

Gomes, L. 2017. Neuromorphic chips are destined for deep learning—or obscurity. *IEEE Spectrum.* https://spectrum.ieee.org/neuromorphic-chips-are-destined-for-deep -learningor-obscurity

Google. 2021. Google privacy & terms. https://policies.google.com/technologies /partner-sites?hl=en-US

Grauer, Y. 2018. What are "data brokers," and why are they scooping up information about you? https://www.vice.com/en/article/bjpx3w/what-are-data-brokers-and -how-to-stop-my-private-data-collection

Gray, C. 2021. *Data dispossession.* https://www.thesociologicalreview.com/data-dis possession/

Green, B. 2021. Data science as political action. *Journal of Social Computing* 2 (3): 249–265.

Gutierrez, M. 2018. *Data activism and social change.* New York: Palgrave Macmillan.

Guyan, K. 2022. *Queer data: Using gender, sex and sexuality data for action.* London: Bloomsbury.

Hacking, I. 1990. *The taming of chance.* Cambridge: Cambridge University Press.

Halford, S., C. Pope, and M. Weal. 2013. Digital futures? Sociological challenges and opportunities in the emergent semantic web. *Sociology* 47 (1): 173–189.

Halpern, O. 2014. *Beautiful data: A history of vision and reason since 1945.* Durham, NC: Duke University Press.

Hamraie, A., and K. Fritsch. 2019. Crip technoscience manifesto. *Catalyst: Feminist, Theory, Technoscience* 5 (1): 1–33. https://doi.org/10.28968/cftt.v5i1.29607

Hearn, A. 2010. Structuring feeling: Web 2.0, online ranking and rating, and the digital "reputation" economy. *Ephemera: Theory & Politics in Organization* 10 (3/4): 412–438.

Heath, S. B. 1982. What no bedtime story means: Narrative skills at home and school. *Language in Society* 11 (1): 49–76.

Hern, A. 2014. eBay study warns search ads have 'no measurable benefit." *The Guardian.* https://www.theguardian.com/technology/2014/jun/05/ebay-search-ads -no-benefit-google-brands-berkeley-chicago

Hintz, A., L. Dencik, and K. Wahl-Jorgensen. 2019. *Digital citizenship in a datafied society.* Cambridge: Polity Press.

Ho, C., and T. Chuang. 2019. Governance of communal data sharing. In *Good data*, ed. A. Daly, M. Mann, and S. Devitt, 202–214. Amsterdam: Institute of Network Cultures.

Hoeyer, K. 2023. *Data paradoxes: The politics of intensified data sourcing in contemporary healthcare.* Cambridge, MA: MIT Press.

Hunter, M. 2013. Imagination may be more important than knowledge: The eight types of imagination we use. *Review of Contemporary Philosophy* 12:113–120.

Hutt, R. 2015. What are your digital rights? *World Economic Forum Articles.* https:// www.weforum.org/agenda/2015/11/what-are-your-digital-rights-explainer/

Iliadis, A., and F. Russo. 2016. Critical data studies: An introduction. *Big Data & Society* 3 (2). doi:10.1177/2053951716674238

Introna, L. D., and H. Nissenbaum. 2000. Shaping the Web: Why the politics of search engines matters. *The Information Society* 16 (3): 169–185.

Ivarsson, J. 2017. Algorithmic accountability. *Lärande | Learning & IT Blog*, May 2. http://lit.blogg.gu.se/2017/05/02/algorithmic-accountability/

Jakobsen, J. 1998. Queer is? Queer does? Normativity and the problem of resistance. *GLQ: A Journal of Lesbian and Gay Studies* 4 (4): 511–536.

James, P., and Van Seters, P. 2014. Global social movements and global civil society: A critical overview. In *Globalization and politics, vol. 2: Global social movements and global civil society*, eds. P. James and P. Van Seters, vii–xxx. Thousand Oaks, CA: Sage.

Jones, K., and C. McCoy. 2019. Reconsidering data in learning analytics: opportunities for critical research using a documentation studies framework, *Learning, Media and Technology* 44 (1): 52–63.

Jones, R. H., A. Chik, and C. A. Hafner. 2015. Introduction: Discourse analysis and digital practices. In *Discourse and digital practices: Doing discourse analysis in the digital age*, ed. R. H. Jones, A. Chik, and C. A. Hafner, 1–17. Abingdon: Routledge.

Kazansky, B., and S. Milan. 2021. Bodies not templates. *New Media & Society* 23 (2): 363–381.

Kennedy, H., T. Poell, and J. van Dijck. 2015. Data and agency. *Big Data & Society* 2 (2): 1–7.

Kitchin, R. 2014. *The data revolution: Big data, data infrastructures and their consequences*. London: Sage.

Kitchin, R. 2017. Thinking critically about and researching algorithms. *Information, Communication & Society* 20 (1): 14–29. https://doi.org/10.1080/1369118X.2016.11 54087

Kitchin, R. 2021. *Data lives: How data are made and shape our world*. Bristol: Bristol University Press.

Kitchin, R., and T. P. Lauriault. 2018. Towards critical data studies: Charting and unpacking data assemblages and their work. In *Thinking big data in geography*, ed. J. Thatcher, A. Shears, and J. Eckert, 3–20. Lincoln: University of Nebraska Press.

Komljenovic, J. 2021. The rise of education rentiers. *Learning, Media and Technology*. https://doi.org/10.1080/17439884.2021.1891422

Koops, B. J. 2021. The concept of function creep. *Law, Innovation and Technology* 13 (1): 29–56.

Korstanje, J. 2021. Machine learning on sound and audio data. *Towards Data Science*. https://towardsdatascience.com/machine-learning-on-sound-and-audio-data-3ae03b cf5095

Langlois G., J. Redden, and G. Elmer, eds. 2015. *Compromised data: From social media to big data*. New York: Bloomsbury.

Lata, T. 2018. Getting your text data ready for your natural language processing journey. *Towards Data Science*. https://towardsdatascience.com/getting-your-text-data -ready-for-your-natural-language-processing-journey-744d52912867

Latour, B. 2004. Why has critique run out of steam? From matters of fact to matters of concern. *Critical Inquiry* 30 (2): 225–248.

Lazarus, D. 2019. Column: Shadowy data brokers make the most of their invisibility cloak. *Los Angeles Times*. https://www.latimes.com/business/story/2019-11-05/column -data-brokers

Lemke, T. (2021). *The Government of Things: Foucault and the New Materialisms*. New York: New York University Press.

Levin, S. 2017. Facebook told advertisers it can identify teens feeling "insecure" and "worthless." *The Guardian Australian*. https://www.theguardian.com/technology /2017/may/01/facebook-advertising-data-insecure-teens

Lewis, T., S. P. Gangadharan, M. Saba, and T. Petty. 2018. *Digital defence playbook: Community power tools for reclaiming data*. Detroit: Our Data Bodies.

Lindner, P. 2020. Molecular politics, wearables, and the Aretaic shift in biopolitical governance. *Theory, Culture & Society* 37 (3): 71–96.

Livingstone, S., M. Stoilova, and R. Nandagiri. 2019a. *Children's data and privacy online: Growing up in a digital age.* London: London School of Economics and Political Science.

Livingstone, S., M. Stoilova, and R. Nandagiri. 2019b. *My data and privacy online: A toolkit for young people.* http://www.lse.ac.uk/my-privacy-uk

Loukissas, Y. 2019. *All data are local: Thinking critically in a data-driven society.* Cambridge, MA: MIT Press.

Louridas, P. 2020. *Algorithms.* Cambridge, MA: MIT Press.

Lovink, G., and Rossiter, N. (2015). Network cultures and the architectured of decision. In *Critical Perspectives on Social Media and Protest: Between Control and Emancipation*, eds. L. Dencik and O. Leistert, 219–232. London: Rowman & Littlefield.

Luke, A. 2000. Critical literacy in Australia: A matter of context and standpoint. *Journal of Adolescent & Adult Literacy* 43 (5): 448–461.

Luke, A., and P. Freebody. 1999. Further notes on the four resources model. *Reading Online.* https://www.semanticscholar.org/paper/Further-notes-on-the-four-resources -model-Luke-Freebody/a9160ce3d5e75744de3d0ddacfaf6861fe928b9e?p2df

Lupton, D. 2013. Swimming or drowning in the data ocean? Thoughts on the metaphors of big data. *The Sociological Life.* https://simplysociology.wordpress.com /2013/10/29/swimming-or-drowning-in-the-data-ocean-thoughts-on-the-metaphors -of-big-data/

Lupton, D. 2017. Personal data practices in the age of lively data. In *Digital sociologies*, ed. J. Daniels, K. Gregory, and T. McMillan Cottom, 339–354. Bristol: Policy Press.

Lupton, D. 2020. *Data selves.* Cambridge, UK: Polity.

Lupton, D., and M. Michael. 2017. "Depends on who's got the data": Public understandings of personal digital dataveillance. *Surveillance & Society* 15 (2): 254–268.

Lyall, B. 2021. "Build a future champion": Exploring a branded activity-tracking platform for children and parents. *Media International Australia.* https://doi.org/10.1177 /1329878X211007167

Mac, R. 2021. Facebook apologizes after AI puts "primates" label on video of a black man. *New York Times.* https://www.nytimes.com/2021/09/03/technology/facebook -ai-race-primates.html

Macgilchrist, F. 2021. Theories of postdigital heterogeneity: Implications for research on education and datafication. *Postdigital Science and Education* 3 (3): 660–667.

Marcus, G., and E. Davis. 2014. Eight (no nine!) problems with big data. *New York Times*, April 6.

Mayernik, M., and A. Acker. 2018. Tracing the traces: The critical role of metadata within networked communications. *Journal of the Association for Information Science and Technology* 69 (1): 177–180.

Mayer-Schoenberger, V., and K. Cukier. 2013. *Big data: A revolution that will transform how we live, work and think*. London: John Murray.

McCosker, A. 2017. Data literacies for the post-demographic social media. *First Monday* 22 (10). http://firstmonday.org/ojs/index.php/fm/article/view/7307/6550

McGlotten S. 2016. Black data. In *No tea, no shade: New writings in black queer studies*, ed. P. Johnson, 262–286. Durham, NC: Duke University Press.

McManus, J. 2016. What is a Facebook dark post? *Medium*. https://medium.com/@MrJamesMcManus/what-is-a-facebook-dark-post-7e6513666d12

McNeil, J. 2022. Crisis text line and the silicon valleyfication of everything. *Vice*, February 11. https://www.vice.com/en/article/wxdpym/crisis-text-line-and-the-silicon-valleyfication-of-everything

Means, A. 2018. Platform learning and on-demand labour. *Learning, Media and Technology* 43 (3): 326–338.

Micheli, M., M. Ponti, M. Craglia, and A. Berti Suman. 2020. Emerging models of data governance in the age of datafication. *Big Data & Society* 7 (2): 2053951720948087.

Mills, C. W. 1959/2000. *The sociological imagination*. Repr., Oxford: Oxford University Press.

Minelli, M., M. Chambers, and A. Dhiraj. 2013. *Big data, big analytics*. Hoboken, NJ: Wiley.

Morrell, E. (2003). *Writing the word and the world: Critical literacy as critical textual production*. Paper presented at the Annual Meeting of the Conference on College Composition and Communication, New York, NY.

Morozov, E. 2013. *To save everything, click here*. New York: Public Affairs.

Morozov, E. 2020. Don't say: "Technology is not neutral." Twitter, February 12. https://twitter.com/evgenymorozov/status/1227496657756901377

Neff, G., A. Tanweer, B. Fiore-Gartland, and L. Osburn. 2017. Critique and contribute: A practice-based framework for improving critical data studies and data science. *Big Data* 5 (2): 85–97.

Ng, A. 2015. Why deep learning is a mandate for humans, not just machines. *Wired*. https://www.wired.com/brandlab/2015/05/andrew-ng-deep-learning-mandate-humans-not-just-machines/

Ng, A. 2020. Teens have figured out how to mess with Instagram's tracking algorithm. *CNET*, February 4. https://www.cnet.com/culture/teens-have-figured-out-how-to-mess-with-instagrams-tracking-algorithm/

Noble, S. 2018. *Algorithms of oppression: how search engines reinforce racism*. New York: NYU Press.

Nordmann, A. 2007. If and then: A critique of speculative nanoethics. *Nanoethics* 1 (1): 31–46.

Obar, J. 2015. Big Data and The Phantom Public: Walter Lippmann and the fallacy of data privacy self-management. *Big Data & Society* 2 (2). https://doi.org/10.1177/2053951715608876

Office of the eSafety Commissioner. 2018. Digital parenting: Supervising preschoolers online. https://www.esafety.gov.au/research/digital-parenting/supervising-preschoolers-online

Office of the eSafety Commissioner. 2020. Protect your personal information. https://www.esafety.gov.au/young-people/protecting-your-identity

Ortutay, B. 2021. Facebook shuts out NYU academics' research on political ads. *Associated Press*, August 4. https://apnews.com/article/technology-business-5d3021ed9f193bf249c3af158b128d18

Pangrazio, L. 2019. Technologically situated: The tacit rules of platform participation. *Journal of Youth Studies*. doi:10.1080/13676261.2019.1575345

Pangrazio, L., and J. Sefton-Green. 2020. The social utility of "data literacy." *Learning, Media and Technology* 45 (2): 208–220.

Pangrazio, L., and L. Cardozo-Gaibisso. 2021. "Your data can go to anyone": The challenges of developing critical data literacies in children. In *Critical digital literacies: Boundary-crossing practices*, ed. J. Avila, 35–51. Boston: Brill.

Pangrazio, L., and N. Selwyn. 2018. "It's not like it's life or death or whatever": Young people's understandings of social media data. *Social Media + Society* 4 (3): 1–9.

Pasquale, F. 2015. *The black box society: The secret algorithms that control money and information*. Cambridge, MA: Harvard University Press.

Pasquale, F. 2020. *New laws of robotics: Defending human expertise in the age of AI*. Cambridge, MA: Harvard University Press.

Peacock, S. 2014. How web tracking changes user agency in the age of big data: The used user. *Big Data & Society* 1 (2): 1–11.

Pink, S., M. Ruckenstein, R. Willim, and M. Duque. 2018. Broken data: Conceptualising data in an emerging world. *Big Data & Society*, January–June, 1–13.

Poell, T., Nieborg, D., & van Dijck, J. 2019. Platformisation. *Internet Policy Review* 8 (4). doi:10.14763/2019.4.1425

Poli, R. 2017. *Introduction to anticipation studies*. New York: Springer.

Popkewitz, T. 1987. *Critical studies in teacher education: Its folklore, theory and practice*. London: Falmer Press.

Press, G. 2020. 54 predictions about the state of data in 2021. *Forbes*, December 30. https://www.forbes.com/sites/gilpress/2021/12/30/54-predictions-about-the-state-of -data-in-2021/?sh=36aa5bcf397d

Puschmann, C., and J. Burgess. 2014. Metaphors of big data. *International Journal of Communication* 8 (2014): 20.

Raji, D. 2021. AI critics and PR hype. Twitter, April 24. https://twitter.com/rajiinio /status/1385935151981420557

Renieris, E. 2019. Distracted by data. October 26. https://medium.com/berkman -klein-center/distracted-by-data-dbe40033591c

Renieris, E. 2023. *Beyond data: Reclaiming human rights at the dawn of the metaverse*. Cambridge, MA: MIT Press.

Renzi, A., and G. Langlois. 2015. Data activism. In *Compromised data: From social media to big data*, ed. G. Langlois, J. Redden, and G. Elmer, 202–225. New York: Bloomsbury.

Reventlow, N. 2017. Digital rights are human rights. *Digital Freedom Fund*. https:// digitalfreedomfund.org/digital-rights-are-human-rights/

Reyes, I., P. Wijesekera, J. Reardon, A. Elazari, A. Razaghpanah, N. Vallina-Rodriguez, and S. Egelman. 2018. "Won't somebody think of the children?" Examining COPPA compliance at scale. *Proceedings on Privacy Enhancing Technologies* 2018 (3): 63–83.

Ricaurte, P. 2019. Data epistemologies, the coloniality of power, and resistance. *Television and New Media* 20 (4): 350–365.

Roberts, L., J. Howell, K. Seaman, and D. Gibson. 2016. Student attitudes toward learning analytics in higher education: "The Fitbit version of the learning world." *Frontiers in Psychology* 7:1–11.

Roddel, V. 2006. *Internet safety parents' guide*. Morrisville, NC: LuLu Press.

Rosenberg, A., and G. J. X. Dance. 2018. "You are the product": Targeted by Cambridge Analytica on Facebook. *New York Times*. https://www.nytimes.com/2018/04 /08/us/facebook-users-data-harvested-cambridge-analytica.html

Ross, A. 1991. Hacking away at the counterculture. In *Technoculture*, ed. C. Penley and A. Ross, 107–134. Minneapolis: University of Minnesota.

Ruppert, E. 2018. Big data economies and ecologies. In *An end to the crisis of empirical sociology? Trends and challenges in social research*, ed. L. McKie and L. Ryan, 12–26. Abingdon: Routledge.

Sadowski, J. 2019. When data is capital. *Big Data & Society* 6 (1): 2053951718820549.

Sadowski, J. 2020. *Too smart*. Cambridge, MA: MIT Press.

Sadowski, J., and R. Bendor. 2019. Selling smartness. *Science, Technology, & Human Values* 44 (3): 540–563.

Schellewald, A. 2022. Theorizing "stories about algorithms" as a mechanism in the formation and maintenance of algorithmic imaginaries. *Social Media + Society*, January–March, 1–10.

Shepard, M. 2022. *There are no facts: Attentive algorithms, extractive data practices, and the quantification of everyday life*. Cambridge, MA: MIT Press.

Siles, I. 2023. *Living with algorithms: Agency and user culture in Costa Rica*. Cambridge, MA: MIT Press.

Siles, I., A. Segura-Castillo, R. Siolis, and M. Sancho. 2020. Folk theories of algorithmic recommendations on Spotify: Enacting data assemblages in the global South. *Big Data & Society* 7 (1). doi:10.1177/2053951720923337

Solsman, J. E. 2018. YouTube's AI is the puppet master over most of what you watch. *CNet*. https://www.cnet.com/tech/services-and-software/youtube-ces-2018-neal-mohan/

Spade, D. 2011. Laws as tactics. *Columbia Journal of Gender & Law* 21:40.

Stevens, N., and O. Keyes. 2021. Seeing infrastructure. *Cultural Studies*. https://doi.org/10.1080/09502386.2021.1895252

Steyerl, H. 2013. Too much world: Is the internet dead? *e-flux*. https://www.e-flux.com/journal/49/60004/too-much-world-is-the-internet-dead/

Street, B. 1995. *Social literacies: Critical approaches to literacy in development, ethnography and education*. Abingdon: Routledge.

Street, B. 2001. *Literacy and development: Ethnographic perspectives*. London: Routledge.

Suckert, L. 2021. The coronavirus and the temporal order of capitalism: Sociological observations and the wisdom of a children's book. *The Sociological Review* 69 (6): 1162–1178.

Taffel, S. 2021. Data and oil: Metaphor, materiality and metabolic rifts. *New Media & Society*. https://doi.org/10.1177/14614448211017887

Taylor, L. 2017. What is data justice? The case for connecting digital rights and freedoms globally. *Big Data & Society* 4 (2). https://doi.org/10.1177/2053951717736335

Thompson, D. 2014. A dangerous question: Does internet advertising work at all? *The Atlantic*. https://www.theatlantic.com/business/archive/2014/06/a-dangerous -question-does-internet-advertising-work-at-all/372704/

Turow, J. 2011. *The daily you: How the new advertising industry is defining your identity and your worth*. New Haven, CT: Yale University Press.

Urry, J. 2016. *What is the future?* Cambridge: Polity Press.

Van Dijck, J. 2014. Datafication, dataism and dataveillance: Big Data between scientific paradigm and ideology. *Surveillance & Society* 12 (2): 197–208.

Van Dijck, J., T. Poell, and M. de Waal. 2018. *The platform society: Public values in an online world*. Oxford: Oxford University Press.

Van Ooijen, I., and H. U. Vrabec. 2019. Does the GDPR enhance consumers' control over personal data? An analysis from a behavioural perspective. *Journal of Consumer Policy* 42 (1): 91–107.

Varah, S. 2014. Video: The next frontier for big data. *Wired*. https://www.wired.com /insights/2014/09/video-big-data/

Viljoen, S. 2020. Democratic data: A relational theory for data governance. *SSRN*. https://papers.ssrn.com/sol3/papers.cfm?abstract_id=3727562

Vincent, J. 2018. Google "fixed" its racist algorithm by removing gorillas from its image-labeling tech. *The Verge*. https://www.theverge.com/2018/1/12/16882408 /google-racist-gorillas-photo-recognition-algorithm-ai

Vinsel, L. 2021. You're doing it wrong: notes on criticism and technology hype. *STS News*, February 2. https://sts-news.medium.com/youre-doing-it-wrong-notes-on -criticism-and-technology-hype-18b08b4307e5.

Walter, M. 2016. Data politics and Indigenous representation in Australian statistics. In *Indigenous data sovereignty: Toward an agenda*, ed. T. Kukutai and J. Taylor, 79–97. Canberra: Australian National University Press.

Walter, M., and M. Suina. 2019. Indigenous data, indigenous methodologies and indigenous data sovereignty. *International Journal of Social Research Methodology* 22 (3): 233–243.

Williams, S. 2022. *Data action: Using data for public good*. Cambridge, MA: MIT Press.

Wynne, B. 2014. Further disorientation in the hall of mirrors. *Public Understanding of Science* 23 (1): 60–70.

Zhu, P. 2014. *Digital master: debunk the myths of enterprise digital maturity*. Morrisville, NC: Lulu Press.

Zuboff, S. 2019. *The age of surveillance capitalism: The fight for a human future at the new frontier of power*. New York: Public Affairs.

Index